T0313264

'Paul Donovan clearly demonstrates a critical issue for economic policy makers and investors. Even if inflation remains contained, specific groups in society will have a very different inflation experience from that portrayed by aggregate consumer price data. Understanding why and how inflation experiences differ from group to group will be increasingly important in creating a fairer society.'

Right Honourable Danny Alexander MP,
Chief Secretary to the United Kingdom Treasury

'Inflation is a topic that can become deeply embedded in a political culture, as Paul Donovan makes clear. Properly understanding the politics as well as the economics of inflation is critical to investment success.'
Gerd W. Hintz, CIO Aequitas, Allianz Equity Advisors (Allianz Global Investors)

'Unveils the ins and outs of inflation – always with the investor and practitioner in mind. The author's sense of humour makes reading the book a real pleasure.'
Bo Bejstrup Christensen, Head of Asset Allocation, Danske Capital

The Truth About Inflation

Inflation is a simple topic, in that the basic concepts are something that everyone can understand. However, inflation is not a simplistic topic. The composition of inflation and what the different inflation measures try to represent cannot be summarised with a single line on a chart or a casual reference to a solitary data point. Investors very often fail to understand the detail behind inflation, and end up making bad investment decisions as a result.

The Truth About Inflation does not set out to forecast inflation, but to help improve its understanding, so that investors can make better decisions to achieve the real returns that they need. Starting with a summary of the long history of inflation, the drivers of price change are considered. Many of the 'urban myths' that have built up about inflation are shown to be a consequence of irrational judgement or political scaremongering. Some behaviour, like the unhealthy veneration of gold as a means of inflation protection, is shown to be the result of historical accident. In the modern era of lower nominal investment returns, inflation inequality (whereby some groups experience persistently higher inflation than others) is a very important consideration.

This book sets out the realities of price changes in the modern investing environment, without using economic equations or jargon. It gives investors the framework they need to think about inflation and how to protect themselves against it, whether the aggregate inflation of the future rises or falls from current levels.

Paul Donovan joined UBS in 1992 and is a managing director and global economist. Paul is responsible for formulating and presenting the UBS Investment Research global economic view.

The Truth About Inflation

Paul Donovan

Routledge
Taylor & Francis Group

LONDON AND NEW YORK

First published 2015
by Routledge
2 Park Square, Milton Park, Abingdon, Oxon OX14 4RN

by Routledge
711 Third Avenue, New York, NY 10017

Routledge is an imprint of the Taylor & Francis Group, an informa business

Disclaimer: The opinions and statements expressed in this book are those of the author and are not necessarily the opinions of any other person, including UBS AG. UBS AG and its affiliates accept no liability whatsoever for any statements or opinions contained in this book, or for the consequences which may result from any person relying on such opinions or statements.

Trademark notice: Product or corporate names may be trademarks or registered trademarks, and are used only for identification and explanation without intent to infringe.

British Library Cataloguing in Publication Data
A catalogue record for this book is available from the British Library

Library of Congress Cataloging in Publication Data
Donovan, Paul, 1972–
The truth about inflation / Paul Donovan.
    pages cm
    1. Inflation (Finance) I. Title.
    HG229.D636 2015
    332.4´1–dc23   2014041863

ISBN: 978-1-138-02361-1 (hbk)
ISBN: 978-1-315-77629-3 (ebk)

Typeset in Times New Roman
by HWA Text and Data Management, London

To my father, Roy Donovan, who gave me my first economics book and who bore the spiralling cost inflation of supporting a son who wanted to be the economist, with remarkably little complaint.

Consider this the real return on your investment, Dad.

Contents

Illustrations

Boxes

Acknowledgements

I have long wanted to write a book on inflation; economists tend to have the strangest desires. Several things provoked my interest in the topic. Perhaps being a child of the 1970s, and British to boot, has meant that inflation is something always lurking in the background of my subconscious. Even as a child I was aware that prices changed. I can remember the creeping cost of the mid-morning milk-and-biscuit at school, and the point at which the two pence coin that had previously bought me a chocolate biscuit on a Friday was no longer sufficient, creating an early and powerful form of the 'loss aversion' theory that pervades this book. (Believe me, the loss of that chocolate biscuit was very, very keenly felt. Do not let anyone tell you that a small piece of shortbread is an adequate substitute.)

More recently, sitting on the investment committee of St Anne's College, Oxford, has made me very aware of the problems of relying on headline inflation as a generic statistic. The inflation in costs faced by the college bears little relation to the headline UK consumer price index for much of the time, and the investment committee spends a great deal of effort trying to overcome the differences. The discussions of my colleagues on the committee, who have a truly frightening depth of experience and wisdom, have always proved a source of stimulation for my work. I always feel my membership of the committee is fraudulent, for I take away infinitely more than I contribute to the committee meetings. Though it will not compensate for everything St Anne's has given me over the years, the royalties from this book are being donated to the college.

Working at UBS Investment Bank has also been a huge source of intellectual stimulus. Over two decades of discussions with colleagues have led to countless instances where my views have been corrected, adjusted and polished. Larry Hatheway, chief economist of UBS, deserves special mention as heading a department that not only allows economists to pursue their own projects, but provides an environment in which proper discussion and constructive criticism can take place. George Magnus, Larry's immediate predecessor, set that environment in place and it has been a privilege to be able to argue repeatedly with George on a wide range of economic (and other) issues over the years. The views of other current and former colleagues have been very helpful: whether wittingly or unwittingly provided, I must acknowledge a real debt to Maury Harris,

Reinhard Cluse, Tao Wang, Duncan Wooldridge, Scott Haslem, Andy Cates, Jeff Palma, Erika Karp and Justin Knight.

Other colleagues very kindly gave up their time to read and check various chapters. Edel Tully, one of the most experienced minds on the topic of precious metals, very kindly looked over the chapter on gold. Ramin Nakisa, an accomplished author on financial assets, took time from his more cerebral reading to look over the chapter on inflation history.

I should also give a word of thanks to Julie Hudson, UBS's head of Socially Responsible Investment, who co-authored two books with me (what books, you ask? Why, *From Red to Green: How the Financial Credit Crunch Could Bankrupt the Environment* and *Food Policy and the Environmental Credit Crunch*. Both still available from all good booksellers and suitable purveyors of e-books.) Julie's hard work as an author, her patience as a colleague and her superior command of the English language made the last two books far easier to write than this.

Ruth Ridout, with considerable bravery, agreed to edit the text of this book, and with considerable tact pointed out the many glaring errors that cropped up (she has the nicest way of indicating when something is complete gibberish). Philip French of UBS also reviewed the text in its entirety with his customary good humour and great eye for detail.

I also have the great fortune to have had the support of friends and family, who have sat listening to my rambling pontification with tolerance, or at least without throwing things at me (most of the time). My nieces Louise, Emma and Sammy are always willing providers of honest criticism – a sample being, 'That's just my uncle: he's on TV and writes books and stuff, but he's really boring', which seems a pretty succinct description of who I am. David Wareham, Alison Wareham, Ciara Wells, Peter Wells, Bhauna Patel, Mark Shepherd and Trish Shepherd have consistently exhibited the enormous depths of tolerance that is a necessary condition of being a friend of mine, and have made valiant efforts not to shut me up when I hold forth on loss aversion and similar fascinating subjects. Chris and Judith Trimming have, as ever, provided a refuge from the pain of writing and editing.

Despite all the support and help, the responsibility for any errors or omissions must be my own, I suppose. Believe me, if I could find a way of blaming someone else, I would. But it seems if the reader has reason to disagree with anything that follows, it must be my fault.

1 What is inflation?

The attempt to understand money has made more persons mad than love.

(Benjamin Disraeli)[1]

In 1795, in Fordingbridge, Hants, England, one Sarah Rogers was tried, convicted and sentenced to three months' hard labour in prison. Today, a three-month jail sentence (without the hard labour) is handed down for a crime like assaulting a police officer. Back in 1795, Sarah Rogers had done something that was considered far more serious in the eyes of the law to warrant her incarceration. Sarah Rogers was convicted of campaigning for cheaper butter. Sarah Rogers was imprisoned for complaining about a very narrow form of price inflation.[2]

Sarah Rogers was imprisoned because the government was afraid it might lose control of society if inflation got out of hand. There had been an assassination attempt against the king in October of the same year, amidst a London riot over food price increases (price increases for which the king and government were blamed). Clearly, inflation and government were assumed to be intimately associated, even in the late eighteenth century, and inflation was taken seriously as a threat to the stability of the realm.

The importance of inflation has not diminished. There were riots over the price of rice in Japan in 1918.[3] Social order disintegrated in Germany during the hyperinflation of 1923, with the state of Bavaria effectively seceding (briefly) from the country. In 1951, the US House of Representatives' Committee on Education and Labor felt itself able to declare that the consumer price index was 'the most important single statistic issued by the government'.[4] A generation later, in the 1970s, some quite polemical ideas were being voiced. The British journalist William Rees-Mogg supported the 1973 Chilean *coup d'état* as a price worth paying for the control of inflation in that country. Samuel Brittan (now columnist at the *Financial Times*) and *The Banker* magazine both warned that democracy in developed economies might not be able to handle inflation and that inflation may in turn undermine democracy. Margaret Thatcher, as British leader of the opposition, declared in 1975 that 'rampant inflation, if unchecked, could destroy the whole fabric of our society'.[5] This is all powerful stuff.

Over two centuries after Sarah Rogers's trial, ninety years from the (first) German hyperinflation and more than a generation on from the fears of the 1970s, and concerns about price changes are still around (although expressing such concerns is not generally considered worthy of a custodial sentence, at least not in democratic countries). Indeed, one might say that concern is too small a word for the sentiment. Inflation provokes a more powerful, passionate response than almost any other concept in economics; and economics is a pretty passionate subject, as everyone knows. Unemployment is perhaps the only other economic issue that pushes the laity of non-economists to such heights of emotion.[6] Investors express indignation about inflation, consumers express concern about the cost of living, workers express worries about real wages. For some the fear of inflation has risen exponentially in the wake of the global financial crisis, as central banks have printed significant amounts of money (in a process known as quantitative policy). And yet in spite of all the talk and concern about inflation, and in spite of the attempts to protect against inflation's supposed corrosive effects, inflation is something that is often wildly misunderstood by investors, the general public and a truly alarming number of politicians.

This misunderstanding of inflation is not helped by modern media. In the past, economic analysis was conducted by trained economists who would hand down their pronouncements (shrouded with an appropriate degree of Delphic obscuration) to be reverentially received by the mass of the population with all the appropriate awe and deference that an economist's views deserve. Today, economic analysis has become economic anarchy. The amateur and unqualified economic pundit of the investment blog writes about consumer price inflation without actually grasping either its composition or its purpose. Business television channels want a simple, single-line graph that they can post on screen for thirty seconds, not a complex mass of numbers that are hedged with qualifications and 'yes, but…' caveats at every turning point. Our understanding of inflation is not helped by a world increasingly dominated by 'sound-bite economics'. Inflation as a concept is simple in that it is something that anyone of normal intelligence should be able to readily understand. However, inflation is not *simplistic* in that it cannot be reduced to a single number or applied indiscriminately. Inflation is at once simple and multifaceted.

The purpose of this book is to redress the balance a little. The aim is not to present a means of forecasting inflation as such. Economic models abound regarding inflation prediction; most of them are relatively dreary, many are far too mathematical in their approach, and few are of any real use to the investor or consumer trying to think about inflation. Instead of presenting a model for *forecasting* inflation, therefore, this book tries to present a means for *understanding* inflation. Understanding what inflation is, and what it is not, is something that is increasingly missing from investment decisions. A proper understanding of why inflation cannot and should not be reduced to a simplistic single figure will prevent investors making potentially damaging decisions. It also identifies some of the challenges policymakers face in balancing the competing forces of perception and reality.

This opening chapter therefore aims to set out what inflation actually is. Like any good economics student, it is as well to begin by defining the terms that are to be used. Once we have established what the word 'inflation' really means, we can get down to the serious business of debunking the myths that surround the idea, and end up by trying to consider inflation in a way that is useful.

So what is inflation?

At its most crude, inflation is the rate of change in prices. Which immediately raises the question: what is a price? A price represents a standardised and mutually agreed measure of what one person is prepared to receive in exchange for whatever goods or services that they can provide. Nowadays we tend to standardise prices in terms of money (meaning notes and coins, or more likely their virtual, electronic equivalent) but it could be anything. The cow has been a medium of exchange for millennia, perhaps for longer than any other form of physical currency. Sea shells, cigarettes, split lengths of a stick – anything will do, and all in their turn have been major forms of currency (in America, Germany and England, respectively). Price is just a convenient shorthand means of summarising the relative value of different goods and services. Price is needed as a metric because those values shift – a point which is absolutely critical to understanding inflation.

Prices change all the time. The price of any good is, broadly speaking, determined by the demand for the product and the amount of supply that exists for that product. The fickleness of fashion means that demand for goods will change over time. The marketplace of the school playground shows this as well as anything: stickers displaying airbrushed images of the latest boy band will command a healthy premium while the band is in fashion, but as the fortunes of the band ebb and their fans emerge from the ether of their influence (or 'grow up' and acquire a more sophisticated aural taste) so the price of such products will decline – until, of course, the band reforms a couple of decades hence and the products assume value as memorabilia. What we have here is demand driving up price in the early stage, prices falling as demand fades without any corresponding reduction in supply, and then finally a constrained supply giving scarcity value at a time when demand, albeit possibly misguided demand, re-emerges.

We should expect individual product prices to change frequently *relative to other prices*. Fashion, seasonal supply and demand patterns, the need to manage warehouse space for retailers – all of these things will cause specific prices to fluctuate. As any parent knows, the price of taking a vacation will tend to rise during the school holidays. This is a seasonal demand-driven price shift (demand rises, when the supply of hotel rooms and flights cannot rise, or at least cannot rise too drastically). There is no reason why the seasonal surge in demand for vacations should lead to an increase in the price of bread. Rising vacation costs represent a relative price shift, not a general increase in prices.

The price change of one product *relative to other products* is not inflation. Sarah Rogers's period in prison was not really the result of protesting about inflation, although that was probably of scant comfort to her. Sarah Rogers was incarcerated

Box 1.1 Let them buy bread

One of my earliest recollections, as a small child, was being entrusted with the task of going to the local shop to buy a loaf of bread. I was given a fifty pence coin, which was a great curiosity to me as my handling of money up until that point had tended to be confined to the smaller denominations – the coppers of one and two pence coins, and the five pence pieces that were still largely the pre-decimalisation shilling coins. I can remember the value of this being earnestly impressed upon me; a fifty pence coin represented a considerable sum of money, at a time when a loaf of bread cost sixteen pence. I was instructed to go to the shop, buy the loaf, and return with bread and change.

Inevitably, I dropped the coin on my way to the shop. The loss of something as valuable as a fifty pence piece was traumatising, so much so that I can still remember roughly where I must have dropped the money – it is somewhere around N51:38:17, E0:25:38 if anyone wants to go and look for it. Of course, nowadays, looking for a fifty pence coin may not seem to be worth the effort. Back when I lost the money, fifty pence was wealth beyond the dreams of avarice (at least, beyond the avaricious dreams of a small child). Fifty pence then was the equivalent of three loaves of bread. Today fifty pence will purchase half a loaf of bread. However, adjusting for the general rate of inflation the fifty pence I lost many years ago is worth around three pounds sixty-five pence today (in 2014). That equates to three and a half loaves of bread (currently retailing for around a pound a loaf).

The trauma of decades past demonstrates an important point. Within a general price rise (to hold the spending power of fifty pence then requires over seven times as much money today), relative prices will still shift (the price of a loaf of bread is six times what it was). Bread is relatively speaking cheaper today. The price of everything has risen, but the price of bread has risen by less than the price of other things.

as the result of protesting a single price change (albeit an important price change, and at a time of general inflation). But, as a general rule, policymakers should not seek to intervene as prices change relative to one another. To legislate that a packet of butter must always have the same price as a loaf of bread would be ridiculous. What if demand for butter falls because people switch to low-fat spreads? Should the policymakers of a more health-conscious nation intervene in the free market because the price of butter falls under such circumstances? Or because the relative price of bread has risen (if one were to barter for it, one would have to offer more butter to obtain a loaf of bread)? This would be an absurd state of affairs. In this example people have chosen to demand less butter, so there is no need for the price of butter to remain as high as it once was.

In spite of the patent absurdity of mandating that the price of a loaf of bread must always equate to the price of a packet of butter, policymakers have repeatedly been drawn to the siren calls of just such regulation. Medieval Europe is littered with examples of governments trying to hold back the incoming tide of relative price shifts by insisting that fixed prices be maintained. The fact that governments continually had to issue edicts on prices suggests quite strongly that none of these edicts were ever observed; the repeated failure of such policies did nothing to stop the attempt to legislate again. More recently, the Soviet Union's economy is a strong propaganda point for an economist arguing against relative price controls, with the resulting frequent shortfalls of specific products as fixed prices fail to balance supply and demand. US President Nixon's presiding over price controls (once as a bureaucrat during the Second World War, and once as president) was ultimately a failure on both occasions – in that relative price shifts were simply delayed, not prevented. Even in the twenty-first century we still find relative price shifts targeted by the media or politicians, provoking the general cry of 'something must be done'. Energy prices often provoke particularly shrill cries for regulation, and in many countries food prices are also regulated as a matter of course. Policymakers should guard against the siren calls of these attempts to brand relative price adjustment as a policy objective – and should politicians give way and confuse relative pricing with inflation, the consumer or the investor should be prepared to bet that the politicians will ultimately fail in any attempt at *relative* price control.

Relative prices are not therefore inflation and thus not a suitable objective for policymakers to pursue – with one caveat that we will come to. We should accept that not only *will* prices change with the ebb and flow of consumer demand (and product supply), but that prices *should* in fact change over time. What matters to policymakers, investors and consumers is not what one specific price is doing, but what prices overall are doing: inflation, in other words.

To qualify for the title 'inflation', any increase in prices needs to be across a broad range of products. This is because a broad-based increase in prices is likely to affect the quality of life of the average consumer in some way. Indeed, the modern concept of inflation originates in concerns about the 'cost of living' and the related concept of a 'living wage' (i.e. a wage that allows its recipient to maintain a stable quality of life over time). The idea that a government should intervene to target broad prices under the concept of the 'cost of living' is old; the concept of 'cost of living' dates to the early nineteenth-century debates about the Corn Laws in the United Kingdom (whereby the government intervened in the market for cereals, distorting the price).

It would be a sad outcome for humanity and, indeed, economists if the quality of life were held hostage to the relative shifts in price of boy band collectibles, or even the price of bread and butter. It is not single price changes that matter to the quality of life, but the broad range of price adjustment. If the price of a wide range of goods and services is rising, then people will be worse off – in that they will be able to purchase fewer goods and will enjoy a lower material standard of living, in the absence of an improvement in their income.

It could be added that a broad-based price change is indicative of some underlying economic shift, beyond the fickleness of fashion or seasonal demand. If the prices of disparate and unrelated products are all increasing at the same time, that would seem a reasonable indicator that some broader macroeconomic force is at work behind the scenes. The underlying economic trends are a legitimate concern for policymakers.

The caveat to the idea that relative price changes do not constitute inflation is that there is one relative price that *does* matter. The astute reader of this book will have spotted that if the price of *money itself* has changed, that is a relative price shift that would and indeed should also be considered a measure of inflation. As prices are determined by supply and demand balances, if the supply of whatever is the medium of exchange (notes and coins, sea shells, cattle, gold, cigarettes, etc.) were to increase *relative* to the supply of everything else, and increase relative to the demand for whatever is the medium of exchange, then the price of all goods would rise in money (medium of exchange) terms. This is a relative price shift that policymakers have a duty to control, because it is inflation. In many, though not all, instances policymakers will also have a duty to control such inflation because very often it is the government that controls the relative supply of money (the medium of exchange). That has not always been the case, as we shall see in the next chapter, but in modern economics it is generally the case.

Real and nominal

This brings us then to the related concept of real and nominal measurement. Because so much in the world of economics is about the 'value' of things, and that value is nowadays calculated in terms of money, it is important to distinguish between times when something has become more valuable (desirable, essential), and times when the price of something has changed because of inflation. To go back to the example of a loaf of bread – the rise in the price of a loaf of bread from sixteen pence to one hundred pence does not mean that bread is nearly six times as valuable, or six times as important, or six times as desirable as it was in the past. The nominal price of bread has gone up, but the real price has in fact gone down (bread prices have fallen *relative* to the prices of other goods and services). Bread is actually less important or less desirable to the British consumer today than it was in the past.

Real measures therefore give us data adjusted for inflation and as such reflect the value or importance of a product or service. Nominal measures make no allowance for inflation. This distinction is generally well understood, though often misapplied, in the modern environment. The high inflation episodes of the 1970s and 1980s have caused people to learn how to distinguish between real and nominal. If wage increases fail to keep pace with inflation, for example, workers will soon identify the fact with almost as much readiness as any economist. However, the distinction between real and nominal is a relatively new distinction. Although there were attempts to distinguish the concepts in the 1920s and the 1930s (principally in France, where the economy suffered a significant bout of inflation after the First World War), as late as the 1950s the Bank of England did not often make the distinction between real and nominal economic variables.

So, if nominal is the face value, and real is the face value adjusted for inflation, what inflation rate should be used to create the real figure? This, as we shall see, is one of the great problems with inflation in the modern world. All too often inflation is taken as meaning the headline consumer price data that is published by most governments, and it is the consumer price index (often abbreviated as CPI) that is subtracted from nominal data to calculate the underlying real value. However, this is not necessarily the right index to be used when trying to calculate real values. Indeed, from an economic point of view, the headline consumer price index is almost certain to be the *wrong* index to be using in calculating the real value of anything. And if the wrong price index is used, then investors, or consumers, or writers of investment blogs will end up miscalculating changes to their standards of living. Real will not, in fact, be real; using the wrong inflation index makes real data a fantasy.

Different measures of inflation

Officially there is a multitude of statistics that measure inflation. The economist is spoilt for choice when it comes to pricing information. Broadly speaking, however, the price data that is available will come into one of four generic categories.

The first and broadest measure of inflation is the gross domestic product deflator. Gross domestic product, generally known as GDP, is an attempt to measure all the economic activity that takes place in an economy in a three-month period. This is done, essentially, by adding up the value of all economic activity (goods and services) that takes place. However, the notion that GDP measures what is happening in an economy is hindered by price movements. Economists want to know if more physical goods are being produced, or more valuable services are being consumed. If prices rise, the nominal value of economic activity is going up, but in fact there may be no increase in actual (real) economic activity – no more goods made, no more services performed. So a deflator is used to strip away the effect of price changes, and allow the economist to determine whether or not more things are happening in an economy.

The deflator is therefore an attempt to measure all prices in the economy; the price of every good and every service. It has to measure the price of every good and every service, at least every legally supplied good and service, in order to be able to tell if economic activity is really changing. So why not just stick with this as the inflation rate to use? If this is measuring the price of everything in the economy, surely that is the best way of determining whether living standards are rising or not?

The problem with using a deflator is that it is too broad for some measures. Does an individual person's standard of living suffer because the price of a gas turbine rises? As most people do not use gas turbines around the home, and will therefore never purchase a gas turbine, they do not really care what happens if the price of a gas turbine changes. The price of a gas turbine is a matter of supreme indifference to most right-thinking consumers. To say that the general population is worse off because gas turbines are more expensive is not terribly helpful, nor is it likely to be particularly true. Thus, using the GDP deflator is not appropriate as an inflation indicator for living standards (for example). GDP deflators have a role, and it is a valuable role, but it is not much use in terms of day to day investor or consumer decision-making.

The next set of prices is producer and wholesale prices, which as the name suggests are the prices charged by the producers (or wholesalers) of goods. Producer and wholesale price indices are what have traditionally formed the basis of inflation calculations – for much of the nineteenth century these prices were the only prices that were regularly reported in the media. Producer prices were popular with economists and statisticians because they were quite easy to observe. In most industries there are a relatively limited number of producers, while there may be hundreds of consumer retail outlets. It is far easier to collect prices of goods as they leave the factory (or the mine, or farm) than to try and calculate the price of the product that the consumer is actually purchasing. Further, in some cases the market where products are traded will be standardised (think of the price of oil, or many food commodities; even something like frozen concentrated orange juice trades in a standardised marketplace at the producer level). The economic historian can indulge in one-stop shopping and acquire a consistent series of producer prices from a single source with minimal effort. Minimal effort is a highly desirable outcome for your average economic historian.

The problem with relying on producer price data is that while it is relatively simple to collect, being standardised, it misses out an awful lot of the price that the consumer ends up paying. A huge amount happens to products after they leave the factory, mine or farm gate. Products have to be advertised, stored, transported, occasionally repackaged, and ultimately sold to consumers. Indeed, in most cases what happens in the final stages of the distribution chain is what matters most to the prices paid by the consumer.

Producer price data can be useful – it can be very important for equity analysts and equity investors trying to estimate the likely outlook for corporate profits, for example, as it represents either the change in revenue received by a company or (if the company is a retail store) the change in some of the costs paid by a company. Of course for most companies, producer price inflation will represent both cost changes and revenue changes. Producer price statistics sometimes make the distinction between input producer prices and output producer prices, or between prices of different stages of production, for this reason. Producer prices can also indicate the presence of inflation risks for the future; if a producer is raising a price today, there has to be an increased probability that the retailer will seek to pass on that increase to the consumer in the future. Nonetheless, because so much that matters to consumers is missed out in the calculation of producer and wholesale prices, the application of producer price inflation must be limited.

So, after a quick tour of the universal concept of the GDP deflator, and the historical but limited concept of producer prices, we can turn to the third set of prices, and to the concept that most people think of when they think of inflation: consumer prices, which are obligingly provided with a monthly or quarterly regularity by virtually every government on the planet. Despite the ubiquitous nature of consumer prices, however, they are not necessarily the best measure of inflation to look at. As later chapters will discuss, the composition of consumer prices means that they may not in fact reflect the cost of living of the typical consumer. Moreover, adjusting the nominal value of certain concepts like debt using the consumer price index is completely wrong.

The misapplication of consumer price inflation is a problem that will crop up repeatedly in the pages that follow. For now, it is sufficient to say that virtually no consumer actually experiences the price inflation rate reported by official consumer price data, and virtually no debtor should care what the official consumer price data tells them.

A further problem around consumer prices is the limited amount of data that economists have to work with. Regularly published consumer price inflation does not have a terribly long history. Before the Second World War, consumer prices did not begin to pretend to reflect the change in price experienced by the 'average' or even the 'typical' consumer in the economy. Early consumer price measures were aimed at the prices of the urban working class (even today the US consumer price data distinguishes 'all urban' consumer price inflation). Generally speaking, we are working with sixty to seventy years' worth of consumer price data. The problem with this is that seventy years or so does not cover that many economic cycles; over the post-war period the United States is generally considered to have experienced twelve economic cycles. Considering inflation over the development of an economic cycle is somewhat hampered by this.

The missing inflation measure from the quartet that we must consider is wage inflation. Wages – or more broadly incomes – are simply the price of human endeavour. Although much of the attention surrounding wage inflation tends to focus on the role wage inflation plays in driving consumer price inflation, this approach underestimates the importance of wage inflation in its own right.

Wage inflation was originally closely tied to the overall concept of inflation – the notion of a living wage was as much about the change in the wage level as it was about the change in the cost of living. Traditionally, economists have referred to the concept as wage inflation, but perhaps we should say 'income inflation' as salaries (monthly fixed payments rather than weekly or daily payments contingent on hours worked) and other forms of income from investments, pensions and benefits play a larger role than they used to. However we refer to it, it is obvious that the affordability of goods and services, or the affordability of a certain lifestyle, will depend both on the cost of the desired lifestyle and on the income that finances it.

Wage or income inflation is particularly important when considering how inflation impacts consumer debt, something that will be examined in Chapter 9. Indeed, the misapplication of consumer price inflation to debt and debt interest rates, when wage or income inflation is the appropriate measure, is one of the more damaging problems that a poor understanding of inflation can produce.

The four broad forms of inflation here fracture into myriad sub-indices. One can manufacture producer prices for different industries. Consumer price indices can exclude certain items ('core' consumer price inflation, excluding food and energy, is a particularly popular concept which will be examined in Chapter 4). Wages or incomes can be subject to all sorts of adjustments. All of these indices can register some form of generalised price increase however – that is to say inflation in some form or another.

What drives inflation?

Having established what inflation is, we should spend at least some time considering what causes inflation. Unfortunately, this is not as easy to do as one might suppose. What causes inflation is a topic that divides both economists and policymakers.

Really, there are two stories that can be told about an inflation episode. A general price increase could either be caused by an increase in the supply of money relative to goods and services, or a general increase in demand for all things relative to supply of all things. The former is a very specific relative price change, changing the price of money itself. The latter is more macro determined and could be caused by a number of factors, for instance a population increase, a natural disaster (disrupting supply), a war, or any one of a number of other disruptions.

Any consideration of the causes of inflation allows the introduction of the sole economic equation of this book. As a general rule there is no need to use equations to understand economics; we all live and act in economies, and relationships should be understandable without dressing economics up with the false façade of mathematical precision. However, this particular equation has entered into, if not the popular consciousness, at least fairly widespread circulation. It is the 'Fisher equation of exchange', named after the economist Irving Fisher.

A couple of thing about the Fisher equation: first it was not discovered by Fisher, second it is not really an equation. The relationship was discussed by John Stuart Mill more than half a century before Fisher, and the concept is not so much an equation as an accounting identity. Fisher was, however, the first to put it into a pseudo-mathematical formula. The identity states:

$$M \times V = P \times Q$$

That rather bald statement perhaps requires a word or two of elaboration. M stands for the money supply. V stands for the velocity of circulation – which is basically how often money changes hands. P stands for the level of prices. Finally, Q stands for the quantity of goods and services sold in an economy. So what the identity is telling us is that the value of goods and services sold in a given time must be equal to the amount of money in circulation multiplied by the number of times money changes hands. The right hand side of the identity is also known as nominal GDP. This is all fairly logical (accounting identities generally are, for one of the few attributes an economist will acknowledge in accountants is their logic). The number of transactions multiplied by the value of the transactions is, indeed, one of the ways that nominal GDP is actually calculated.

No one disputes the identity. The arguments surrounding the Fisher equation arise because of disputes about what drives inflation, and thus what policymakers should do in order to control inflation. The contention of monetarists is that inflation is all about the money supply. This assumes a relatively stable velocity of circulation, and real GDP that is mainly influenced by other factors, which leaves a direct relationship between the money supply and the price level. It has led to a famous dictum from the economist Milton Friedman, to the effect that 'inflation is always and everywhere a monetary phenomenon'.[7]

Those who argue that the level of demand is driving inflation reject these assumptions. If a general increase in demand takes place while the quantity of goods supplied remains unchanged or relatively stable, inflation is the likely result. The money supply can remain stable in such circumstances, but the velocity of circulation will effectively increase (because people are scrambling for goods that are in short supply, and will spend money as soon as they get it). Imagine a frenzy of people spending money as soon as they make it, for fear that the goods will not be available if they do not 'buy now'. The hysterical reaction to the introduction of the latest toy or gadget conjures up some sense of this frantic desire to spend (think of the mob scenes outside stores coinciding with the introduction of the latest smartphone, or on 'Black Friday' after the US Thanksgiving holiday).

So, which side is correct? The honest answer is that there are inflationary episodes that support both sides. Excess money supply has caused some periods of inflation, and indeed the extremes of hyperinflation. On the other hand, there are also instances of general demand driving inflation – prices in a besieged town are a good instance. In the siege of Paris in 1871, food prices rose dramatically because demand outstripped supply, and the contents of the Paris zoos were sold for their meat. The hippopotamus of the Jardin des Plantes at 80,000 francs found no buyer – not because of any squeamishness on the part of the Parisians (with the right sauce, no doubt it could be rendered palatable) – but was because it was too expensive. The elephants, at 27,000 francs for a pair, were less fortunate.[8]

The root cause of inflation is perhaps less important to the investor than being able to identify the early warning signs that inflation is coming. Policymakers, investors, and indeed consumers and business owners, need to spot inflation when it is coming and consider the consequences. This brings us to the next stage in the voyage of discovery about inflation: is inflation really a problem?

What is so bad about a bit of inflation?

In 1933, the American economist Eleanor Dulles boldly asserted with complete self-assurance that 'few, if any, would contend that a continuous rise in prices is a possible basis for economic life'.[9] From the vantage point of 1933, an eminent US economist could not possibly comprehend how civilisation could continue if prices rose year after year after year. And yet, despite Ms Dulles's most powerful of assertions, the world seems to have struggled on with continuous increases in prices for the past seventy years or so. Indeed, the continuous rise in prices that has occurred since the Second World War has not only been possible as a basis for some semblance of economic life, it has been possible alongside the most dramatic increase in global living standards that humanity has ever experienced. It would be going too far to assert that the continuous increase in prices was the *basis* of this prosperity, but the idea of continuous inflation does not appear to have been too economically damaging to living standards. So why is the fear of inflation so great?

Economic theory provides us with one answer through something called 'loss aversion', a concept that will pop up time and again in this modest volume. Loss aversion implies that most people sadly lack the rationality that is the hallmark of every economist. Ordinary people, lacking the impartial detachment that an economics degree instantly confers, irrationally feel more strongly about losing something than they do about gaining the same thing. Give someone $100 and they feel happy. Take the $100 away from them, and they will feel worse than they did before the whole monetary give and take began. The pain of a dollar lost outweighs the pleasure of a dollar gained.

The fact that the loss of x weighs more than gaining x is a key part of understanding why inflation is so often viewed with a kind of horror. Inflation takes away the spending power of money. Imagine working for five years to accumulate enough savings so as to be able to purchase a car (for the benefit of American readers, who may now be exhibiting some confusion, it is actually possible to save money out of income in order to purchase a car – in some parts of the world, purchasing a car using credit is not actually a social requirement). At the very moment of purchase, the price of the car doubles – and thus can no longer be afforded. The halving of the value of one's savings (in real terms) is a significant loss, and the saver will feel it acutely and probably be quite annoyed.[10]

Other features of inflation inspire a sense of fear and loathing. Inflation is quite a subtle form of loss. No one is likely to claim that being robbed at gun point would be a pleasant experience, but it would be a quantifiable experience. One would know what one has lost, and one would know that the loss has happened and is finished with. Inflation is not like that; its criminal equivalent is probably the leaching effects of blackmail rather than the abrupt loss of a mugging. Real losses from inflation can creep up on the consumer or investor unawares. The gradual erosion of spending power may not be immediately evident. When the losses from inflation do become evident (the consumer suddenly notices that it costs an extra $10 to fill up the family sports utility vehicle, or an extra £10 to pay for a week's travel on the London Underground) there is then likely to be a lingering suspicion that the losses may be more than observed. If one has not noticed inflation's corrosive power in the past, perhaps one is still overlooking aspects of the damage wrought by inflation even now?

And then there is the uncertainty about the future. If inflation has already caused losses, what might it do in the future? Will it cause equal losses in the year ahead? Or will those losses be greater? Or could inflation fade away and the losses become less? Uncertainty generally unnerves people, and uncertainty about losses, which assume disproportionate importance because of loss aversion, can bring about a state of nervous collapse.

In fact, the uncertainty about inflation lies at the very heart of the damage inflation produces. At the risk of causing the reader to choke over the pages of this book (it may be a good idea to put down any drink you are holding) let us quickly debunk one of the key assumptions made about inflation.

Inflation itself need not do any economic damage at all.

There are certain conditions attached to this, but under the right conditions inflation of 1,000 per cent per year could be perfectly acceptable, and cause no damage to the economy. The point is that if investors, consumers and workers know *with certainty* that inflation is going to be 1,000 per cent in the coming year, they will adjust their demands accordingly. Workers will insist that their pay adjusts appropriately. Savers will insist that their bank accounts (or other investments) yield them at least 1,000 per cent interest each year – which means of course that the value of their stock of savings and investments adjusts for the rise in prices, and the spending power of their savings is not eaten away by inflation. Borrowers will be required to pay more than 1,000 per cent interest on their loans; 1,003 per cent, for instance, which would equate to a real interest rate of 3 per cent. A 3 per cent real interest rate is perfectly reasonable, and there can be few economists who would suggest that a 3 per cent real interest cost would be significantly detrimental to economic growth. In this instance, the economy can manage to deal with high inflation because it factors inflation in to all of its price contracts – a process that economists refer to as indexation. This is hardly a novel idea. The colony of Massachusetts adjusted the pay of its militia to take account of changes in local prices during the American Revolution.[11]

In the modern age even the consumer can get by without cost or inconvenience in a world of 1,000 per cent inflation. Traditionally, high inflation has produced what economists (ever erudite) called 'shoe leather costs'. This referred to the fact that in a high inflation environment, consumers would have to keep rushing to their bank to withdraw their money and spend it. One could only ever withdraw small amounts of cash at very frequent intervals otherwise inflation would eat away at its value. In a hyperinflation episode to hold cash for a day or even a few hours would be foolhardy. The time and effort of constantly withdrawing cash from the bank, accompanied by the need to keep repairing shoes worn out by the toing and froing from the bank, is a cost.

Nowadays, shoe leather costs are something of a quaint acronym. Everyone can behave like a member of the British royal family, and not carry cash. A debit card, linked to a bank account accruing interest of 1,000 per cent per annum on a daily basis (on an hourly basis, if one desires) removes shoe leather costs entirely. One does not have to carry cash. Indeed, in some economies (those of the Nordic region, for instance), the use of credit and debit cards has become so commonplace as to make physical cash almost redundant – and this without the inflation incentive. In Sweden only around 20 per cent of transactions in shops now involve cash, and between 65 per cent and 75 per cent of *bank branches* refuse to handle cash. Electronic transactions (and not just cards, but mobile phones and direct transfer payments) dominate.[12] It is a similar if less extreme story elsewhere. In the United Kingdom only 53 per cent of real-world transactions in 2013 used cash.[13]

Other costs have fallen before the advances of technology. Germany's hyperinflation led to a surge in employment of bookkeepers, to try and keep track of all of the zeros as the currency lost control. Those bookkeepers cost money, and so inflation added to the cost of doing business. In the 1970s, the tables that calculated bond yields for a given bond price became obsolete as bond yields rose and bond prices fell below the limits conceived by the authors of the reference books, necessitating time-consuming calculations, which cost money to those banks trading in the bond markets. Computers remove both bookkeeper and bond yield problems at the touch of a key. Computerised price displays and bar code scanners remove even the cost of physically re-pricing products by attaching sticky labels to goods – the 'sticker price' cost of inflation has also faded into the obscurity of ancient history.

Doubtless there are still some readers spluttering incoherently at the idea that inflation need not be an economic problem, and it does indeed go against human instincts – this refusal to accept that inflation need not be any trouble in a modern economy is loss aversion bubbling up to the surface of the reader's subconscious. The fear of loss of purchasing power is a potent fear. But this is the point. The key assumption behind the idea that inflation is not a problem was that there was *certainty* in the prediction of future inflation. That certainty allows a society to set up a system that entirely compensates for the inflation. Wage earners, investors, borrowers, consumers – all are compensated or pay compensation for the impact of inflation. No one loses.

The problems with inflation start when there is uncertainty about the future of inflation. A gnawing doubt, an insidious voice in the darkness that malevolently whispers 'what if economists' forecasts of inflation are wrong?' will quickly grow into a fear that creates a significant economic cost. In a perfect world no one would listen to those quiet voices that dare to challenge the omniscience of the economics profession. Unfortunately, we do not live in a perfect world.

The moment uncertainty creeps into the popular consciousness, the costs of inflation start to ratchet up. The saver says 'I want 1,000 per cent interest to compensate me for inflation, but just in case the economists are wrong in their forecasts I want another 100 per cent interest as an insurance policy.' This is known as the inflation uncertainty risk premium. That cost is passed onto the borrower, who has to find an extra 100 per cent interest payment to assuage the fears and insecurities of the saver. If inflation does come in at 1,000 per cent as economists forecast (for how could economists be wrong?) then the real cost of borrowing has gone up to a completely usurious 103 per cent. Inflation uncertainty is a very observable addition to the real cost of borrowing money.

In a more extreme case (often found in hyperinflation episodes), the saver may decide that saving is not worth the risk. Why save, even if the interest rate is 1,100 per cent, if there is a chance that inflation is 1,200 per cent? A small chance that inflation is 1,200 per cent would mean that the saver was worse off by saving. In which case it would be better, perhaps, to buy something now rather than save for the future. Most hyperinflation episodes conclude with a frantic attempt by consumers to convert their currency into tangible goods like canned food or consumer durables, for fear inflation will destroy the value of any money that is held as an asset. But if savers choose to spend rather than save, then there will be no funds for investing – investment collapses, and future growth then suffers.

If absolutely everything could be indexed against inflation, then even inflation uncertainty could also be removed as a risk. In such a world, everything would be quoted in real terms, and the movements of inflation would be of scant interest. But this is impossible. The problem, as we shall come to discover in the coming chapters, is that inflation takes many different forms depending on who is contemplating what inflation is. To index everything would require myriad indices to be created.

So, for an economist, or an investor, or a consumer, the damage that is wrought by inflation is not because prices change per se. The damage wrought by inflation is because people are uncertain about the future path of inflation, and demand additional compensation as an insurance against that uncertainty. Economic growth accelerates when people take risks – the risk to invest, the risk to lend, the risk to borrow. If there is an increase in a risk premium as a result of inflation uncertainty, then taking a risk becomes a more costly operation. That means that fewer risks will be taken, and the economy overall will suffer.

Disinflation and deflation

If inflation is bad not because prices go up, but because it creates uncertainty, can we say the same thing about the other side of the inflation coin? Should we say that falling prices – deflation – are not bad either, except that they may create uncertainty?

Unfortunately, deflation has the potential to wreak more economic damage than does inflation. But before coming to that let us quickly clarify the distinction between the different forms of falling prices.

The first form is disinflation, which is not falling prices at all. Disinflation is when the inflation rate falls but prices do not – when 3 per cent inflation moves to 2 per cent inflation, for example. Note that the price level is rising in that scenario, but rising more slowly than it has done in the past. Unless an economy has embarked on a hyperinflation spiral, disinflation will be a periodic feature of any economy. Of itself, disinflation is not a problem, unless it escapes from the control of policymakers. If that happens there may be a period of deflation.

Deflation is outright negative inflation – the level of prices this year is lower than it was last year. Economists will, as a rule, make a distinction between 'good' deflation and 'bad' deflation. Good deflation will take place if an economy has become more efficient in the production or the supply of a range of products or services. Greater efficiency means that more can be supplied at less cost. Such deflation is likely to be temporary, as the improvement in efficiency is likely to be a one-off structural change rather than a persistent improvement. The key characteristic of good deflation is that consumers will respond to the fall in prices by increasing their demand ('things are cheaper, so we can buy more'). The increase in supply of products or services is then met with an increase in demand, and thus prices stabilise over the medium term.

Bad deflation is the more corrosive form of deflation, and occurs when there is not enough demand in the economy (it is sometimes known as 'demand deficient' deflation for this very reason). This form of deflation can be very long lasting. Consumers effectively say 'I won't buy now, because it will be cheaper next year', and then the following year say once again 'I won't buy now because it will be cheaper next year'. The cycle repeats year in, year out (for more on this, see Japan). A bad deflation scenario is likely to result in negative growth and eventually negative wage or income inflation.

As with inflation, uncertainty about deflation will create a risk. Should a business borrow money at 5 per cent interest to invest in a new factory? If it is certain that it will be able to raise its prices by 3 per cent each year, and the new factory will enable it to increase production 3 per cent each year, then it should. But what if economic circumstances mean that the price of its product falls 1 per cent for a year? Then the income from building the new factory will not cover the debt. If there is a risk of deflation, there is a disincentive to invest.

To the regular distortion of risk there are then the two additional problems, snappily branded 'the zero interest rate bound' and 'the inflation illusion'. The zero interest rate bound is pretty simple. It is difficult to get interest rates below 0 per cent (in nominal terms), at least in the real world. A government or a central bank may lend at negative interest rates and chalk the loss up to policy stimulus, but the private investor generally has no incentive to lend at negative rates. Why should an individual lend money out (taking a risk by doing so) only to get less money back in the future? It is better to keep the money in a bank, or *in extremis* keep it under the mattress or futon or whatever.

An exception to the zero bound on interest rates was in the depths of the financial crisis that began in 2008. When confidence in the banking system collapsed, large investors felt that it was better to invest their cash into very short-dated government debt (Treasury bills) even if those Treasury bills generated negative interest rates. The certainty of a small loss from a negative interest rate was felt to be preferable to the possibility of a cataclysmic loss if the bank holding your deposit failed. Why not hoard the cash at home? Because those who rushed to accept negative interest rates on their Treasury bills were very, very large investors. Hoarding a billion dollars under the mattress would require a very large mattress, and make for a rather uncomfortable night's sleep. Storing a billion dollars in hundred dollar bills beneath a US king-sized mattress would raise the mattress somewhere between nine and ten feet off the ground. One might also suppose that storing a billion dollars under the mattress could also make one's home something of a conspicuous target for local burglars.

Ignoring the exceptional circumstances of extreme financial system distress, when a negative interest rate is viewed as being more like an insurance premium that is worth paying for certainty, the inability of real-world nominal interest rates to move below zero creates further economic problems. The zero rate bound matters to an economy because if interest rates cannot go below zero, and the relevant inflation measure is dropping 5 per cent per year, how do policymakers lower real interest rates to stimulate the economy? Real interest rates are (positive) 5 per cent in this scenario, because zero rates less deflation of 5 per cent will generate a positive real return of 5 per cent.

So a deflation episode encourages savers to hoard cash and keep the money at home. It prevents the central bank lowering the real interest rate on credit to a level that encourages borrowing. The worse deflation is, the greater the disincentive to spend money. The worse deflation is, the greater the disincentive to lend money. The worse deflation is, the higher the real rate of interest on borrowing and thus the greater the disincentive to invest in the real economy. The worse deflation is, the greater the risk of weaker economic growth, and the greater the risk that deflation will get worse.

Thus, zero real-world interest rates in a deflationary environment will lead to cash being hoarded in physical form and investment all but ceasing. This is not generally considered terribly constructive for economic development. As a rule, economists do not *intentionally* advocate policies that encourage an economy to follow a downwards death spiral.

The second problem with negative inflation is the inflation illusion, and in particular what this means for wages and competitiveness. We are going back to that most useful of economic concepts, loss aversion. The irrational wage earner cannot really be distinguished from the irrational consumer (not least because they are one and the same person much of the time). Employees do not like taking pay cuts, because they feel that they are losing something to which they are 'entitled'. The employer who rationally explains that this is due to falling prices and that the employee is just as well off as before in real terms is not likely to be listened to calmly and rationally, no matter how many economic texts are cited in defence of this self-evident truth. This means that in a deflationary environment, it is pretty hard to get workers to accept a nominal (but not necessarily a real) pay cut. In many countries, indeed, cuts in nominal wages are illegal.

The aversion to taking a nominal pay cut, and the ability to prevent nominal pay cuts from being imposed, increased as labour became more organised. This fact was identified by the economist Lord Keynes in the aftermath of the First World War, noting that the more unionised labour market of the 1920s was likely to resist downwards moves in nominal wages. It was an important issue, because the United Kingdom re-established the pound at its pre-war level (against gold), with price levels substantially higher than they had been in 1913. This situation called for at least some downwards flexibility in nominal wages if competitiveness was to be maintained, and the organised nature of the labour market made that unlikely.

It is worth noting in passing that there is some flexibility, if part of the employee's compensation is in the form of a variable bonus. Not paying a bonus is unlikely to be met with much joy on the part of the employee, but the failure to pay a bonus one year will be accepted more readily than the demand that one's basic salary is cut. The reason for this is that the employee never possessed the bonus, so loss aversion does not really apply (one cannot mourn the loss of something that one has never possessed). However, this occurs only when a bonus is never paid and thus never possessed – never 'in one's hands' metaphorically speaking. A bonus clawback where a bonus is paid, and then taken back again after payment, for whatever reason, will be considered in just as negative a light as a cut in basic pay, because this is something where possession has been granted and then revoked.

This means that a deflation environment can damage an economy's international competitiveness (as the real cost of labour remains stubbornly high), while at the same time constraining investment and long-term growth prospects. The costs of 'bad' deflation are at least as damaging, and possibly more damaging, than the costs of inflation.

The truth about inflation

The central point to take away from this chapter is that it is not inflation that is damaging, but the uncertainty about inflation that is damaging. Inflation stability should be the objective of any policymaker, because (providing that they are convincing) making inflation control a policy objective should minimise inflation uncertainty risk, which will then promote investment and economic growth. Policymakers should not worry about individual price movements – relative price adjustment is a sign of a healthy economy.

It is important to stress that none of this is an argument in favour of inflation. If inflation stability is the ideal for economic development, keeping risks to a minimum, then inflation stability is most likely to be achieved in a relatively low inflation environment. The risk of inflation coming in 5 per cent away from forecast is generally going to be greater if inflation is around 100 per cent than if inflation is around 2 per cent. Policymakers therefore need to find some happy medium for inflation. The ideal inflation will avoid the Scylla of a number so high that it creates increased inflation uncertainty, while at the same time skirting the Charybdis of deflation with its attendant additional problems. Modern central banks have tended to settle on a target rate of between 2 per cent and 3 per cent as either an explicit or an implicit target, which seems to steer an appropriate middle course between these twin threats.

In pursuit of a better understanding of inflation and what it means to consumers and investors, the rest of this book is an attempt to destroy some of the myths that surround inflation. It is not a prediction about what is likely to happen to inflation in the coming years, because such a question cannot be answered properly – it is too vague, too imprecise. Inflation could go up or down depending on whether you are rich or poor, young or old, in the UK or Japan, a saver or a borrower. What this book sets out to do is to help give a better understanding of what inflation is (and what inflation is not), which will help the reader to face the future with greater confidence.

The next chapter starts the process by debunking the idea that inflation is a relatively new concept, with a quick tour of inflation through the ages (and a survey of the different causes of the inflation episodes that have occurred). After that we turn with some trepidation to tackle the role of gold and inflation – and why acolytes of the barbarous relic of gold as a form of money or as a store of value are so misguided.

The following set of chapters looks in turn at some of the problems of inflation in a modern industrialised economy, considering what inflation really is and how the perception of inflation can be manipulated. Some of the sacred cows of the economic and investment blogosphere will be gently led to sacrifice on the altar of economic common sense; looking at the relationship of money printing and inflation, quality and inflation, what sort of inflation the official statistics cater for, and how foreigners influence (or fail to influence) inflation.

The final two chapters deal with investment and inflation – tackling one of the most pervasive and most dangerous misunderstandings about inflation (the debt–inflation myth), and considering the investment and policy implications of what inflation truly is.

Whether the headline consumer price index is low or high, we live in a world where inflation matters. In the modern world, understanding that inflation is more complex than the headline consumer price figure implies may be the most important lesson to learn from inflation in the twenty-first century.

Notes

1 Quoted in Sparling (1933) p 3.
2 *Ipswich Journal* (1795).
3 Haupt in Trentman (2012) p 276.
4 Stapleford (2009) p 3.
5 Jackson and Saunders (2012) p 66.
6 Easterly and Fischer (2000) cite a survey of thirty-eight economies that ranks inflation and high prices as the third most important policy priority (out of a range including non-economic policies). Combined with 'having enough money to live on', which is associated with inflation via real living standards, inflation and real living standards were the top policy priorities.
7 Friedman (1970), citing his earlier work *Inflation: Causes and Consequences*, published in 1963.
8 Horne (1967) p 179.
9 Dulles (1933) p 79.
10 Shiller (1996) looked specifically at non-economists' attitudes to inflation and found that the belief that inflation would reduce their real buying power was the main concern by an overwhelming margin. What economists would consider valid concerns (inconvenience, etc.) barely registered with non-economists.
11 Stapleford (2009) p 10.
12 Magnusson and Gustafsson (2013).
13 Data from the British Retail Consortium.

2 A brief history of inflation

> Greet prees at market maketh deere ware, And to greet cheep is holde at litel prys [A great crowd at the market makes wares expensive, And too great a supply makes them of little value].
>
> (Geoffrey Chaucer, *The Wife of Bath*)

All too often inflation is considered as a modern concept. The belief that inflation began at some point in the early 1970s is a misremembering of history, perhaps fuelled by a desire to castigate floating exchange rates or paper currency as the origin of the problem. In fact, inflation is an economic phenomenon that dates back millennia. For inflation to be present, only two conditions really have to be met. The first condition, fairly obviously, is the existence of money; although only the concept of money (as a reference medium of exchange) is strictly necessary. Inflation can take place perfectly easily in the absence of physical money, if credit is available instead. But the general price level must rise, and be understood to be rising, for inflation to be present. Money as a frame of reference is therefore necessary.

The second condition for inflation is perhaps less obvious than the presence of money itself. Let us turn, for one last time, to Sarah Rogers of Fordingbridge – before leaving the poor woman alone. What was the most salient point of Sarah's campaign for cheap butter? The most salient point was that Sarah Rogers was not making the butter herself. Sarah was not out on the streets, protesting over the price of milk (as a raw ingredient for butter). What had got Sarah so upset was the price of the finished product that she wanted to purchase. Sarah was buying the butter, ready-made, from someone else (specifically from one Hannah Dawson, who appears to have been rather upset at having her butter being taken and a below-market price offered in exchange – hence the whole regrettable, and frankly unpleasant, business of the prosecution and jail time for Sarah Rogers). For inflation to have any relevance at all in modern life there needs to be some dependence on the labour or output of others. Self-sufficiency makes inflation an entirely meaningless concept. What this means, in practical terms, is that inflation is an urban concept.

The creation of towns and cities automatically detaches the consumer from the means of directly providing for their needs from their own land and labour.

Urbanisation necessarily means that food, at the very least, must come from outside, beyond what can be produced on the limited amount of land that urban conurbation makes available. Towns also tend to encourage labour specialisation, which the founder of modern economics, Adam Smith, so approvingly referred to as the 'division of labour'. Specialisation goes hand in hand with urbanisation, because it allows groups of specialists to come together to produce a finished product, as well as providing a convenient supply for all those essentials that are not produced in the home of the specialist. But specialisation means that the consumer is also detached from surviving on the product of their own labour alone. If one has become a specialised producer the generality of need cannot be met with one's own physical output. The consumer has to pay for products made by others, and accordingly to pay for their labour, and raises the funds for doing that by selling the product of their own labour in turn (or conceivably finding someone willing to lend the consumer money, in the expectation that future labour will lead to that money being repaid). With specialisation and urbanisation comes the ability for prices to start changing, and at the very least for relative prices, including those of labour, to shift. Is a pair of boots worth two shirts, or three? Are the services of a priest worth more or less than the services of a magistrate?

The more urban, and indeed the more urbane, the consumer becomes, the more important inflation is likely to be as an indicator of the consumer's standard of living. The modern consumer in a developed economy makes very, very little of what they consume at home; and they must pay for all that is manufactured outside the home. If the price of the labour, equipment and so forth is subject to change, then the consumer will face inflationary (or disinflationary or deflationary) forces. The sixteenth-century household, even an urban household, would most often make cloth at home. The eighteenth-century household would not necessarily make cloth, but certainly would make clothes (Jane Austen's novel *Northanger Abbey* talks of the genteel heroine making shirts for her brother, for instance). The nineteenth-century household would have made far more of their prepared food than today's household, and even in the mid-twentieth century it was the norm to make jams and preserves in the home. The modern era, where shop bought (or internet bought) is the dominant means of consumption, is an era where inflation matters more than ever before.

The more developed an economy, the higher the proportion of a consumer's standard of living that depends on goods and services being 'bought in', and thus the higher the proportion of a consumer's standard of living that is subject to inflation.

This helps us in looking for inflation in history. There is no point looking to hunter-gatherer societies for inflation, as these are self-sufficient groups. Instead, it is in the towns and cities of history that we can find inflation, and conveniently these societies are more likely to keep records. In a relatively urban society like that of the United Kingdom it is possible to construct some kind of inflation index going back to the late thirteenth century. Of course, what makes up inflation will have changed over time, but the existence of a large number of town records giving market prices and similar data allows economic historians to approximate appropriately weighted consumer price indices. Indeed, when consumer price indices were first calculated at a national level in the United States, the Federal government did not even bother with rural areas; it was felt that the prices from seventy towns and cities across the country would suffice.

It is also worth observing that in a political sense urban inflation is likely to be more important than is rural inflation. It is relatively easy to riot and protest over a fall or perceived fall in the urban standard of living brought about by higher prices. Population density always raises the risk of social unrest – a riot requires a certain number of people to be present. Rioting on one's own in the middle of a corn field or rice paddy is a little pointless.

Therefore, a brief history of inflation should start with some of the oldest cities for which we have records. Indeed, evidence of inflation can be found in some of the earliest cities in the world. The rest of this chapter looks at the edited highlights of inflation over nearly three millennia.

Inflation in ancient times

Knowledge of some of the earliest recorded inflation comes to the modern economist courtesy of dried mud. The ancient city of Babylon had a habit of recording things of importance on clay tablets (the entries being referred to as diaries) with a remarkable degree of consistency. There are records of price levels dating back to the reign of Hammurapi (circa 1793 BC to 1750 BC),[1] but these are snapshots of price data rather than a long-term series from which we can derive inflation. When it comes to a consistent time series, a run of price records have been recovered on whole or partial tablets for a period stretching from 652 BC to 61 AD, although there is evidence that this particular series was recording events from somewhere around 740 BC to 75 AD. These diaries included astronomical observations, measurements of the height of the river Euphrates, occasional pieces of gossip and news, and the price of six specific commodities. The prices of the same six commodities are reported, in the same order, using the same method, on virtually all the recovered tablets discovered by archaeologists. Eight centuries of price data, consistently reported, is an unprecedented achievement – only English price data stretches over so long a period and that is data that has been reconstructed *ex post* from local records rather than derived from a single consistent source.

Sadly for economists there are a couple of issues in tracking the data. First, while there is evidence of monthly data records over eight centuries, only a fraction of all the tablets inscribed have been recovered. The bulk of the tablets are from 464 BC to 73 BC, and only selected months have been recovered. Second, the diary entries relating to price data came at the bottom of the tablets, and are frequently broken off and lost to history. While economists are used to being relegated to positions far below their true worth, it is a little galling that the vital economic data comes right at the very end of the tablets, below even the measurement of the height of the river Euphrates. In spite of these two challenges, however, there is still a reasonable amount of economic data available.

The six commodities we have evidence for are: barley, dates, cuscuta (a spice), cardamom, sesame and wool. These commodities all appear to have been important to the typical consumer of Babylon. Technically, the six commodities would all be considered as being a mix of consumer prices and producer prices, inasmuch as consumers undoubtedly purchased these goods for consumption at home, but the commodities also served as the raw materials to manufacture other goods. This group of six commodities is probably not that bad an approximation of a price index. It compares pretty favourably to the earliest attempts to come up with consumer prices in the United Kingdom at the start of the twentieth century, where the London prices of just thirty food items were aggregated and thought to be sufficiently representative as to constitute a general inflation measure.[2]

The fact that the prices of these six commodities were recorded at all underscores once again the importance of price in an urban society. Whether the records were made because prices were directly important, or because the scribes were engaged in building a database that would uncover some mystic correlation between the lunar cycle and prices amounts to the same thing. Understanding price movements justified a considerable amount of effort on the part of the Babylonian intelligentsia. One can only imagine the awe and excitement with which an economist's insights would have been received.

So, what of inflation? The tablets that have survived the past two millennia show very distinctly that there were periods of both deflation and inflation in Babylon. In silver shekel terms, Babylon experienced a prolonged period where prices tended to decline, followed by a further period where prices tended to rise. From the start of the 'quality' data available in 464 BC there appears to have been a tendency for prices to decline, into the latter part of the second century BC. In 309 BC, at the peak of its price, barley cost almost forty-five times what it was retailing for in 186 BC, at the low point in its specific cycle. There was considerable movement in all of the commodity prices. The period of deflation was followed by a period of inflation, with prices rising from the mid- to late second century BC, until the end of the price data in the mid-first century BC.

Academic research[3] suggests that the price move of an individual commodity – barley, say – was strongly influenced by the general price level of the Babylonian economy. In other words, this is not all about relative price shifts, which might have been caused by a plague of locusts one year destroying a crop of barley and raising the price of barley compared with other commodities. In fact, almost three-quarters of the variation in the price of a commodity can be explained by the movement of the overall price level of the Babylonian economy. This meets the definition of inflation in the strictest sense. The Babylonian tablets show inflation (and deflation) existed, and that the broader macroeconomic environment had an impact on prices.

While scribes in ancient Babylon were recording their prices in a nice, orderly and, above all, consistent fashion, in the Mediterranean things were a little more chaotic. Greece was an urban society for centuries before Rome had evolved beyond a cluster of villages. However, records of prices in the Greek city states were not consistently kept. There were records of market prices kept by contemporaries, because prices were important, but the ebb and flow of political regimes meant that neat, consistent clay tablets were not part of the process. Nonetheless, Hellenic civilisation has one distinction that is worthy of note for it is a Greek colony that provides us with one of the earliest recorded instances of a government printing money (in a somewhat metaphorical sense), and in doing so almost certainly creating inflation.

The man who set the printing presses rolling was Dionysius the Elder of Syracuse, who ran a Greek colony on the island of Sicily. Dionysius had racked up a certain amount of debt in fighting wars. This was a state of affairs that was not that uncommon in ancient Greece; in the absence of reality television programmes, one had to do something on a Saturday night and fighting with one's neighbours was as entertaining an occupation as anything else that was on offer. Indeed, Dionysius the Elder's first act on assuming political control of Syracuse was to double the pay of the army. He went on to build a navy and, in addition, by all accounts was rather extravagant in his personal tastes.

The problem, as governments ever since have discovered, was how to finance all of the debt once it had been acquired. Creditors are unaccountably keen on having their money repaid; it is one of their idiosyncrasies. As the debt of Syracuse increased, the usual revenue-raising methods of taxation, confiscation, pillaging and so forth were undertaken. In addition, Dionysius the Elder had the bright idea of calling in all the drachmae of Syracuse (the silver coin that was the standard form of currency), and stamping each one drachma coin as being worth two drachmae. This is the ancient equivalent of setting the printing presses rolling – and overnight doubled the money supply of Syracuse in drachmae terms, although not in terms of the weight of silver. The result was that debts contracted with reference to drachmae amounts were halved in terms of the weight of silver rendered in payment.

This was not the only increase in the money supply that Dionysius the Elder instituted. He also made an issue of tin coins, and insisted that they be accepted as having the same value as silver drachmae. Again, the money supply was increased. As long as Dionysius could enforce the acceptance of tin coins, he would have found it easy to increase the money supply of Syracuse and in doing so would have created higher inflation. More money was chasing the same amount of goods and services, so prices would have risen.

To be fair there is some question over whether Dionysius's actions should be considered a default or an inflationary act. However, if all one drachma silver coins were re-stamped as being worth two drachmae, then presumably the new face value would have had to have been accepted in exchange for private debts as well as those of the tyrant. If so, this is a general inflation, albeit one that helped the ruler avoid paying his debts 'in full' in the context of the weight of silver that was owed. Perhaps the best thing to suggest is that Dionysius demonstrated the principle of a government inflating its way out of debt, by ensuring that it contracted debts that were specified in currency terms and not in weight of silver terms. If so, Dionysius has much to answer for, for he founded the myth that governments can always inflate their way out of debt – a myth we will need to examine in detail in Chapter 9.

Elsewhere in the Hellenic world prices were considered sufficiently important that they were inscribed on monuments, and referenced in the popular culture of the day. Specifically, the prices that garnered most attention were the prices of the various forms of labour. Unlike the records from Babylon, Greek records detail wages and an economist can get a sense of service sector inflation quite clearly. Athenian inscriptions and other sources give evidence of waves of inflation pressures hitting the shores of the Greek economy over the course of the fifth and fourth centuries BC.

What the data from Athens demonstrates is a period of (wage) inflation in the two decades that preceded the Peloponnesian War, from 450 BC to 432 BC, when there was a 50 per cent increase in public sector wages.[4] This rise was spread out over nearly twenty years, we must remember, but it is still a reasonable increase in incomes. There are a couple of theories as to the cause. One is the flow of tributes (paid in silver) due to Athens each year, increasing the Athenian money supply. Another possible cause is an increase in public spending caused by the temporary period of peace that Athens enjoyed. This is an early instance of the dispute between economists as to the causes of inflation identified in the last chapter; on the one hand, a monetary phenomenon, on the other hand an increase in demand.

The initial wage inflation gave way to stagnation during the period of conflict, and then a brief period of falling wages. From 403 BC, wage inflation was back on track, although it was not a uniform increase. Public sector workers and professors saw wages rising, but those in the military did not.

What the Athenian data indicates is at least two periods of general wage inflation, within which there were relative price shifts (wages of public sector officials versus the military for instance). That argues for a degree of economic sophistication, inasmuch as relative wage changes take place, but also underscores the long history of inflation in its various forms.

Moving on a couple of centuries, and slightly to the west, and Rome comes into view as an urban society with inflation issues. However, economists find that measuring Roman inflation is somewhat hampered by the size of the Empire. There was not really a single price for a good or a service (even though there was a single currency) because transport costs could make it impractical to export goods from low-price areas to high-price areas, especially if sea transport was not an option. Moving bulky goods like grain more than a couple of days' journey away was expensive enough to maintain distinct prices in different markets. Further, cyclical movements in price related to agricultural production could cause significant (localised) shifts in price. The Roman Empire was only just about self-sufficient in food, and so disruptions to food supply would have dramatic consequences for food prices.

Nevertheless, there is more than enough evidence of inflation in Roman times, in specific areas of the Empire. Roman emperors discovered, or rediscovered, Dionysius's method of printing money. The silver denarius was the main coin of the Roman Empire, and it was steadily reduced in value. The Emperor Nero seems to have started the practice of reducing the silver content of what was notionally a silver coin, but the process was continued by several of his successors.[5] One of the problems was that the state revenues tended to be relatively fixed, so a government that needed to raise revenues had three choices: sell state property, seize private property or debase the currency – that is to say, reduce the precious metal content, without changing the value stamped on the face of the coin. The third option was favoured several times, and as a result prices increased (in terms of denarii). Emperors either reduced the silver content of coins, or made the coins smaller (without reducing the face value of the coin).

The repeated debasements meant that prices rose. By 301 AD the Emperor Diocletian had had enough, and issued a detailed edict that specified the prices of certain products. Prices of goods and services were fixed in absolute and relative terms. This imperial inflation temper tantrum followed a century and a half during which prices had risen by a little under 20,000 per cent (cumulatively).[6] The Diocletian price fixing was about as effective as such price fixings normally are – products with fixed prices simply disappeared from the markets as producers refused to sell at the new lower prices. Moreover, either because of a woefully incomplete understanding of economics or as the result of an egotistical assumption that the imperial will on pricing would be obeyed, the process of debasement that lay behind the inflation carried on. By the year 306 AD the number of denarii minted from a pound of silver was eighty-six times the number that had been minted two centuries earlier. Less than two decades later the denarius was one-third the weight it had been under Diocletian.

Inflation of 20,000 per cent sounds horrific, but what it actually means is that prices rose around 3.6 per cent a year in the century and a half before the Diocletian edict. That is still a relatively high rate of inflation by the modern standards of an advanced economy, but not quite as shocking a concept as the cumulative figure perhaps suggests.

Time passed, the Emperor Constantine came along, embraced Christianity, and saw an opportunity to seize the gold and silver of pagan temples. This was melted down and the money supply increased again (effectively the silver in the temples was 'sterilised' in economic terms, meaning it was not used as money until Constantine reissued it as coin). The increased number of coins in circulation led to higher prices – evidence from Egypt suggests substantially higher prices – over the subsequent years. It was not until the very end of the fourth century AD that the habit of debasing the denarius or issuing new coins disappeared. As the increase in the number of denarii in circulation was checked, so prices started to stabilise in denarii terms.

What the Babylonian, Greek and Roman examples illustrate is that inflation and urban culture seem to go hand in hand. General increases in the price level, which went beyond the swings caused by the agricultural cycle, seem to have been perfectly normal over two millennia ago. The fact that policymakers sought to remedy these problems (albeit through the highly imperfect medium of price controls) implies awareness of the inflation reality and of its potential social consequences. What was missing was a contemporary understanding of how best to control inflation. This ignorance around inflation control continued into medieval times, but as time progressed a rather important new development took place. Ancient civilisations were often still dealing with physical money that was based on precious metals (and where debasement was the main mechanism for increasing the money supply). By the medieval period some cultures were discovering new and exciting ways of creating inflation.

Inflation in medieval times

The Ancients had already experienced inflation, and of course once the inflation genie came out of the bottle it proved rather difficult to put it back. The last millennium provides us with further evidence of inflation, and further methods by which inflation could be created – several of them almost identical to the forces that create inflation today.

China has left economists with evidence of a series of inflationary episodes, which arose from the fatal combination of too much paper money and too few economists. China appears to have invented paper currency – a curiosity remarked upon with appropriate wonder by the Venetian Marco Polo when he travelled there. There is evidence that paper money circulated from the ninth century onwards.[7] The heyday of Chinese government-issued paper currency was from the eleventh to the sixteenth centuries (paper currency persisted beyond the sixteenth century, but as private rather than government-issued paper). The problem was that, lacking economists on the imperial staff, the Chinese authorities failed to understand the dangers and kept on printing too much money. Time after time China suffered bouts of inflation.

The government of Szechuan was one of the earlier money printers. The currency of Szechuan was iron based, which rendered it rather impractical for transactions of any kind of size (owing, of course, to the weight). Paper money was a convenient solution for all, especially for the government. In the early days there was considerable discipline about how much paper money could be supplied; generally the amount issued was strictly limited over the course of a three-year cycle. By 1072, politicians weakened and started breaching their self-imposed limits. Money supply expanded rapidly, and with it prices (in paper currency terms). By 1200, the supply of paper money had grown to such an extent that it was regarded as worthless and as a result paper currency had all but disappeared from accepted use. The Szechuan dynasty did not survive.

In spite of this rather inauspicious precedent, the Southern Sung dynasty was not going to pass up on the opportunities that paper money offered, and was successfully issuing currency from 1160 onwards. Self-imposed limits were, once again, in place to prevent the downwards spiral to inflation. The primrose path to inflationary perdition beckoned, however, and by 1209 the amount of paper currency in circulation stood at almost four times the original limit. This did not cause inflation (we will look at why this was the case in Chapter 5) – but because prices had initially remained stable the Southern Sung dynasty felt emboldened to carry on printing. The result was inevitable; prices in paper currency terms rose. Over the half century or so in which monetary discipline was lost, prices measured in paper currency terms rose over 2,000 per cent, with an average annual rate of 6.4 per cent.[8] Developed economy inflation in the latter half of the twentieth century was a picture of restraint and moderation in comparison. The Southern Sung dynasty did not survive.

The pattern of issuing paper money with restraint and then that restraint giving way to political pressure was repeated again and again. The Chin dynasty printed enough money to create massive inflation in the early thirteenth century – the money printing being spurred by the need to finance wars against the invading Mongols. Paper money was being accepted at 1 per cent of its face value by 1214. New forms of notes were successively issued, and by 1224 the latest iteration was worth 80,000,000 of the 1214 notes. This is the equivalent of a pretty impressive level of price inflation over the course of a decade. The Chin dynasty did not survive.

After the Chins and their paper currency were brought down, the victorious Mongols printed their own money. With an inevitability that no contemporary seems to have noticed, this started to create inflation from 1276 onwards with prices (in paper currency terms) accelerating in the fourteenth century. In an attempt to force acceptance of paper money and drive up its value, the Mongols banned wooden and bamboo money (generally used as private tokens – the John Lewis voucher or Sears gift card of their day). The use of gold and silver as a medium of exchange was prohibited, and the only permitted use was for the manufacture of jewellery and the like – a situation that was almost exactly mimicked in the United States between 1933 and 1971. None of these measures could stand for long against the power of the printing press, and by 1356 the paper currency of the Mongols was virtually worthless. The Mongol dynasty did not survive.

The successors of the Mongols, the Mings, printed their own currency too – because why would they not? Like all their predecessors they began with restraint around the year 1375. By 1450, the paper was worth less than 0.1 per cent of its face value. The inflation of each preceding dynasty was being repeated with a somewhat relentless monotony. The Mings did break with tradition in one regard, however. The Mings did not keep on printing paper money until the bitter end (which for them came in 1644). From 1500 until the nineteenth century Chinese governments did not print any money at all. Years of successive printing had made the population wary of accepting paper currency, and the cost of raising revenues through printing money was viewed as exceeding the cost of raising revenues through taxation. Prices were still important enough to merit comment, however. The scholar Li Rihua's *Diary from the Water Tasting Studio* periodically records the prices of goods purchased in the twilight of the Ming Empire;[9] the fact that prices were recorded, a century after the paper price inflation episodes, indicates that price sensitivity did not disappear.

In his writings on the Far East Marco Polo had marvelled at the ability of Chinese emperors to persuade their populations to accept paper as a form of currency, comparing the practice to alchemy, but over in Europe governments were also able to create currency (and with it, inflation) relatively easily. The tradition of debasing currency was well established, and the silver content of coinage declined when governments needed to find a source of revenue. This was the metallurgical equivalent of money printing. There was classical precedent for this of course; debasing was a practice that both the Greeks and the Romans had already embraced with vim and vigour. Debasement was one factor that contributed to the Western European medieval inflation.

Western Europe experienced an inflationary wave that corresponded, at least initially, with the earlier episodes of paper inflation in China. From around 1180 (roughly speaking) prices started to increase in Western Europe. Over the course of the thirteenth century the rate of inflation *averaged* something like 0.5 per cent a year,[10] although with sporadic episodes of far higher inflation. Clearly, this was far less onerous than the inflationary episodes of the Chinese, but European inflation in the medieval period had a persistence that was unusual. There was a revealing shift in the language. Price changes were no longer referred to as 'fames' (famines) but 'caristia' (costly). The association of prices rising in tune with the rhythm of the harvest cycle was broken.

The causes of this inflationary episode are complex, and still much disputed by economic historians, but two broad strands can be discerned, with a possible third factor. First, there was an increase in the population of Western Europe. An increase in population meant that there was an increase in the demand for 'stuff', and in particular that there was an increase in demand for the pretty essential 'stuff' that is food and energy. It was difficult to increase the supply of either food or energy given the technologies of the time, and so the prices of these commodities rose. The inflation episode was not only a general rise in prices, it was also a relative price shift. The price of food and energy rose relative to the price of manufactured goods, and to the price of labour.

As Chapter 4 will reveal, wage costs are pretty important for manufactured goods pricing, and thus the pattern of relative wage and manufactured goods prices in the thirteenth century is not surprising.

The second strand was the increase in the money supply. The increase in the money supply came about, in part, because there was not enough cash to start off with. There was a scramble for money as a medium of exchange. As a result, the population of Western Europe began to adopt non-standard forms of money – known as 'mobilia'. Mobilia included furs, jewellery and textiles – essentially high-value relatively portable articles that could be exchanged. Even books were used as a form of currency (something readers may like to consider – the idea of purchasing multiple copies of this book on the off-chance that it becomes a currency in the future is something that the author would wish to encourage, though no guarantees are offered as to the future value of this book as a currency substitute).

As well as the adoption of mobilia, there were two other forces increasing the money supply. The initial shortage of cash in circulation had spurred an increase in silver production through extracting silver from ore and exploiting deposits that were previously not thought worth the effort to mine. European silver production in Europe rose to around 50 tons *per year* by 1300. To put that into context the *stock* of silver in England in 1200 was only 300 tons. The number of coins minted in the UK rose roughly five-fold over the course of the thirteenth century.[11] And then finally we return to our old friend, debasement. Philip the Fair of France was such a reckless debaser that merchants in the early fourteenth century gave up using the French livre and took their silver across the English Channel to have it coined into the still debased but more reliable pound sterling (the effect of this was to increase the money supply of England, with inflationary consequences). Continual debasement or metallurgical money printing shook the faith of the local population to such an extent that those that could afford to abandoned their own currency in favour of the currency of another – a practice still seen today in countries like Argentina.

The third issue is far more uncertain as a cause of inflation, but it is a possibility that should be mentioned. The velocity of circulation of money also increased during the inflationary period. There was a growth in the number of markets and fairs, increasing the opportunities for commerce (and also increasing the number of times coins changed hands). While an increase in velocity does not have to increase the price level, it can do so. To go back to the Fisher identity introduced in the last chapter, if the velocity of circulation rises either prices can rise, or real economic activity can rise, or some combination of the two will take place.

The medieval period therefore gives us two distinct patterns of inflation. The Chinese conform to the classic monetarist view, in that their reckless printing of money *ultimately* created inflation. In Europe, the drivers of inflation seemed to be a mix of factors. There was an increased demand for 'stuff' coming from a population increase (and an inability to increase supplies of food and fuel to match the increase in population). In addition, there was an increase in money supply from debasement and increased mining of precious metals and the introduction of precious metal substitutes as proxies for the more established forms of money.

Inflation from the Renaissance to the Industrial Age

European economies in the sixteenth century witnessed a source of inflation which for the most part was not something individual governments could control. As well as the debasement of existing coins, there was an increase in the amount of silver in circulation as the Spanish invasion and eventual conquest of central and southern America led to the regions' stocks of precious metals being imported into Europe. While technically, if perhaps a little unrealistically, the Spanish could have controlled this flow of metal, once the silver was in Europe it went into circulation. Estimates suggest that the stock of Spanish silver increased to over eight times its mid-sixteenth century level over the course of the subsequent hundred years.[12]

It is tempting to put all the blame for higher inflation entirely on the increase in money supply (silver) coming from abroad. The theory, though good as theories go, does hit some snags. For one thing, modern metallurgical evidence can actually identify the forms of silver that originated in South America. This sort of silver did not arrive in the north of France until the very end of the sixteenth century and does not appear in English coin in the sixteenth century at all.[13] So, the direct impact of Spanish silver cannot be blamed for all of the inflationary episodes of all of Europe. To the extent that the supply of silver did increase because of Spanish imports can be thought of as an event beyond the control of many governments (the Germans, for instance, could not stop the increase in money supply as Spanish silver was circulated through the medium of international trade). This is one of those rare instances of price inflation arising because of events beyond the government's direct control. But there must be other factors behind the price increases of the sixteenth century.

Alongside the introduction of South American silver, Europe experienced the melting down of silver 'plate' (meaning silver products) to produce coin. Melting plate changed silver from a sterilised non-monetary form into non-sterilised money supply as with the earlier actions of the Emperor Constantine. English prices broadly speaking trebled (when measured in silver coin) over the century that preceded the onset of the civil war of the 1630s.

Seventeenth century price increases were further encouraged by poor harvests and the ensuing higher food prices. After years of relatively good harvests, when at least the European population had grown, climate changes reduced the food supply without (initially) reducing the population. When combined with the money supply increases, inflation was the inevitable consequence.

It is true that the price moves of the sixteenth century amounted to a little more than 1 per cent inflation a year, but this was a persistent inflation. At 1 per cent per year average inflation had also accelerated – the medieval inflation had averaged 0.5 per cent per year. This was an inflation that contemporaries were aware of and commented on. It is true that the comments were generally ill-informed, and there was a tendency to focus in on individual prices as being 'unjust', but the increase in the cost of living was understood as it was happening. This century of persistent inflation makes something of a mockery of the statement from Eleanor Dulles that we came across in the last chapter about persistent inflation being incompatible with economic life.

One thing that made debasement and money 'printing' easier in the industrial era was the industrialisation of coinage. Coins could be produced more quickly, allowing a faster increase in the money supply. One quirk of this was evident in North America. The seventeenth-century British colonies used wampum, a form of bead, to trade with the local population. The native population could only make thirty-five to forty beads a day, but the Europeans with iron tools and machinery could make far more. The value of wampum fell as the speed of production increased. Industrialisation of the money supply – any money supply – did not automatically generate inflation, but industrialisation certainly made inflation easier to achieve.

By the time we get to the eighteenth century, the excuses for allowing inflation to take place are starting to wear a little thin. The Age of Enlightenment had been reached, and economists were leading humanity out of the darkness of ignorance and towards a better understanding of the world around them. (It is true that doctors, engineers, physicists and the like played some role in the Enlightenment as well, but it is obvious to any economist that economists were leading the way and the other professions merely trailed in their wake.) At least some of the causes of inflation were better understood at this stage. At the end of the inflationary period, Jane Marcet wrote in the second edition of her *Conversations on Political Economy* (1817) 'An excess of currency produced by an over-issue of bank-notes must therefore remain in the country and cause a depression of the value of money, which would be discovered by a general rise in the prices of commodities.'[14] It is as erudite an explanation of the monetarist concept of inflation as anything that has come out over the subsequent couple of centuries, and follows just over a century when Marcet would have had ample opportunity to witness just that sort of inflation in reality.

The eighteenth century saw various inflation episodes, and offers support to both the idea of monetary forces and demand drivers of inflation. From the start of the second quarter of the eighteenth century food prices in particular began to rise and, in testament to the power of globalisation, prices in North America mirrored those of Europe. This was, at least initially, more of a relative shift (the price of manufactured products did not rise, and in some cases fell as more and more of the household budget was absorbed in paying for food, which reduced demand for manufactured product). This pattern, which mirrors that of the medieval inflation, certainly suggests a strain caused by the increased demands of a growing population.

However, the eighteenth century also witnessed monetary-inspired inflation periods. The French Revolution led to the printing of 'assignats', a form of currency that rapidly lost value through over-supply and a lack of confidence in the revolutionary government. Prices had already been rising in France before the revolution (the price of bread in Paris peaked on the day that the Bastille prison was stormed), and a signal of the political importance of inflation can be seen in the fact that the revolutionary government attempted to stop further increases by diktat – its price controls working as well as these things normally do (i.e. not at all). Inflation continued, and the assignats (created in 1792) lost over 80 per cent of their value by the end of the eighteenth century.

The nineteenth century was the first time since Babylon that governments started to collect price data in a systematic manner, mainly in the form of wholesale and producer prices. The century witnessed several inflation episodes. The price increases of the Paris Commune, and the unfortunate consequences for the Parisian elephants, were remarked upon in the last chapter. Inflation was also a feature of the US Civil War, the result of increased demand, reduced supply and money printing. Both Union and Confederacy printed paper money,[15] and both suffered high inflation. Confederacy inflation was significantly higher than that of the Union because the government had little access to international credit or markets, and because the bank notes were easily forged (increasing the money supply beyond even the inflationary tendencies of the Confederacy). The value of the Confederate dollar was buoyed by a patriotic demand for the currency until the Battle of Gettysburg. After that, things went down. By 1863, a Confederate dollar was worth 6 per cent of a gold dollar, and by May 1864 a pound of bacon cost $9 using Confederate dollars. (In August 2014 Fox News ran a story claiming that bacon prices had hit an all-time high of $6.11 per pound in the US. This is only true if one is selective about the currency one chooses.) The Confederacy was not alone in creating inflation – prices in the Union greenbacks rose by around 50 per cent over the course of the conflict.

The Renaissance and the industrial era again show us periods of inflation driven by money supply, and periods driven by a general imbalance of supply and demand (especially in the sixteenth century and in times of war). They also show us the power that mechanical production of money can have, with the use of paper money and the increased speed with which even specie can be produced. The speed with which money could be generated, if governments so desired, was something that was to have profound implications in the twentieth century.

The twentieth century

The twentieth century is when inflation comes into focus as a concept in its own right. The end of the nineteenth century and the start of the twentieth saw large-scale urbanisation in a number of economies, and with it concerns about the cost of living. Urbanisation allows inflation, and mass urbanisation (combined with either democracy or the threat of an urban mob) pushed the 'living wage' concept to the top of the political agenda. The nineteenth century saw the first systematic attempts at collecting price data since ancient Babylon with producer and wholesale price series; the twentieth century saw very deliberate attempts to collect price data as it pertained to consumers and specifically working class, urban consumers.

Twentieth century inflation clusters into two distinct episodes – the first broadly focused on the 1920s, and the second the 1970s and 1980s. There were other inflation episodes, and some hyperinflation episodes – the late 1940s, for instance – but these two periods are what tend to capture popular attention.

In the wake of the First World War, a spate of hyperinflation episodes swept across several advanced industrialised economies. The word 'hyperinflation' tends to be used loosely. Like many terms in economics, 'hyperinflation' is a word that defies absolute definition, and instead tends to be applied indiscriminately by journalists seeking to sensationalise. Inflation of over 100 per cent per year is sometimes classified as hyperinflation, although strictly speaking it would be considered 'high' inflation. One oft-used definition, proposed by Professor Phillip Cagan, characterises hyperinflation as a period when inflation exceeds 50 per cent per month, that is, prices are 50 per cent higher in February than they were in January. The hyperinflation episode is characterised as lasting from the first month inflation exceeds 50 per cent until the month it falls below 50 per cent, with the caveat that it must stay below 50 per cent for a year.

The 1920s saw a cluster of hyperinflation episodes in Europe. Austria, Soviet Russia, Germany, Poland and Hungary all had hyperinflation (using the Cagan definition). Austria was first, starting in October 1921, and Hungary concluded the process in February 1924. Russia and Hungary are worth a quick look, but the star of the hyperinflation show is undoubtedly Germany.

Soviet Russia's hyperinflation, from December 1921 until January 1924, followed a prolonged period of high inflation that inspired the famous comment from Keynes: 'Lenin is said to have declared that the best way to debauch the capitalist system was to destroy the currency. By a continuing process of inflation, governments can confiscate, secretly and unobserved, an important part of the wealth of their citizens.' Keynes's citation appears to have been based on a newspaper report of an interview with Lenin in 1919, in which Lenin went on to suggest that the Soviet printing presses were 'printing rouble notes, day and night, without rest',[16] to achieve the policy goal of creating inflation. Confiscating the wealth of the middle classes was a deliberate objective of the Soviet government, and it seemed to have pursued the policy with a single-minded purpose. From the start of the First World War until 1924, the Russian currency collapsed in value by a factor of five billion – a fairly debauched way of living by any standards. Marxist theory suggested that in the Communist state money would be redundant, but in the interim taking away its value was advocated as a laudable objective. This is the first recorded instance of inflation as a policy tool, rather than as the consequence – often the unintended consequence – of other policy measures.

The Hungarian hyperinflation, from March 1923 until February 1924, also offers some interesting, novel features. The ravages of war and its aftermath had already led to high inflation across the former Austro-Hungarian Empire; an inflation that was understated in the official price statistics, as many transactions took place on the black market at prices significantly above those that were officially recorded. The defeated Austro-Hungarian Empire had initially maintained its monetary union in the wake of the political separation of the component states. However, in the absence of fiscal and banking union this obviously proved unsustainable. States began to secede from the monetary union. The point was that as each state seceded, the new currencies tended to lose value, and canny investors began to appreciate this fact. There was therefore an opportunity for investors to take their Austro-Hungarian money into Hungary (particularly smaller denomination notes) and to convert their money into dollars (or any other sound currency) at an advantageous rate. Money poured into Hungary while the monetary union lasted, with investors in Austria and elsewhere hoping that they would be able to profit from the fact that Hungary's currency had kept its value better than their own.

The unfortunate consequence of this from Hungary's perspective was that Hungary's domestic money supply grew dramatically. Essentially, the money supply from other parts of the Austro-Hungarian Empire drained into Hungary, which meant that when the Hungarians converted their currency (by stamping over the old imperial bank notes) in 1922, they found that they had more than three times the value of notes that were circulating in 1919 – a far greater amount of money in circulation than the economic activity of Hungary could possibly justify. The result was the same as if there had been a massive printing of money in Hungary and, aided by further domestic policy errors, the situation fuelled hyperinflation. There may be lessons here for those Germans who are so passionate in their desire to break up the euro. Being perceived as the strong currency in a collapsing monetary union is not necessarily a good thing.

This brings us then to the German hyperinflation of July 1922 to November 1923. The risk of hyperinflation was known and understood, and yet still one of the most advanced industrialised economies in the world succumbed. One illustration of the comprehension of inflation risks can be seen in a children's book, *The Gold Seekers*, published during the First World War. The aim of the book was to get children to inform the authorities about those economically wise citizens who were keeping hold of their gold and refusing to exchange it for bank notes. One of the remarkably precocious children of the story reasons with the unpatriotic gold hoarder:

> What would happen if the Reich began to print money without paying attention to its gold stock? It would immediately suffer a loss of confidence. The notes would no longer be accepted, especially abroad, or if accepted, then it would be like those profiteers who supply 750 marks of goods for the 1000 marks you pay them.[17]

This was a specious argument for why paper notes would keep their value. Sadly, the custodians of the country's printing presses did not appear to have read the right sort of children's stories when growing up, and in spite of the risk of a loss of confidence, money was printed without paying attention to pretty much anything at all.

There were many facets to cause the hyperinflation episode, but basically they are different aspects of the same thing; political necessity triumphed over economic good sense. During the First World War the German government had effectively resorted to printing money as a means of financing the conflict. While the British government had been able to sell overseas assets to finance at least part of its war effort, Germany did not have this option, and as a result the mark had already lost three-quarters of its pre-war value by 1918. Somewhat prophetically, in 1919 finance minister Erzberger declared 'whether rich or poor we all have too much paper money in our pockets'.[18] At the same time, production in Germany was constrained by the loss of the Ruhr to France, reparations demands from the victorious Allies, and problems in obtaining the foreign currency with which to import raw materials. Thus, the monetarist crisis of too much money chasing too few goods came about.

By May of 1922, only around a fifth of the German government's revenue came from taxation. The rest was borrowed money, and printing money financed much of the borrowing. Initially, the printing of money helped the German economy export more. The value of the mark fell against other currencies, and exports were boosted. Wages failed to keep up with prices, so the real cost of labour was lower (helping German companies' competitiveness). Of course falling real wages are not a good thing for workers, and by mid-1922 inflation expectations were being built in to pay demands. Germany's competitive advantage was lost. In July 1922, prices rose 50 per cent compared with the previous month, and the starting pistol for a hyperinflation race was fired.

The occupation by France and Belgium of the German industrial heartland of the Ruhr accelerated German inflation in two ways. First, of course, Germany lost access to the raw materials produced by the Ruhr, in particular coal. Second, the German government in Berlin advocated a passive resistance to the occupation, and sought to compensate business owners and citizens of the Ruhr. This the government did by providing marks to the Ruhr population, but of course the only way it could produce those marks was to print the money. Less was produced, money supply rose, and hyperinflation received another shot of adrenaline.

The scale with which money was printed is quite staggering. At the height of the hyperinflation 1,783 printing presses were in operation, twenty-four hours a day, to supply the requisite amount of paper money.[19] Notes were eventually printed on one side only to speed up production. The director of the Reichsbank, Havenstein, repeatedly cited the increased speed with which the central bank was able to print money as evidence that it was handling the situation. The price consequences were inevitable. The German hyperinflation introduced the word 'quintillion' to the world, to express the collapse of the currency. In November 1923, two weeks before the introduction of the new Rentenmark, the Reichsbank issued a 100 trillion mark bank note.

Why has the inflation of the German Weimar Republic assumed such prominence in economic folklore? The price change was dramatic, but other economies also experienced hyperinflation episodes. No doubt the fame of the German hyperinflation arises because of the background, and because of the consequences of the price increases. Germany was, as late as 1922, the second largest economy in the world. Even with the ravages of war and the loss of the Ruhr it was still a considerable industrial force. Hyperinflation was not supposed to happen to economies like Germany.

The consequences of the hyperinflation were profound. The middle class, who tended to live on fixed incomes, was devastated. After the currency reform there was some attempt to restore values – but bonds were converted at 12.5 per cent of their pre-inflation value, a huge loss of income to those dependent on their investments. In 1913, 15 per cent of German national income went to rentiers (people living off of investments). By 1925, that figure was 3 per cent. The number can be taken as an index of the well-being of the middle class. On the other side, the working class received some benefit in that spending on rents fell from 19.3 per cent of their incomes in 1913 to 0.3 per cent of their incomes at the height of the crisis. That benefit must be offset by the fact that unemployment hit 23.4 per cent in November 1923.

The hyperinflation generated malnutrition. Food imports ceased (for Germany had no money with which to purchase foodstuffs). Although the harvest was good in 1923, farmers had no intention of selling food to market for a currency that was falling so fast, and so they kept their produce back. The urban citizen therefore suffered considerably – so much so that gangs of urban dwellers went to the countryside to seize food from farmers.

Finally, there were the political consequences. Bavaria disregarded the powers of the Weimar president, and vested them instead in a local Bavarian who declared martial law, effectively (if temporarily) seceding from the Republic. The authority of the government broke down; municipalities and companies began producing their own money, as there was no faith in the money printed by the central government. A rise in the price of bread in November 1923 led to anti-Semitic riots in Berlin which only ended when the army was called in.

The hyperinflation was brought to an end by currency reform. The Reichsbank continued to exist, as did the old mark, but a new currency (the Rentenmark) was introduced alongside it with a limited circulation. The Rentenmark stabilised in value, and prices normalised.

Weimar Germany's hyperinflation looms so large in the popular economic memory because it took place in a highly advanced economy, because the economic consequences were so drastic and because of the political aftermath to which it contributed. Nevertheless, it was hardly the last hyperinflation of the twentieth century. It was not even Germany's last hyperinflation. The 1940s saw hyperinflation in several economies, including Germany. Hungary introduced the word 'octillion' to the world in 1946 – the price level of its wonderfully named currency, the pengő, rose 400 octillion or 400 multiplied by 10^{27}. These are numbers that are too tiring to contemplate, never mind type out. In Nationalist China the government faced inflation that was nine hundred times the rate of Weimar Germany, and started taxing 'in kind' (3 per cent of the wheat crop and 5 per cent of the rice crop had to be physically handed over).

The hyperinflation episodes have had lingering effects on attitudes to inflation. Research by the World Bank has tentatively concluded that the population or diaspora of those countries that experienced hyperinflation in the 1940s were more likely to say that they were concerned by inflation risk even two generations later. The experience of hyperinflation can be especially scarring.

In the latter part of the twentieth century inflation continued to be a feature of developed and emerging economies alike. A survey of one hundred and thirty-three economies in the years after 1957 found that over two-thirds had experienced inflation rates of over 25 per cent per year at some point, and over a third had experienced inflation in excess of 50 per cent per year.[20] For many countries these inflationary episodes took place in the 1970s and the 1980s, and it is this era that is perhaps the most important for investors today. Many of today's investors will have first-hand experience of the inflation at this time, and that experience will shape current attitudes around the risk of inflation.

The inflation of the 1970s actually began in the 1960s. The oil price shock of October 1973, when the Organization of Petroleum Exporting Countries (OPEC) embargoed the export of oil, is important too. This quadrupled the price of crude oil from $2.90 per barrel prior to the embargo to $11.65 per barrel in January 1974. The circumstances around the collapse of the dollar-pegged foreign exchange rate system in 1971 also contributed to the inflation episode. The key point is that inflation pressures were already mounting before either of these events. The acceleration of inflation was due to the fact that pretty much everything that could go wrong, did go wrong.

Much of the story must focus on the economics of the United States. The US was a more important economy in the late 1960s than it is today in terms of both its size and its role in the global foreign exchange system. In the late 1960s, President Johnson had pursued a policy of 'guns and butter' – continuing with the war in Vietnam and simultaneously promoting Great Society at home. This led to an increase in demand in the US that was felt in global commodity markets. Commodity prices started to rise.

America's central bank, the Federal Reserve, tightened monetary policy in 1966, and there was an economic slowdown from 1968 to 1971, in an attempt to get this demand-pull inflation under control. However, this ran into problems in 1971 as the dollar-gold standard collapsed, President Nixon imposed a 10 per cent import tariff (obviously inflationary), and wage and price controls were put in place in spite of Nixon's personal antipathy. Economically the president was sceptical of controls; politically he saw the controls as an opportunity. Perhaps more importantly, President Nixon began to fear that the state of the economy might damage his chances of a second term as president; Nixon blamed his electoral defeat in 1960 on a failure to offer economic stimulus before the election, and he had been shaken by Republican losses in Congress in the 1970 mid-term elections. Nixon started to apply pressure to the Federal Reserve and in particular to its chair, Arthur Burns. Burns, incidentally, was the author of a book back in 1957, *Prosperity without Inflation*. There is a certain irony in the title, as Arthur Burns's time at the Federal Reserve was marked by a decline in prosperity and a dramatic rise in inflation.

Stories were leaked to the American press suggesting that the administration might increase the number of positions on the Federal Reserve policymaking committee to allow the president to 'pack' the committee with his own supporters who would vote for policy accommodation. (The strategy was not original; similar threats over different economic policies were used by the British Prime Minister David Lloyd George in his fight with the House of Lords at the start of the twentieth century, and by Democrat President F. D. Roosevelt in his struggles with the US Supreme Court in the mid-1930s.) Imposing wage and price controls, which had been advocated by Arthur Burns, reduced the resistance of the Federal Reserve. The US central bank was cowed, or sort of cowed, and eased monetary policy by cutting interest rates and allowing the money supply to grow.

In 1971, the mix was therefore a backdrop of increased aggregate demand from US fiscal expansion of the later 1960s, wage and price controls, and easier monetary policy. The Federal Reserve did begin to tighten policy just ahead of the 1972 election, when Nixon (and Burns) seemed confident of Nixon's re-election. The noted economist Milton Friedman was not a fan of the policy, and told *Newsweek* in August 1971 that Nixon's price controls 'will end as all previous attempts to freeze prices and wages have ended, from the time of the Roman emperor Diocletian to the present, in utter failure'.[21] Friedman's intellectual bias made it perhaps predictable that he would not be an enthusiastic supporter of wage and price controls, although he deserves kudos for slipping an accurate historical reference into a *Newsweek* article.

In 1973, the situation unravelled, and unravelled rapidly. The initial wage and price controls had worked in that they had reduced the rate of inflation between their imposition and the presidential election (if we assume that the objective of the policy was to create the right economic climate for Nixon's re-election). After the election, 'Phase Three' controls on wages and prices were introduced, and were an effective easing of controls. The result was inevitable. Inflation rocketed upwards like a startled pheasant. The desire to change wages and prices had not dissipated during the freeze – both companies and employees were biding their time, and the pent-up inflation was released with explosive force. In early 1973, there was a scramble to purchase, and consumers rushed to the shops. While this could have been the latent hedonism of the American consumer exerting itself in the traditional manner, in fact it appears that consumers were buying before prices rose further, in a manner characteristic of high and hyper-inflation episodes.

Food price inflation rose so rapidly that in June 1973 the government tried a sixty-day freeze on food prices. There was a sad predictability about the consequences. Food disappeared from stores and there were shortages until the price freeze was lifted in July, thirty-five days after the freeze was implemented. Friedman was right. Diocletian's price fixing 1,672 years earlier had caused Roman producers to refuse to sell their products at the imperially fixed price.

Note that all of this chaotic price action was taking place before the first oil price shock of 1973. The rise in energy prices exacerbated an already poor inflation environment. The energy price shock was a relative price shock and need not have been a general inflation shock. The price of oil rose; other prices could have fallen in absolute or relative terms. However, the climate in which the energy shock occurred meant that the relative price move provoked other price actions that pushed the economy into a more general inflation crisis.

The British inflation experience was particularly severe in the 1970s, with retail price inflation peaking at 26.9 per cent in 1975. The British government, like President Nixon, tried a wage and price control policy. As with the US policy it did not seem to work very well although the British persisted with variations on the policy for some time. Ahead of the second general election of 1974, the Conservative Party manifesto declared '…inflation at its present pace threatens… the survival of our free and democratic institutions… inflation and rising prices tear society apart'. Reading this one gets the impression that the British Conservative Party was not a fan of inflation. However, the Labour Party, which won this particular election, also opposed inflation. In 1975, the British government issued a pamphlet to every household in the Kingdom entitled *Attack on Inflation: A Policy for Survival*. Remarkably, some people read it (around a third of the population, apparently) – a sign of the seriousness with which the government viewed the inflation problem, and the seriousness with which inflation was viewed by the general population. It takes a lot of determination and a strong stomach to read a British government pamphlet on anything.

The British experience of inflation in the 1970s was a mix of accommodative policy, the commodity price shock and inflationary wage claims. There was a perception that wages were not keeping up with prices (70 per cent of the population thought real wages were falling in a 1972 survey). The government deliberately sought to emphasise the role of unions in creating inflation, a view which became more prevalent in the popular perception. While there were inflationary pay claims, creating this image must also be considered a matter of policy; the government wanted wage restraint, and the only way to create a climate where that might happen was if the government emphasised the links between wages and inflation.

Inflation in the 1970s was by no means an exclusively Anglo-Saxon phenomenon. Japan and Korea had inflation rates of over 20 per cent. Price levels in France and Denmark rose by two and a half times from 1970 to the end of 1980. Over the same period, prices trebled in Finland and Ireland, rose more than three and a half times in Italy, more than quadrupled in Spain and rose to five and a half times the 1970 level in Portugal.[22]

What the 1970s show is a mix of forces driving inflation higher. The legacy of demand exceeding supply in the 1960s was felt via global commodity prices – and global commodity prices were more important to inflation in the 1970s than they are today. Wage and price control policies failed, in that the attempts to restrict relative wage and price adjustment just delayed wage and price increases – and the built-up pressure on wages and prices was all the more explosive when it happened. Monetary policy was also loosened, particularly in the United States, which created localised inflation problems.

Other factors can be added into the mix. The recycling of petrodollars from oil-producing countries that had more money than they knew what to do with led to explosive credit growth in Latin America. This fuelled demand, but ultimately inflation (and a debt crisis). Trade unions bargained for higher wages to protect their members' real incomes, without consideration for the unemployment consequences for the wider population.

The inflation episodes of the 1970s matter today, in part because of what they can tell us about how policy contributed to inflation, but also because of how they influenced the psychology of those who lived through them. The World Bank survey about the lingering psychological scarring of hyperinflation has already been mentioned. The 1970s were not, for the most part, a hyperinflation episode under the definition used here. However, they were a high inflation episode. Today's generation of investors and policymakers grew up during the 1970s. We must suppose that investor and policymaker attitudes towards inflation will have been shaped, at least in part, by the experiences of the 1970s.

The common threads of history

What can history teach us about the cause of inflation? The most salient point of this chapter is that inflation is a repeated feature of the world economy, at least once urbanisation has started. It is also clear that inflation can be driven by a surge in demand that the economy is unable to meet – a consumer boom.

Inflation can be caused by a contraction in economic supply against unchanged demand – a famine (not necessarily confined to food of course). Inflation can also be caused by an excessive increase in the money supply as in the ancient world, or in hyperinflationary episodes, or *exacerbated* by an excessive increase in the money supply as with the inflation of the Renaissance or the US in the 1970s.

This chapter has only touched on a small number of inflation episodes. The problems of Latin America or the inflation of Eastern Europe after the fall of communism have been overlooked, as have the struggles of Asia in the 1950s, or conflicts over inflation in UK policy in the 1980s. That, however, is rather the point. A brief history of inflation must be highly selective, because inflation is a constant thread running through human history. With money and urbanisation comes the possibility of inflation, and with the possibility comes the probability that at some point inflation will be allowed to develop.

One of the common themes from history is that inflation, and particularly episodes of high inflation or hyperinflation, comes about through either economic ignorance or through the wilful disregard of economic reality. In other words, armed with basic economic knowledge and reliable data, it should be perfectly possible to keep inflation within acceptable bounds through preventing excess money supply or adjusting the balance of supply and demand in the wider economy. Fail to understand economic relationships and inflation readily results; the assorted inflations of the Chinese medieval period demonstrate this. Governments hit on an idea – paper money – that seemed to work, but lacked the economic understanding that would have allowed paper money to flourish without creating inflation (or excessive inflation).

This is not to say that inflation will not fluctuate. Small changes in the inflation rate on a year to year basis are always likely as relative prices move around. However, persistent high inflation must be considered to be avoidable with the proper policy restraint. Historically, persistent high inflation has arisen either because policymakers chose inflation as the lesser evil (prioritising other policy objectives) or because they did not understand what they were doing.

The damage wrought by economic ignorance has stretched far into modern times. Despite economics having been established as a profession since the Enlightenment, Havenstein, president of the German Reichsbank during the hyperinflation period, was not an economist. Astonishing though it is to contemplate, the Weimar Republic entrusted its central bank, the sanctity of its currency, and ultimately its inflation rate to a *lawyer*. How a civilised nation could commit so fundamental an error as putting in place a lawyer to do an economist's job is almost beyond comprehension. The failure to understand economics, and the failure to heed the advice of those that did understand economics, led to a hyperinflation episode that has scarred the collective memory of Germans for four generations.

One would have hoped that the precedent of the German hyperinflation, combined with even a cursory trawl of the internet, would have rendered significant inflation episodes a thing of the past; and yet the late twentieth century witnessed Zimbabwe's hyperinflation.

The historical persistence of inflation as being an economic feature that exists beyond relative price changes naturally leads to a desire on the part of investors to insure themselves against inflation. Inflation means real losses, and inflation always seems to be a risk somewhere in the world. The problem with this desire is not that it is wrong to try and protect against inflation, but that investors seek too simple a solution to the threat of inflation. Investors want a 'magic bullet' to protect against inflation increases. Some investors go further, and suggest that the 'magic bullet' might be a 'golden bullet'. It is time to turn to the topic of gold and inflation.

Notes

1   Fischer (1996) p xvi.
2   Stapleford (2009) p 56.
3   Slotsky (1997).
4   Loomis (1998).
5   Nero's coin was 94 per cent silver. Taking Nero as our benchmark (Nero = 100) the silver content of the denarius moved as follows:

Emperor	Year	Silver content relative to Nero
Nero	54	100.000
Vitellius	68	86.170
Domitian	81	97.872
Trajan	98	98.936
Hadrian	117	92.553
Antoninus Pius	138	79.787
Marcus Aurelius	161	72.340
Septimius Severus	193	53.191
Elagabalus	218	45.745
Alexander Severus	222	37.234
Gordian	238	29.787
Philip	244	0.532
Claudius Victorinus	268	0.021

Source: Adapted from Michell (1947).

6   Fischer *et al.* (2002).
7   The Mediterranean city of Carthage had used stamped leather as a medium of exchange at one point in the ancient period, but the prize for the consistent use of paper as a form of currency should really be awarded to China.
8   Fischer *et al.* (2002).
9   Clunas in Trentman (2012) p 58.
10   Fischer (1996) p 17.
11   Fischer (1996) p 24.
12   Brenner (1962).

13 Fischer (1996) p 82.
14 Marcet (1817) p 354.
15 In fact, three dollars circulated. The Greenback of the Union, the Grayback of the Confederacy (so called because of the colour of the bank notes) and the Goldback of California. As its name suggests, the Goldback was backed by gold.
16 White and Schuler (2009).
17 Taylor (2013) p 14.
18 Taylor (2013) p 106.
19 Fischer (1996) p 193.
20 Fischer *et al.* (2002).
21 *Newsweek* 30 August 1971, cited in Bowles (2005) p 128.
22 Mitchell (2003), Table H2, p 867.

3   All that is gold does not glitter

When… a paper currency is divorced from gold every intelligent man and woman is confronted with serious doubts and troubling uncertainty.

(Eleanor Lansing Dulles, American economist, 1933)[1]

They [rulers and subjects] have clung pertinaciously to the belief that gold was really stable and have treated it as stable in all their monetary dealings, and have accepted avidly all kinds of explanations of their economic sufferings rather than the true one that their money was not a stable measure of value.

(Sir Basil P. Blunkett, Director of the Bank of England, 1933)[2]

If there is one topic which economists have reason to fear, it is the topic of gold. There is something about gold that seems to cast rationality into the outer darkness and replace it with an almost fanatical passion from a subsection of society – gold bugs, who believe that gold is in some way the only proper currency that exists, has ever existed or ever will exist. Whenever gold is discussed, gold bugs will emerge like creatures from Tolkienian nightmare, alternating a crooning solicitous cry of 'my precious' with vicious shrieks of defiance at the tricks of economists who are merely trying to point out the facts and uncover the absurdity of the gold bug position. The advent of the internet has made this worse, for gold bugs now cluster together on blogs and websites, fuelling their delusions by sharing misinformation with one another and in doing so constructing a fantasy realm far more elaborate than anything Middle Earth had to offer. The quote from Eleanor Dulles which heads this chapter gives some hint of the emotional *cri de coeur* that the topic of gold can evoke from some.

In writing about gold, therefore, economists are taking their lives into their hands. But truth must out. Arguments about the role of gold as a medium of exchange are often intimately associated with ideas about inflation. Any attempt to examine the concept of inflation must consider the role of gold and its partners in the various forms of the gold standard. Gold as a currency comes in three basic forms: gold specie, a gold standard, a derived gold standard. The first gold currency is the physical circulation of gold coin (specie), and realistically has never lasted terribly long. Gold as a physical currency is not very convenient, especially when trading over any distance. Credit and gold proxies tend to supplement specie, and this means that gold is but one form of currency in circulation at any moment. It is true that gold may be the only legal tender (and thus the only form of currency acceptable for paying taxes, or the form that a creditor can insist upon receiving in settlement of a debt) but other forms of currency will circulate.

The second form of gold currency, a gold standard, does not require physical gold coins to be in circulation at all. A gold standard simply requires that whatever currency form is in circulation as a medium of exchange can in theory be converted into gold at a certain fixed rate. The British abortive return to a gold standard in the 1920s withdrew gold coins from everyday circulation, whereas gold specie had been a part (albeit a very small part) of the nineteenth century gold standard. The link to gold was kept in the 1920s as the new system theoretically allowed gold to be exchanged at a fixed rate for the notes and coins that were in use – hence the legend 'I promise to pay the bearer on demand the sum of...' which appears on British bank notes to this day. The 'sum' cited is notionally the sum in gold. The statement is nowadays nothing more than a nostalgic fiction.

It is also worth pointing out that the traditional aim of the gold standard system of currencies was not inflation control, but ease of convertibility of currencies across international boundaries. The world's first proper gold standard, established by the British in the nineteenth century, had the pound defined in terms of a fixed quantity of gold (specifically a troy ounce of gold was worth four pounds and five shillings, so a pound sterling was the equivalent of 113.0016 grains of gold).[3] As other currencies came to be defined in terms of fixed quantities of gold (the US dollar eventually defined as 23.33 grains, for example, making one troy ounce the equivalent of twenty dollars and sixty-seven cents), this meant that the ratio of one currency to another was also fixed and it gave certainty about the number of pounds sterling it would take to purchase a foreign currency. Under this gold standard, one pound sterling was worth just under four US dollars and eighty-seven cents ($4.8665 to be precise).

The gold standard mechanism was maintained as a means of automatically balancing international trade balances in the first instance, and that was the focus of the academic literature surrounding the gold standard. A country that ran a persistent trade deficit would ultimately have to export gold to pay for the goods it was importing. The loss of gold would force the central bank to raise interest rates to stem the loss of gold, slowing the domestic economy. Demand for imports and thus the outflow of gold to pay for imports would decline as the economy slowed, and gold would also flow back into the economy attracted by higher interest rates. That was the theory, at any rate. The dominance of the gold standard as a monetary system means that a lot of the economic literature referencing inflation in the nineteenth and early twentieth century used language that a modern readership would tend to associate with foreign exchange markets. Inflation 'devalues' and 'depreciates' a currency and real values (adjusting for inflation) are often made with reference to foreign currency values. The use of foreign currencies as a proxy for real values meant that the values may not have been real at all, if the foreign currency used in the comparison has also experienced inflation or deflation.

The final form of a gold currency is a gold-derived standard, as with the Bretton Woods exchange rate system that existed from 1946 until 1971. This system allows only indirect conversion into gold, and in the case of Bretton Woods only allowed that conversion into gold for specific investors (central banks). The idea is that currencies trade with fixed exchange rates to one another, and the reference currency is convertible into gold at a predetermined price. Under Bretton Woods a dual market for gold emerged, with the private sector price of gold for jewellery and the like different from the official price of gold, which converted $35 for a troy ounce.

The misconceptions about gold, currency and inflation are legion, and it is hard for an economist to know where to begin. However, braving the inevitable wrath that will be heaped upon this book for the attempt, let us examine a couple of the key misconceptions about gold before getting down to the serious business of the relationship between gold and inflation.

The gold myths

One of the biggest challenges to rational good sense that an economist comes across is the notion that gold has an intrinsic value – the idea that gold is worth something *because* it is gold. This is complete nonsense. Gold is only worth whatever other people are prepared to give in exchange for it. Gold has the same intrinsic value as Bitcoin, or any other of the virtual currencies that have sprung up. If no one else wants to own gold, the gold bug will be left with a big pile of inedible, non-combustible scrap metal that has no worth at all. If no one else wants to own a virtual currency, then the electronic bug is left with a collection of virtual binary code that equally has no worth at all.

We have excellent evidence of this fact in history. When British settlers first sailed off to Massachusetts Bay, they went armed with various impractical items (and neglected to take many things that might actually be worth having in a potentially hostile environment). Some of the most impractical things that they brought with them were coins, including gold coins.

After having settled into the neighbourhood, the Massachusetts Bay settlers came to realise that they lacked several of those things that make life worth living; food, for instance, as well as goods like furs that could be traded for profit with people back in England. So the settlers had the intelligent idea of purchasing some of these things from the local tribes that formed part of the indigenous population. We have enough historical accounts to be able to reconstruct what happened.

The settlers sought out the local tribes, full of bright enthusiasm, and suggested that they might purchase some of the things that they needed. The local tribes agreed to trade, and everything was going fine until it came to payment. The settlers handed over their gold coins (and no doubt their silver coins too), only to be met with incomprehension and indeed incredulity on the part of the local population. The settlers assumed that the coins would be accepted because they themselves accepted them in exchange for goods and services. The local population, quite understandably, asked what the use of such tokens was to them. They were not edible, they did not serve as a source of fuel, they did not keep the bearer warm, and they had no significance in the local religions. The local tribes owed no taxes to the English Crown (taxation can be a powerful reason for holding coin). Why on earth should the local population desire to own coin?

The settlers may have tried to make the argument that the coins could be used to purchase goods and services from the settlers. Indeed, this is the only argument that the settlers *could* have made. No doubt the shouts of derisive laughter from the local tribal population could be heard up and down the Eastern Seaboard – for, of course, the settlers had very little that the native population was interested in purchasing at that time (this changed later; firearms being an early desirable purchase and marking the start of gun culture in the United States).

The point of this abortive attempt at trade using gold is to underscore the point that gold is only worth something because other people accept it as a medium of exchange. If a group does not accept gold as a medium of exchange, then it has no worth. The English settlers accepted gold coins (and silver coins too, of course) because they had confidence that they could surrender those coins in exchange for things of practical worth in the future: food, clothing, books on inflation, shelter and so forth. The local tribal population of Massachusetts Bay had no such confidence, and were not going to surrender things that actually had a value (like food and furs) for misshapen discs of shiny metal. Gold had, and has, no intrinsic value.

The solution to the Massachusetts Bay dilemma, at least initially, was that the settlers started trading using wampum as currency (wampum are beads made from shells formed into belts). The industrialisation of wampum manufacture and its impact on prices was mentioned in the last chapter. Interestingly, the local tribes did not use wampum as a currency. While wampum belts had value to the local tribes and were presented to mark specific occasions, wampum was only traded with the settlers. An exchange rate came into being, and initially six white beads or three black beads were worth one English penny (a silver penny, in those days).[4] The local tribes accepted the beads as having value because they could be used to create belts that had religious or cultural significance. Indeed, the settlers realised that anything perceived as a medium of exchange would do for currency amongst their own population, and they rather practically made beaver fur a form of legal currency for local transactions. Beaver was far less susceptible to significant increases in supply than was wampum.

This history of the Massachusetts Bay settlers describes a situation that is in all economic respects identical to the virtual currencies that exist today. A seller may accept a virtual currency because they believe that they will be able to exchange it for something that they desire or need in the future. The virtual currency has no intrinsic value (just as gold has no intrinsic value) – the value is *derived* from the value of the useful goods or services that the holder anticipates the virtual currency will be able to purchase in the future. Thus, the value of the virtual currency, like the value of gold, is a *derived* value.

Even if one can convince a gold bug that gold has no intrinsic value, the next line of resistance is that 'gold has been the world's currency for thousands of years', which the gold bug will take as irrefutable evidence that gold is the only currency worth holding, and the only 'safe' currency. This argument is as nonsensical as ascribing gold an intrinsic value. As the previous chapter has demonstrated, many things have served as a currency in various parts of the world at various times in human history. As long as there was confidence that the currency would be accepted as a medium of exchange by someone else in the future, anything would do.

The ancient world used silver rather than gold as the main medium of exchange. This was for practical purposes as much as anything else. Gold was too scarce to be a useful medium of exchange for the ordinary citizen. An historical example shows this. In the first century of the Roman Empire, before inflation really got going, a Roman soldier would receive annual pay of 225 silver denarii. The Roman Empire had (at least theoretically) a gold coin, the aureus, although this was not really used. With 25 denarii exchanged for one aureus, this meant that a Roman legionnaire would receive the equivalent of 9 aurei per year, and at least in theory could have been paid in gold. Of course, to pay the salary of a legionnaire in gold would have been impractical – imagine trying to buy daily necessities with a coin that represented the equivalent of 11 per cent of your annual income? It would be like asking a US soldier today to undertake a weekly food shop at Walmart when the smallest medium of exchange they have to offer the checkout operator is a Rolex watch. (A US E5 enlisted soldier with ten years' service earned around $37,000 per year in 2014, and in 2014 $4,100 would purchase a Rolex at the cheaper end of the range.)

The Athenians did use gold on one occasion, but it was an extreme event. Besieged in 407 BC and running out of silver they melted a golden statue of Nike (symbol of victory) to produce an emergency currency. Otherwise the irrelevance of gold to Greek society can be seen by the fact that Alexander the Great's capture of booty in the form of gold and silver from around 330 BC was inflationary only to the extent that it contained silver. The more prevalent gold had no impact on the Athenian money supply. We have already seen that the Szechuan dynasty of China based its currency on iron coins before discovering the delights of paper, and the Southern Sung dynasty used copper coins (which for larger transactions were massed together on strings – the coins having holes in their centre to facilitate this purpose). No gold coin was minted in Italy from the decline of the Roman Empire until the mid-thirteenth century, and even then the creation of gold coin was seen as a response to extreme monetary conditions.[5]

The English, and then later the British, monetary system used silver as the main medium of exchange for most of its history (hence the pre-decimal symbol for a penny being 1d – a reminder of the Roman denarius). Britain only truly operated a gold standard for its currency in 1821 with the lifting of the Bank Restriction Act, although silver coins had effectively disappeared from circulation around a century earlier. The gold standard, defining sterling in terms of gold, was formally adopted five years earlier in 1816, though the legislation drew very little comment in the local media. Silver was used as the dominant form of currency by most of the rest of the world until the late nineteenth century, sometimes alongside gold (as in France), and sometimes as the sole medium of exchange (as in China).

Interestingly, there is an argument that for much of human history the main medium of exchange was not gold, silver or even iron, but credit. In a world where small change was hard to come by, the best way to solve the problem was to allow credit to build up between traders in a small community. There would be a notional unit of account, which could be anything. Cattle were frequently used, and indeed still are in some societies. One could also make a claim that the cow is the one true physical form of currency that has been consistently used by humanity over the millennia. But rather than having to keep passing a cow back and forth across the garden fence every time one made a transaction with one's neighbour, a system of credit would be used and a final reckoning would tally up who owed what every once in a while – once a quarter was a common system. This is a practical example of electronic money before electronics – what is sometimes referred to in older economic texts as 'book money'.

So, why have these myths around the value and role of gold sprung up? One issue, surely, is our old friend 'loss aversion' that was introduced in the opening chapter. Gold-based currency systems are normally abandoned as a result of economic stress (war in 1914, economic stress in the UK in 1931, recession in the US in 1971). As a consequence, ending a gold-pegged system will often coincide with either currency depreciation or inflation – the sort of loss that the theory of loss aversion abhors. The losses caused by the economic distress surrounding the change of currency regime induce a sense of nostalgia for times past, and a convenient veil is cast over the fact that the use of gold may have caused the economic distress in the first place.

In addition, the undue reverence that is ascribed to gold might be attributed to the dominance of Anglo-Saxon economists in the early nineteenth century, who advocated gold seemingly because it was the British standard and therefore must be superior. There was actually considerable disagreement over the introduction of a gold standard at the time. Over eight hundred pamphlets, the blogs of their day, were published on the topic between 1797 and 1821. *The Edinburgh Review*, one of the leading journals of its day, covered the topic of money more than any other issue in the early years of the nineteenth century.[6] This vigorous debate about the use of gold was ignored in subsequent analysis of the introduction of gold, because it did not conform to the idea of gold as a natural, inevitable currency. The climate of intellectual economic nationalism has lingered on with the idea that 'gold is best'.

Gold and inflation

As economic facts defeat the gold bugs on the arguments of value and history, the last refuge of the defenders of gold is that 'gold stops inflation'. It is on this point that things start to get serious, for even today there are investors who believe that holding gold will in some way grant them guaranteed insurance against the ravages of inflation (what market practitioners call a 'perfect hedge').

The principle of gold as an anti-inflation strategy has some sound economics behind it, in that the supply of gold is less easily increased than is the supply of paper money or indeed the supply of some other forms of currency. This means that reducing the relative price of money by increasing its supply is more difficult if gold is used as the basis of an economy's medium of exchange. However, this does not mean that inflation episodes are *impossible* under a gold standard currency system. While long-term inflation is relatively unlikely (indeed, as we shall see, deflation is more probable *in the long run*), quite prolonged interludes of inflation are perfectly possible and indeed have occurred frequently under gold-based currency systems. Gold is not a guarantee against inflation in the short or medium term. Investors tend to care most about the short or medium term.

There are two obvious ways in which inflation can occur under a gold-based currency system. The first is that the supply of gold in an economy is not necessarily fixed. If gold is scarce, and gold is a medium of exchange, then efforts will likely be made to find more gold either through better extraction methods, recycling or through the discovery of new sources. This will make the supply of gold, and thus the 'price' or derived value of gold, unpredictable, as the supply of gold can and will fluctuate relative to the supply of other goods. The most basic way of increasing prices through increasing gold supply is to simply dig more of the stuff out of the ground. The late 1890s saw rising inflation, even under a global financial system that had largely (although not universally) adopted gold as its currency basis, because significant gold discoveries were made in Australia, Canada and South Africa. This was an inflationary episode that all countries had to accept, because it was the global supply of gold that rose.

Gold supply can also adjust in other ways. Gold that is held as jewellery or ornament can be melted down to provide an increase in supply (the Emperor Constantine's melting of temple ornaments is an example), or gold can be put into wider circulation. One of the critical reasons behind the failure of the short-lived gold standard of the 1920s was that around half the world's monetary gold (i.e. bullion and coin, rather than jewellery and ornament) was held by the central banks of France and the United States. Their failure to put that gold into circulation in a gold currency system contributed to unacceptable deflationary pressures in the global economy. Had they put the gold into circulation, prices would have risen.

There are those who wonder whether people would really be willing to sacrifice their jewellery and ornaments in order to monetise gold. Aside from the historical parallel of the seventeenth century, when silver plate was readily melted as economics dictated, our current time gives ample example of gold being thrown into the melting pot. In 2012, around 36 per cent of the world's gold supply came not from holes in the ground, but from recycling.[7] It seems that when there is the scent of monetary gain on the air people can be remarkably unsentimental about the artistic merit or even the emotional significance of their jewellery.

The second means by which inflation can occur even with a gold-based currency is by adjusting what are sometimes called the 'rules of the game'. The pure gold bug may object that this is cheating, in that this is a form of breaking the strict rules which are supposed to govern a gold standard currency. This is true, but the fact that such cheating is possible under a gold-based currency system prevents gold being a perfect hedge against inflation.

Cheating is possible because gold coins are rarely the only form of currency in circulation in a gold-based currency system. We have already seen that in medieval times the shortage of precious metal (then mainly silver) led to the use of 'mobilia' as substitute forms of currency. The survival of the gold-based currency system in nineteenth-century Britain depended in part on the use of non-gold substitutes for currency. Bills of exchange and promissory notes (formal, tradable, but personalised forms of credit that formed key plot points in the works of Dickens, Trollope and other writers of the time) meant that credit was becoming as important for large transactions as it had always been for small transactions. Cheques could be drawn on bank deposits. Bank notes circulated as well. All of these instruments were accepted as forms of payment on the assumption that they could be converted into the gold coins that formed legal tender if the bearer desired. Most of the world's gold-based currencies have actually operated on a Rumpelstiltskin principle. The systems work by spinning something like straw into a gold proxy. The systems depend on maintaining the belief that the gold proxy could be converted into gold on demand – but if confidence in convertibility collapsed there would be a rush to trade in these other forms of currency in order to hold physical coin.[8]

If the ratio of non-gold currency to gold currency was held rigidly constant, then there was no opportunity for 'cheating' on the gold standard. Adam Smith, with a certain Scottish dourness, used to advocate an eighteen to one ratio for non-gold currency to gold currency. However, if the authorities or banks or issuers of non-gold currency forms felt that the chances of a panicked demand for gold were limited, then they could increase the ratio of non-gold currency to gold. This allowed for an increase in the money supply in the near term, and thus raised the potential for inflation. To give an idea of the scale, bear in mind that the British economy of the nineteenth century was not built on a solid foundation of gold at all. Instead, the British economy was covered by what the economist Brigitte Granville cites as being described as a 'thin film of gold'.[9] For much of the latter part of the nineteenth century gold coins and bullion held in the United Kingdom formed less than 2 per cent of the deposits and notes in circulation, and even after the gold discoveries of the late nineteenth century the ratio only rose to 3.8 per cent in 1913. This was nothing like what Adam Smith advocated. This was not even a gold-plated monetary system; the pound sterling was a currency that was merely gilded with the thinnest possible layer of gold leaf.

The ability to cheat on the gold standard (and in doing so create inflation) could not go on indefinitely. If the relationship of non-gold currency to gold currency veered too far from what was perceived as a 'safe' ratio then either the gold-based currency system would collapse, or there would have to be a reduction in non-gold currency in circulation (reducing the total money supply, and therefore tending to produce deflation in the economy). The point here is not that inflation would become a permanent feature of an economy that cheated on the rules of the game; the point is that inflation could be a quite long-lived feature of an economy that cheated.

The devastating damage of gold as a currency

The potential for bouts of inflation in a gold-based economy highlights one of the most damaging features of a gold-based system – a problem emphasised by the quote from Sir Basil Blunkett at the start of this chapter. Gold may (or may not) create stable prices over the long term, but in the short and medium term a gold-based currency creates inflation instability.

The long gold standard experience of the United Kingdom superficially appears to argue that inflation is kept in check by the use of the yellow metal. From 1830 until 1913, a relatively broad measure of prices in the UK saw an increase of 0 per cent, as Figure 3.1 demonstrates. The figure is an index of the consumer price level, not the consumer inflation rate. The consumer price *level* in 1913 was pretty much the same as the price level of 1830.

This demonstration of price stability over the course of a century no doubt has gold bugs buzzing with triumph. However, it is worth noting what happened over shorter time periods during that century. Inflation rose and fell, and there were inflation and deflation episodes lasting several years. Any investors looking for a home for their money would not take much comfort from the fact that inflation was stable over a century, if they experienced a cumulative inflation of 28 per cent from 1851 to 1873. Indeed, inflation totalled 30 per cent from 1851 to 1856 (followed by deflation, followed by inflation). It is no good consoling such investors with the fact that deflation in their children's or their grandchildren's lifetime will compensate for the loss of living standards that they themselves are suffering at that particular moment. Altruism and goodwill towards future

Figure 3.1 A broad price index in the UK from 1830 until 1913

Source: Bank of England.

generations will only take one so far. From the perspective of the 1851 investors, the real value of their investments has been eroded by inflation, and that is all there is to it.

The fact that very few investors make investment decisions with an eye to the likely returns that can be earned a century hence means that we must focus on shorter episodes of inflation to gauge investors' likely reactions. With the shorter-term volatility of inflation under the gold standard investors were inevitably uncertain about the likely path of prices over the course of their investment. They would require compensation for this uncertainty. This, of course, is the inflation uncertainty risk premium that we encountered in the first chapter. The gold standard could create a decade of inflation or a decade of deflation, and unless an investor was going to adopt the recklessness of a gambler at the gold standard inflationary roulette wheel they would demand an additional rate of return to compensate for the risk they undertook in committing their money to an investment.

Inflation uncertainty persists even today. Using not inflation, but the relative price of gold and milk (as a widely consumed commodity), we can see that prices can still rise in gold terms. Figure 3.2 compares the dollar price of a gallon of full milk in the United States with the gold price of a gallon of milk (assuming the Bretton Woods standard of a troy ounce of gold being worth $35).

Two things are evident from this. First, there was a relative price move between the price of milk and the price of gold between 1996 and 2002 that was not matched in the dollar price. Using gold would have created a price increase over a length of time that would exceed many investors' definitions of 'long term'. Second, the price of milk denominated in gold dollars is a lot more volatile than

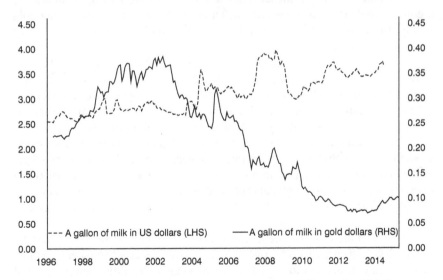

Figure 3.2 The price of a gallon of milk in the US, in paper dollars and gold dollars

Source: US Bureau of Labor Statistics and author's calculations from World Bank data via Haver Analytics.

the price of milk denominated in paper currency, in spite of the significant printing of money by the US Federal Reserve.

The damage of this volatility was highlighted in the dying days of the gold standard. Professor Jacob Viner stated: 'The price of gold has been less stable than the price of eggs. A standard of value fluctuating in its own value must be an important factor in initiating and accentuating the recurrent cycles of expansion and depression from which the modern world has suffered.'[10] Sir Basil Blunkett of the Bank of England, who seemed to be leading a particularly spirited campaign against the absurdity of gold as a currency eighty-odd years ago, declared that gold was a standard that could 'at one time measure an inch and at another a hundred or more inches'.[11] The most cursory of glances at the previous inflation chart confirms this, and leaves the rational economist cheering Sir Basil on, and wishing him every success in his endeavours.

Because the relative price of gold is not stable, and because there can be relatively long periods of inflation under a gold-based system, real borrowing costs will be higher than they would be under a system that generated relative certainty about the rate of inflation over the investable time horizon. The inflation uncertainty caused by fluctuations in the relative price of gold in turn reduces investment below the level that could potentially be achieved, and that reduced rate of investment ultimately lowers the trend rate of growth of an economy.

Gold, trade and deflation

That gold does not create inflation stability in the short to medium term is relatively clear from the historical evidence. However, *over the longer term*, the bias is for a gold or gold standard to generate deflation in the absence of increasing gold supply. There are two stories to be told here: global trade volumes and the bias of correcting imbalances.

The trade volume story is one of simple mathematics; the supply of gold cannot grow fast enough to meet the potential growth of the world economy and world trade. The gold bug advocate of a gold standard makes a virtue of the fact that gold supply cannot increase terribly quickly. To the rational economist this fact is one of the most fatal of flaws in the arguments of the gold peddlers.

A quick examination of the numbers should make this point. The world economy today probably has a trend rate of growth of somewhere between 5.5 per cent and 6.0 per cent per year in nominal terms. If we assume that international trade is stable as a share of global economic activity, and that trade protectionism is contained, then international trade should also increase by around 5.5 per cent to 6.0 per cent per year. So far, so good.

However, if the value of international trade is rising by 5.5 per cent to 6.0 per cent each year, then the world economy will need 5.5 per cent to 6.0 per cent more money each year in order to engage in international trade. If, through some act of economic madness, the world were to attempt a gold standard system, then the increase in international trade would require an increase in gold supply of 5.5 per cent to 6.0 per cent per year.

The stock of gold today is increasing at a rate of no more than 3.0 per cent per year; that is to say, mining will increase the gold stock by something like that amount. A figure of 3.0 per cent can be considered to be the upper limit of the gold supply increase through mining. Clearly, 3.0 per cent is not quite the same thing as 5.5 per cent to 6.0 per cent. There is something of a gap.

The gap between the growth in gold supply and the growth in the value of international trade means that in the long term there are only two options for the world economy if it adheres to a gold standard. First, and most obviously, global trade grows more slowly. This would mean either that the volume of global trade slows so that it grows at 3.0 per cent, and thus globalisation reverses sharply with all the attendant inefficiencies that suggests, or alternatively the global economy grows at 3.0 per cent in nominal terms and global trade maintains its share of economic activity. The idea that the world economy grows at 3.0 per cent in nominal terms would find relatively few advocates, as with a global population that is continuing to expand it would mean, on average, a fairly sharp reversal of the standard of living for each person.

The alternative way of squaring the circle in the long term is to introduce deflation. If the volume of trade (real trade) grows at 6.0 per cent, and prices fall by 3.0 per cent, then an increase in the global money supply (gold) of 3.0 per cent will be enough to finance global trade, because the value of global trade (nominal trade) is growing by 3.0 per cent. Nominal 3.0 per cent growth less −3.0 per cent inflation gives 6.0 per cent real growth. This is, however, a fairly aggressive form of deflation. As discussed in the opening chapter, deflation is not generally considered a desirable situation for a modern economy to find itself in.

As we have already discovered, there are things that can be done in the short term to help offset this situation. Possibly new sources of gold could be identified, although this has to be considered relatively less likely nowadays than was the case in the nineteenth century. Ultimately, even gold bugs must accept that gold is a finite resource – indeed it is that which lures advocates of gold to the yellow metal in the first place.

If physical gold supply cannot be increased further, then an alternative solution may be to increase the circulation of other forms of money – bills of exchange, mobilia or whatever. This is valid in the short term and the medium term, and of course has happened historically. However, if the gold-based system is to survive, a continual increase in the ratio of gold substitute currencies to gold cannot persist indefinitely. At some point the inexorably increasing supply of non-gold currency will raise the question in the mind of the holder as to whether they will really be able to get gold in exchange for whatever substitute they are holding. As soon as the seed of doubt has been sown, the rational thing to do is to refuse to accept the substitutes and only accept gold. The gold substitute to gold ratio falls, and we are back to where we started with a currency that is not increasing with sufficient speed to lubricate the wheels of commerce.

Indeed, exactly this problem occurred under the Bretton Woods exchange rate system in the 1960s. The Bretton Woods system introduced US dollars as a non-gold form of international currency, with dollar holders required to believe that they could convert those dollars into gold at a rate of $35 per ounce. Rather unsportingly, President de Gaulle of France observed that the supply of dollars was going up, and the supply of gold held in Fort Knox was not, and that as a result it might be rather difficult in the future to convert holdings of dollars into gold at will. This was all perfectly true, but not something that should really have been mentioned in polite society. Having declared that the Bretton Woods exchange rate emperor was not fully clothed, de Gaulle insisted that the French receive gold and not dollars for their foreign exchange reserves, and by doing so hastened the ultimate demise of the Bretton Woods exchange rate system. In fact, de Gaulle's observation was not an original thought. An economist called Triffin had noted the broader problems of the Bretton Woods standard in a testimony to Congress in 1960, identifying a problem that was forever immortalised as 'the Triffin Dilemma'. Going even further back in time, at the outset of the Bretton Woods exchange rate system Keynes had advocated a very different structure to avoid this problem, but the Americans had pushed for the dollar-based system (and as they were the ones with the money, they won out).

So, the long-term big picture options for a gold currency system are that it will tend to be deflationary as a trend (with bouts of inflation in between), or the gold system itself will give way under the strain, or there will be very little economic growth. None of these are very enticing options.

There is a second deflationary impulse that comes from a gold-based system, which is less big picture (but still longer term). This deflationary force comes from the skewed pressures around economic policy under a gold standard system. As already mentioned, a gold-based currency system is supposed to regulate international trade imbalances by shifting gold from countries running trade deficits to those running trade surpluses. The debtor country is supposed to pay in gold to make its international purchases, and so the domestic money supply goes down and interest rates will go up. This will deflate domestic prices and slow domestic activity, and if carried on to a sufficient degree will create a recession or a depression.

Thus far the gold-based currency standard has produced a deflationary impulse. But what of the creditor country? For every debtor there must be a creditor sitting on the other side of the ledger, after all, and the creditor will be receiving gold inflows. Those gold inflows should increase the domestic money supply and by doing so stimulate domestic demand and create inflation. That, at least, is the theory.

The difficulty with this argument is that the advantage lies entirely with the creditor in a gold-based system. The creditor does not have to increase the amount of gold in circulation. The creditor could hoard the gold, miser-like, in the vaults of its central bank. By doing so it would not permit the domestic money supply to rise. This is what policymakers in France and the United States did during the 1920s; economists call this policy 'sterilisation' (we saw in the previous chapter how the Emperor Constantine reversed the sterilisation of gold and silver by melting down pagan temple treasures and turning them into coin). The process of sterilisation is simple enough; it can be put into effect through the management of short-term interest rates, or by the regulation of the financial sector. The problem for the economist is that sterilisation can continue without limit. There is nothing to stop a creditor country accumulating an ever larger stockpile of gold, but only allowing an ever diminishing proportion of that gold into the domestic money supply. The result is no inflation, no domestic economic stimulus, and no offset to the economic circumstances of the debtor country.

The debtor country, of course, does not have this luxury. When the gold is gone, it is gone. As gold stocks diminish the debtor country is forced into ever more deflationary policies, while as the creditor's gold stocks increase they have no compulsion to pursue a stimulatory policy at all. Therefore, while there is no necessity for a gold-based currency system to introduce a deflationary bias through the process of trade imbalance adjustment, the fact that the system is skewed in favour of the creditor country and against the debtor country does give a deflationary bias to the global economy.

The clear long-term, multi-year risk of a gold-based system is that it will create price deflation. The United Kingdom-led gold-based currency standard of the nineteenth century only avoided this outcome through the fortuitous discovery of additional gold deposits at the end of the century. Had those deposits lain undiscovered the deflation effect would have been overwhelming.

The buzzing of the gold bugs should by now have faded to nothing, but occasionally one hears the argument that this deflationary fear is overdone; the nineteenth century was a period of abundant prosperity, after all. The counterarguments to this are succinct. The nineteenth century was not a gold standard – the majority of the world did not use a gold-based currency for the majority of the century (or anything like). The country that did use gold as its currency basis for the nineteenth century, the United Kingdom, saw real economic growth per person of roughly 1.1 per cent between 1820 and 1870 – a relatively poor improvement in living standards when compared with the growth per person of between 1.8 per cent and 1.9 per cent per year that the Group of Seven (G7) economies experienced between 1972 and 2012 under a paper currency regime.[12] Note too that the later series includes the various oil price shocks, and the bulk of the impact of the global financial crisis.

The unpleasant squelching noise that the reader may now be able to detect is the sound of a gold bug being squashed beneath the force of economic logic.

Tarnished gold

The fascination that surrounds gold and its relationship with general inflation is a dangerous romanticism of a world that never really existed. Gold is one of many currency forms that have existed over the centuries, and we should not be seduced by British economic nationalism into believing that gold is in any way superior to any of the other currency forms humanity has used. Above all else the idea of gold as having intrinsic value needs to be rejected for the fairy tale that it is. Gold has the same intrinsic value as a Bitcoin – that is, none at all. Gold is worth only what it can purchase; which means it is worth only what other people will willingly surrender in exchange.

A gold-based currency is ultimately likely to be deflationary over the very long term, just because of the constrained supply of gold and what that will imply for the relative price of the metal when compared with goods and labour that are not so supply constrained. However, moving from the multigenerational long term to any realistic investment time horizon means that gold is no guaranteed hedge against inflation, and there can be absolutely no certainty as to price stability. Investors should not depend on gold to preserve the real value of their portfolios; they may strike lucky and preserve their real worth, or even increase it, but by the same token they may strike lucky in the casino at Monte Carlo.

This does not mean that investors should disregard gold as an asset – it has attributes that allow it to diversify risk in a portfolio. The problems of gold are simply that it does not now provide, and never has, an adequate guaranteed hedge against the effects of inflation.

Notes

1　Dulles (1933) p 1.
2　Sparling (1933) p 33.
3　This was the world's first gold standard because it specifically and legally defined a currency in terms of an amount of gold. Prior to that, a currency was worth what the government (generally the monarch) said it was worth. Debasement was not possible under the British gold standard, because the UK government had committed to a pound being worth a measurable amount of gold. The United Kingdom was either on the gold standard or off of it. Prior to that, debasement was possible because the government simply declared what the value of the currency was, and could change it at whim – which, as the previous chapter demonstrated, was a remarkably regular occurrence.
4　Sparling (1933) p 80.
5　Fischer (1996) p 25.
6　Dick (2013) p 36 and p 59.
7　World Gold Council (2013) p 8.
8　One natural desire for a proxy arose because, as long as confidence in the convertibility of substitutes could be maintained, the substitutes were more convenient to use than gold specie. Witness the evidence of the Somerset banker Mr Stuckey, complaining in 1819 to the House of Lords about the cost of using gold. 'In 1817, we had a circulation of guineas, which we found very inconvenient. It cost us near 100*l* [pounds] to transmit gold and silver to London in the first six months of the year 1817.' Quote from Tooke (1838) Volume 1 p 133.
9　Granville (2013) p 20 citing Sayers.
10　Sparling (1933) p 34.
11　Sparling (1933) p 9.
12　UK historical data from Broadberry *et al.* (2011), Table 25. G7 data from the Organisation for Economic Co-operation and Development database.

4   What makes up inflation?

The CPI [consumer price index] as calculated may not be a conspiracy but it's definitely a con job foisted on an unwitting public by government officials...

(Bill Gross)[1]

It is time to move away from the comfort blanket of economic history and embrace the realities of inflation in the modern world. This chapter examines what goes into inflation to try to understand what inflation actually is, before going on to consider over the subsequent chapters what inflation most emphatically is not. This is not to retrace the journey taken in the earlier chapters. Inflation is a general increase in prices, not a relative increase in prices – we have already established that much. The Fisher equation of exchange that establishes the relationship of money supply, velocity, prices and transactions still holds. Neither the relative price nor the Fisher equation concept needs to be revisited. Instead, this chapter will break down the specific components of inflation, and consider the way in which spin (and the media) can manipulate our misunderstanding of what causes inflation so as to create an unnecessary acceptance of price changes. The serious risk of politicians mismanaging inflation in response to a popular misunderstanding of it is also examined. This is a passionate issue, as the quote from Bill Gross that heads this chapter makes clear. Gross, at the time he made the quote, was rarely cited without the suffix 'manager of the world's largest bond fund', and his complaints about the construction of consumer price inflation should be addressed.

The simplistic breakdown

The modern consumer price indices that measure inflation are supposed to approximate the typical 'basket of goods and services' that is purchased by an average household. Statisticians nowadays look at all the broad categories of goods and services that are legally consumed by the consumer in an economy, and try to form a representative sample of the average consumer's expenditure. Taking a large sample of goods and services means that the statistic should capture general price increases, and that any relative price change will be averaged out in the scale of the index. Thus, the first definition of inflation from the first chapter is satisfied, and we have a general index of prices with which to work.

The earliest consumer price indices were mainly focused on goods, and primarily on the very narrow category of food products at that. The Labour Bureau within the UK's Board of Trade produced an index of thirty food items in the late nineteenth century, while in 1891 the US Senate Finance Committee ordered the Bureau of Labor Statistics to produce an index that turned out to be just over two hundred items, mostly food and clothing. These first indices did not actually aim to replicate the average household's spending, but instead were focused on lower-income groups that spent most of their income on food, energy and rent (because it was the standard of living of lower-income households that was the focus of political concern). Such indices would not be much use in gauging the average household's cost of living nowadays. Services have a larger weight in modern spending baskets, and consequently must carry greater weight in modern consumer price indices for developed economies if they are to accurately reflect the cost of living in such an economy. However, the precise components of each idealised consumer basket will differ from economy to economy, because, of course, different economies have different consumer tastes and cultural patterns. For example, sushi will play a larger role in the Japanese consumer price basket than it will in the Italian. The purchase and leasing of vehicles is extremely important in the United States (where the right to drive a sports utility vehicle was only omitted from the Constitution through some terrible lack of foresight on the part of the Founding Fathers); it is far less important in Japan. In the US, vehicle purchase and leasing weighs in at 5.8 per cent of the consumer price basket, while in Japan it is a mere 1.8 per cent of consumer spending.

The European Union produces a series of consumer price indices that go under the name of 'harmonised' consumer prices, but this harmonisation does not mean that each component has the same weighting across the European Union. Rather, the broad methodology is harmonised, and the weightings vary from economy to economy according to cultural taste. Table 4.1 summarises the weightings of some of the very broadest categories of inflation components (the table does not sum to 100 per cent).

It seems a fairly pertinent question to ask whether it is fair to make a comparison of consumer prices between economies, when the weightings applied to the different categories differ. Can we really say inflation in Germany is higher than inflation in the United States, if the German inflation is caused by an increase in the price of alcohol which carries greater weight in Germany than it does in the United States? The answer to this question is generally 'yes'; we need to remember what consumer prices are trying to measure. The point of consumer price indices is to try to get a handle on whether the cost of living has been rising in an economy over time. What we want to know is whether the expense of living a German 'lifestyle' is rising more rapidly than is the expense of living an American 'lifestyle'. International comparisons of consumer prices

Table 4.1 Inflation weights in different advanced economies today

	United States	United Kingdom	Germany	France	Japan
Food	8.2	9.9	11.0	15.1	17.3
Alcohol	1.0	2.0	4.4	1.9	1.3
Clothing	3.6	6.2	5.1	5.1	4.1
Education	3.2	2.2	0.9	0.4	3.3
Health	7.6	2.4	0.5	4.2	4.3
Transport fuel	5.1	3.5	4.2	4.4	2.3
Energy for the home	4.0	4.5	7.7	5.5	5.4
Shelter	32.0	9.0	11.4	8.6	18.7
Vehicles	5.8	4.4	3.7	3.6	1.8
Furniture	3.4	4.7	4.8	4.5	3.5

Source: Bureau of Labor Statistics, Eurostat, Statistics Japan, via Haver Analytics.

should be considered as an 'apples to apples' comparison, in that the economist is comparing 'lifestyle to lifestyle'. The precise details of what makes up that lifestyle are not normally very relevant for the purposes of international comparison.

Asset prices and inflation

Before getting down to the details of what makes up inflation, it is worth taking a moment to consider an omission. Inflation, at least consumer price inflation, is supposed to be a rough proxy for the cost of living. It is all about lifestyle. That means, critically, that asset prices are not a part of consumer price inflation. Asset prices should not be a part of consumer price inflation. In fact, asset prices are, for the most part, the antithesis of what consumer price inflation is supposed to measure.

Assets are not the same thing as the goods and services consumers use to create a specific lifestyle. Purchasing an asset *today* does not increase a consumer's ability to spend money or enjoy goods and services *today*. Assets are things that represent the potential to generate a *future* income stream. If an investor buys equities, they are hoping to earn dividends as income in the years ahead, and maybe some capital gains in the future if they choose to sell the equities. If an investor buys a house, they could at least in theory derive an income from renting out that house in the future, or possibly realise a capital gain by selling it at a higher price. In short, acquiring an asset is about providing for a future standard of living by acquiring a future income or capital gain; owning an asset says nothing about a consumer's *current* standard of living. Consumer price inflation is all about how price changes are affecting a consumer's real current standard of living. Asset price inflation relates to future income; consumer price inflation relates to current spending.

This does not mean that policymakers should necessarily ignore asset prices. Asset price changes can have economic consequences. If asset prices rise above fair value, there are potentially significant consequences. This, incidentally, is why investors should be very wary of the idea that rising asset prices are a 'good' thing. Asset prices that are fair value are 'good'. Rising asset prices that take an asset further and further away from fair value and more and more into 'bubble' territory are absolutely not a good thing. Asset prices that inflate too quickly can lead to a misallocation of resources in an economy, financial instability, excessive borrowing and excessive consumption – all things policymakers should be concerned about. Policymakers can react to asset price inflation while recognising that asset price increases are not inflation in a consumer price, cost-of-living sort of a way. They may be relevant but they should not be considered inflation in the sense that most investors understand the term.

The obvious problem arises when something can be thought of as an asset and as an item that enhances one's standard of living. In consumer price terms this essentially comes down to housing, and that is a key part of what is put in and what is left out of consumer price calculations.

The inflation hokey cokey

So far the composition of inflation statistics seems to be relatively simple, and the investor should have little trouble in tracking the headline cost of living. Unfortunately, this simplicity is deceptive. No sooner is the headline consumer price basket published than we immediately enter into an economic hokey cokey dance, with a frenetic process of adjustment that is forever putting things in and taking things out of the headline index. There is also quite a lot of 'shaking all about' involved in the process as well. It is this continuously changing composition of consumer prices that has drawn the criticism of the likes of Gross, but it does have a purpose.

There are two important problems around the reported breakdown of the basic consumer price index into component subcategories: housing, and food and energy. The nature of each of these problems is somewhat different, but both cause considerable difficulty in generating a 'clean' cost of living index.

The observant reader will have noticed that housing is weighted very, very differently among the various economies summarised in Table 4.1. Housing is a problem in societies where a reasonable proportion of the population live in a home that they own. What is the cost of housing in such a society? Obviously, or seemingly obviously, the cost of owning a property is the monthly mortgage payment. This is the sum of money that has to be paid to have the right to live in a house, and it is a regular monthly outgoing. The problem with this is that in paying for a mortgage, the homeowner is actually getting two things. The homeowner is getting to enjoy the lifestyle benefits of living in a home ('shelter', to be all economist-like about the terminology), and they are acquiring an asset or paying off the debt used to acquire an asset. Furthermore, someone who has paid off their mortgage is still getting the economic service of 'shelter', even if they are no longer paying anything towards it in monthly outgoings beyond maintenance costs. In comparison, someone who is just renting the place where they live is paying for the comfort and benefits of 'shelter', which is what dictates their standard of living, but they are not acquiring an asset in the process. Indeed, the earliest price statistics in the US and the UK dealt with the problem of housing by simply ignoring it, even though the cost of housing would often be the largest single purchase a household made each week.

The complications of housing are not a small problem because housing can carry a considerable weight even in modern consumer price indices. 'Shelter', which includes hotel accommodation, accounts for almost a third of the consumer price basket in the United States. How the cost of housing is calculated can therefore make a pretty big difference to the level of inflation.

For the most part consumer price data exclude mortgage payments from homeowners and instead concentrate on measuring the cost of the lifestyle benefit that is associated with owning a house. After all, if we are trying to measure the cost of a lifestyle with consumer price data, then it seems only fair to focus on the cost of enjoying 'shelter' rather than capturing any future financial income stream that may come from the ownership of an asset. How is that cost of 'shelter' calculated so as to exclude the benefits of asset ownership?

The European harmonised inflation data (which include the consumer price index for the United Kingdom) get around the problem of housing as an asset versus housing as part of a standard of living by ignoring it. Never let it be said that the statisticians of the European Union are not pragmatic when it comes to difficult issues. Housing costs are included where rent is paid, because paying rent does not lead to the acquisition of any asset. Maintenance costs for property owners are also included, quite rightly. However, payments made by owners of property related to the purchase of the property are entirely ignored in European inflation statistics, on the grounds that owning a property is entirely about the acquisition of an asset. The fact that the property owner lives in the asset is considered to be incidental.

The UK Retail Price Index, which still forms the basis of much of the UK's inflation-linked contracts, does include mortgage payments. The instance of home ownership in the UK is so high that the UK is more adversely affected than other European economies by the failure to include home ownership costs in the consumer price index.

Elsewhere, most notably in the United States, the concept of 'shelter' is calculated by working out what rent homeowners would have to pay if they were renting the property rather than owning it. If one is renting, clearly one does not enjoy the benefit of owning an asset, only the benefit of having a roof over one's head. Therefore, if statisticians can approximate the rental value of the property a person is living in, they have an idea of the cost of enjoying that 'shelter' without the complication of asset acquisition. This statistic is known as implied rent, sometimes owners' equivalent rent, and the idea is that the homeowner is renting the property from themselves – at once a tenant enjoying the benefits of shelter, and a landlord enjoying the income stream of an asset.

This is by no means a perfect solution, for a couple of reasons. As should be obvious, if there is a high instance of home ownership there will only be a small sample of rental properties statisticians can use to approximate the cost of enjoying shelter. This small sample may be biased as a result of its size, and the true rental value of a home may be distorted; the whole assumption about housing costs is like an inverted pyramid, resting on a very narrow foundation. The second problem with measuring lifestyle costs using an implied rent rather than the actual monthly mortgage outgoings for a homeowner is that it is perfectly possible that the expense of the household will be changing by more than the consumer price basket implies. Mortgage payments could easily increase more quickly than rental payments (or vice versa). Of course, for those homeowners who have completed their mortgage payments, the cost of living index using implied rents may make their cost of living appear higher than it actually is, although (again) if inflation numbers are inflated relative to reality people tend not to complain so much.

The problem with the way housing is treated in consumer price inflation is that in many cases the homeowner will have outgoings that exceed the spending implied in the consumer price index. The UK retail price measure will reflect consumer spending in reality, but also capture asset price effects. The European consumer price measures simply ignore a part of the cost of living because it is deemed to be all asset price effects. The US method tries to separate the asset price and the non-asset price components of the housing spending. In all cases, bar the UK retail price calculation, there is a risk that the housing cost reality will differ from the reported housing cost, because of the asset component embedded in housing.

Telling homeowners that their cost of living is not really increasing as much as they think because they are actually acquiring an asset is likely to be met with a fairly pithy response. The counterargument hurled into the face of the long-suffering economist will be 'my mortgage costs me more, and I have less money'. This is true, and the economist's justification of 'you have less money because you are acquiring an asset' is likely to be of little comfort to mortgage payers who are scrambling to meet increased monthly outgoings from their income. Mortgage payers are obviously going to believe that their standard of living is lower if they are able to purchase fewer smartphones, takeaway pizzas or bottles of wine as a result of an increase in their mortgage payments. Surely reducing the ability to consume the things that make life worth living is the very definition of a falling standard of living? What is objectively a necessary solution to the problem of housing in consumer price measures is something that to most consumers intuitively seems to be a statistical-economic fraud.

Unfortunately, there is no perfect solution to the problem of housing. Implied rent is generally considered to make the best of it. The most troubling result of this compromise is that if there is a divergence between the growth of implied rent and the growth of mortgage payments, or any housing measure in CPI when compared to the outgoings of a homeowner in reality, homeowners will begin to distrust the accuracy of consumer price data. Indeed, *in extremis*, homeowners could even begin to distrust economists at central banks for using consumer price data (and distrusting economists is a circumstance that would hasten the collapse of civilisation as we know it). This loss of confidence undermines central bank credibility in a way that could actually make controlling inflation more difficult.

So much for housing. The second adjustment that is frequently made to modern cost of living indices is the exclusion of food and energy prices. Consumer prices excluding food and energy are often referred to as 'core' inflation. The exception to this relatively sensible rule is Japan, where core inflation is consumer prices excluding food alone. The inflation rate excluding food and energy in Japan is helpfully known as core-core inflation.

Excluding food and energy from the consumer prices immediately provokes a shrill cry of objection from many consumers and investors. After all the earliest indices were pretty much nothing but food, and now statisticians and economists are trying to cut food out altogether. Food and energy prices tend to move around a great deal, and there is therefore a supposition that by excluding food and energy, statisticians are in some way manipulating inflation to keep the official data lower than it should be. The question 'why are you excluding everything that is pushing inflation higher?' is often asked of an economist, generally in a slightly resentful tone. (The reverse complaint is not normally raised when food and energy prices are reducing inflation and the headline rate is lower than the core.) However, there is a justification for excluding food and energy from consumer prices for policy purposes. Investors, however much they may object to the loss of food and energy from the consumer price basket, should still pay attention to core data as a useful indicator.

Fundamentally, a central bank is capable of controlling domestic money supply or interest rates. Economists at a central bank can, with their special superhero-like powers, manipulate money supply or interest rates so as to manage many forms of inflation. What economists are not able to do is control the weather. A bad harvest reducing the supply of agricultural commodities will have a positive influence on food prices (not as much as one might think, as we shall see a little later on, but it will have an impact). A cold winter, increasing demand for energy, will drive up energy prices. These are factors beyond even an economist's control. Changing interest rates will not cause crops to grow faster, nor can adjustments in the domestic money supply alter the amount of snowfall over the course of a winter. It is also worth noting that food and energy prices are at least partially determined by global market conditions, and the central bank of a small economy has little chance of influencing global prices through domestic monetary policy.

Excluding food and energy to get a core (or core-core) inflation rate is not, therefore, an attempt to suggest that food and energy do not matter to the standard of living in an economy. If one is trying to assess whether one's lifestyle is more or less expensive than it was in the past, then the core inflation rate is no use. However, if policymakers are trying to decide whether they should be taking action and changing interest rates or other policy measures on the back of inflation, then there is an argument for using core inflation. Core inflation is more susceptible to the influence of policymakers, as it reflects inflation causes that they can actually control.

The arguments around the use of core inflation are not too dissimilar from those that surround the way in which house prices are measured in inflation. Core inflation is not an accurate measure of how the cost of living has changed for a typical family, but it may nevertheless be politic to use this in the setting of policy, as this is the core inflation measure that represents the bit of inflation that policy can actually influence. On the other hand, if central banks and other policymakers have as their objective the stabilisation of the cost of living, why should one not use the true cost of living? If a bad harvest has helped to drive the price of vegetables higher, should not the central bank tighten monetary policy to drive other prices (smartphones or whatever) lower, in order to offset the effects of higher food prices on family budgets? But if a central bank is slowing an economy with tighter monetary policy today to offset higher food prices, in the knowledge that a better harvest or a warmer winter next year will completely reverse the position, could they not be accused of acting impatiently and increasing economic volatility and uncertainty (especially as the impact of monetary policy in an economy operates with relatively lengthy lags)? And so the arguments go back and forth.

The pragmatic policymaker (if such creatures exist) will target headline consumer price inflation as reflecting an approximation of the standard of living, while monitoring core inflation as a source of additional information to be used in determining whether or not to tighten policy. A sensible approach may be to ignore short-term fluctuations that are beyond the central bank's direct control, but react when core and headline consumer price measures are signalling a similar message. Even this approach is not perfect, however. If a central bank ignores a headline consumer price move on the grounds that it is a temporary effect, then as with housing consumers may start to question the central bank's credibility: consumers have been promised a stable level of inflation, and patently a change in the headline inflation rate for whatever cause means that the promise is not being kept in the short term, whatever may happen in the long term. Investors are also likely to feel that short-term volatility in the headline inflation rate may be a problem – think of the issue of inflation volatility under the gold standard, and the inflation uncertainty premium that this introduced into investors' perceptions of risk. Although the episodes of inflation volatility may be more short-lived than the volatility experienced under the gold standard if it is just seasonal fluctuations in food and energy prices that are driving the change, the element of inflation uncertainty is likely to concern at least some investors, as well as undermining the credibility of the central bank.

Excluding or recalculating certain components from inflation may be desirable, but with both the housing measure and the food and energy measures there is a risk that consumers feel 'short-changed' by the adjusted inflation measure. In both cases the threat to the credibility of the central bank has been highlighted. The credibility of the central bank matters because it can be influential in how wages are set in an economy. One important factor in determining wages is what workers believe will happen with inflation in the future. If the central bank is credible and has a clear inflation target, then that inflation target is likely to form the basis of pay negotiations. If the central bank's credibility has been undermined then workers are likely to regard the inflation target as a starting point for negotiations, to which an inflation uncertainty risk must be added. That inflation uncertainty risk will put upwards pressure on wages, and as we shall now see the role of wages in feeding back into inflation is absolutely critical.

The true breakdown of inflation

So far we have considered inflation by looking at the components that make up the index. This is fine, as far as it goes, and it can be quite useful in identifying when 'Acts of God' (like bad weather) are creating temporary distortions. Breaking inflation into its separate components can also help with assessing relative price changes that may result from industry-specific rather than macroeconomic problems (for example, industrial action reducing the supply of one sort of product, raising its price). However, considering inflation as merely a mix of specific categories of goods and services is a rather superficial way of thinking about price change and what drives general rather than relative or industry-specific price shifts. More importantly, it is not terribly helpful from the perspective of the policymaker (seeking, one hopes, to manage inflation), nor the investor (seeking, one assumes, to avoid inflation ravaging the real value of their portfolio).

The alternative way of breaking down inflation is to consider what goes into each of the goods and services that makes up inflation. How much of this is labour? How much of it is commodities? Breaking down inflation in this way allows the economist to try to predict where inflation is going. If the oil price rises, what does that mean for inflation? The starting point is to ask the question as to how important oil is to the price of goods and services in an economy. Oil is directly represented in the consumer price basket by the weightings given to heating oil, gasoline or petroleum and other such products. Table 4.1 showed that the fuel for cars weighted between 2.3 per cent and 5.1 per cent of the consumer price basket in the sampled economies. Summing all of the various, specific weightings for fuel would appear to give an idea of the importance of oil to consumer prices – but there is more to oil than that. Oil may be present in many forms in the consumer price index, without physically being purchased as a barrel of liquid Brent crude and appearing as a direct component of the index. If oil is used in generating electricity then all things being equal a rise in the price of oil will have an impact on electricity prices. The impact of oil on electricity prices will not be included in an assessment that just considers the weightings for heating oil and gasoline.

Very well, we can add the weightings of electricity to our calculations of the importance of oil to inflation. But this is not really accurate. Electricity prices are about more than just oil, and electricity prices might not rise in lock-step with the rise in oil prices. And then we need to go even further in understanding the role of oil; if oil prices do cause an increase in electricity prices, that might cause an increase in fertiliser prices, and an increase in fertiliser prices might in turn cause an increase in food prices. The impact of oil on the consumer price index has spread throughout the economy via a plethora of products that all have some oil relationship – even if that relationship is several times removed. The weighting for what might be considered 'pure' oil products in the consumer price basket is incapable of capturing these disparate forces.

To describe the role of oil in an economy as 'complex' rapidly becomes a polite understatement. Peeling away the layers of each product in the consumer price basket, we find further layers demanding their own exposure. At this point an investor may be tempted to bury their head in their hands and start to weep, but for an economist the way to simplify this onion-like economic exercise is to take a step back and consider the big picture. How much of a country's overall economic activity is due to labour? How much is due to oil? How much is due to copper? The process can be repeated for almost any input into the production process. These different levels of importance can be calculated readily enough: if economists wish to calculate the true impact of labour across the entirety of the consumer price basket we can measure the wages, salaries and benefits paid by employers for all the labour used in an economy over any given time frame, we can measure the size of economic output of those employers over the same time frame, and we can compare the two. The same process can be gone through for various commodities, and this will allow the economist to develop a picture that represents the relative importance of labour, commodities, or anything else that one wishes to disaggregate. The process will capture the impact of labour and commodities on the price of exports as well as on the price of domestically produced goods, but with trade a relatively low share of most developed economies' economic activity this is unlikely to be too significant a distortion.

So what does this approach reveal about consumer price inflation? In an advanced industrialised economy inflation is overwhelmingly a matter of *domestic* labour costs. There may be periods when the ratios change, but on average inflation is around 60–65 per cent labour (because payments to labour are the equivalent of around 60–65 per cent of corporate value added in an economy). The importance of oil varies from economy to economy, but it should be assumed to be somewhere between 2 per cent and 4 per cent in the Organisation for Economic Co-operation and Development. We know how much crude oil an economy consumes in a year (nearly nineteen million barrels per day in the US). We know what the price of crude oil is, and therefore what the value of crude oil consumed is. We know what the value of all economic activity in the United States is – the ratio between the two comes out at around 4 per cent as the US is quite an intensive consumer of oil by developed economy standards (all those sports utility vehicles). This is a lot lower than the consumer price weighting for oil, but remember that the consumer price weighting represents the price paid by the consumer, not the price of crude oil. A lot of the price paid by the consumer for oil will be labour cost, retail margins and taxation. If an investor is trying to consider the importance of *crude oil prices* to inflation, then none of the price consequences of labour, retail margin and taxation will matter.

The dominance of domestic labour costs to inflation in a developed economy should not really occasion much surprise. The importance of the labour of others as opposed to self-sufficiency was one of the factors identified in the second chapter as a necessary condition for creating inflation. In a sense, inflation is founded on the idea of people being paid to labour on behalf of others. As societies become more sophisticated and less self-sufficient (at an individual level) then the role of labour in driving prices will necessarily become increasingly important – a sentiment pithily summarised two centuries ago by Jane Marcet: 'no sooner does the labour of man become necessary to procure us the enjoyment of any commodity, than that commodity acquires a value'.[2]

It is critical to note that the important drivers of the labour portion of inflation are not wages and salaries. What economists are trying to find is how labour costs will affect prices, and this is about more than just wages and salaries. For one thing, there may be other costs associated with employing labour like taxes or welfare costs. If those costs rise, then the costs of operating a business increase, and if labour costs amount to 60–65 per cent of the operating costs of a business then the business has a relatively strong incentive to raise prices as an offset. But perhaps more importantly there is the issue of how hard the workforce works, as that determines the amount of goods or services that are actually produced.

If a smartphone manufacturer pays its workforce 10 per cent more, but by doing so incentivises the workers to work 20 per cent harder (in effect to produce 20 per cent more smartphones), then the owner of that firm has made a pretty good bargain. The more productive the workforce, the more it is worth paying it. What is happening in this example is that what economists call 'unit labour costs' are falling (the phrase comes about because we are measuring the cost of labour required to produce one unit of output – one smartphone in this example). If spending 10 per cent more on wages means that 20 per cent more smartphones are produced, then the labour cost to make a single smartphone is coming down. If the labour costs account for 60–65 per cent of the cost of manufacturing a smartphone, then the manufacturer can readily reduce the price of a smartphone if it wishes.

What this means is that monitoring domestic unit labour costs should give a reasonable idea of the inflation pressures that exist in an economy. However, the relationship is not perfect. After all, around 35 per cent of a product's price is made up of other costs (commodity prices being one of the higher-profile instances). There is also the question of whether manufacturers will choose to pass on lower labour costs, or whether they will seek to increase profit margins instead. The correlation of consumer prices and unit labour costs will not be perfect, but it is well for policymakers and investors to remember the importance of unit labour costs in determining prices. It is one of the reasons why labour market data is treated so reverentially when inflation is forecast. Failing to remember the importance of labour costs to overall inflation can lead to more acceptance of inflation than is actually warranted, and this is the next issue to address.

Spin and sound-bite economics

The fact that prices are mainly about domestic labour costs is something that is frequently not properly recognised in everyday economics. This allows a rather toxic combination of sound-bite economics and profit maximisation to creep into issues around modern inflation. This in turn potentially allows the consumer to be manipulated into believing that price increases are justified when economic reality suggests that they are not.

One of the most glaring instances of this problem arises with food. The great problem with popular perceptions about food pricing is that consumers do not live in the real economic world, but instead inhabit some nostalgic fairy-tale-like existence which has not been economic reality for at least a couple of centuries. Consumers in developed economies cling tenaciously but entirely erroneously to the quaint notion that the price of what they are eating is in some way related to what happens on a farm. Nothing could be further from the truth. In modern economies, food is not 'food' at all.

Imagine that there is an increase in the price of agricultural commodity prices, like wheat. Media outlets will assume the appearance of concern in their reporting. Television news reports will show farmers talking about poor crop yields, and then cut away to supermarket shelves of bread with alarming graphics demonstrating the extent to which bread prices are rising. Newspaper articles about food prices will discuss the impact of climate change, and predict whether food prices will continue to rise as wheat prices reach record highs (in a foreign currency, on a foreign bourse). Meanwhile the economist, their face suffused with a dark purple hue, will be pounding their breakfast table almost incoherent with rage and yelling 'what the [expletive deleted] has the price of wheat got to do with the price of bread?' It takes a lot to make an economist even slightly incoherent, and so this reaction is worth probing in some depth.

Food producers are keen to promote the idea that what they are selling is largely a farm product. Consumers don't like to think of food as an industry, and so supermarkets put pictures of farmers on the packaging of their meat, advertisements from bread producers will show waving fields of wheat. Soft drink producers present natural products being carefully selected, even hand-picked, before going into their product. What is almost never shown is everything that happens after the crops leave the farm gate.

The pastoral idyll of farmers lugging sacks of wheat to the local windmill, to be ground into flour that would be collected by the local baker to make into bread is a complete nonsense. The nursery rhymes of our childhood have lied to us. Instead what we have is a lengthy and complex supply chain that converts agricultural commodities into food that we can actually consume. The loaf of bread that we purchase, be it pre-sliced and packed with preservatives or 'baked for you today in-store', is actually predominantly labour.

For most advanced economies, food purchased for home consumption is around 80 per cent labour cost after the farm gate. Only around 20 per cent of what we pay for food actually goes to a farmer (and that 20 per cent will have to cover the cost of land, labour, fuel, fertiliser and so forth – and fertiliser itself is a mix of energy, labour and chemical costs).

This situation describes a developed economy. Emerging markets will have a lower labour content in their food (because consumers in an emerging market are likely to consume food that has had less processing done to it before it gets to the home, and the consumer's own labour in processing food in the home is considered to be 'free' labour for the purposes of calculating inflation). In a developed economy the consumer is paying for the wheat in bread, but also for the manufacture of the wheat flour, the manufacture of the bread itself, the labour involved in distributing the bread, the labour involved in actually selling the bread (someone has to put the bread on shelves, even if the checkout is increasingly automated). The advertising of the bread, the lawyers involved with the various companies along the bread supply chain (lawyers get everywhere), even potentially a crumb or two for an economist involved in the advising of companies – all of these forms of labour are packaged up into the loaf of bread that the consumer is handing over money to purchase. 'Give us this day our daily bread' has never been more labour based than it is today.

Breaking down food prices today reveals a very labour-intensive industry; indeed food is a more labour-intensive industry than most. The most extreme instance of this is the milk industry. In the United Kingdom around 72 per cent of the price of a pint of milk actually goes to a farmer (what is known as the farm gate price) – the remaining 28 per cent mainly goes to labour costs incurred after the farm gate.[3] Milk is, after all, milk – and as a purchased foodstuff it is a product that is as close to the raw agricultural commodity as one can reasonably get nowadays; and yet in reality the milk that we buy is less than three-quarters milk.

So, what does this all mean? It means, self-evidently, that the price of a loaf of bread should not just reflect the price of wheat, but must also reflect the price of a complex system of labour that goes into getting bread to the consumer in the form that we now consume bread. Therefore, if labour costs are relatively stable, and the price of wheat rises 10 per cent, then the price of bread should not rise by any more than 2 per cent. Similarly, if the price of raw milk rises by 10 per cent then the price the consumer pays should not rise by more than 7 per cent.

The problem with this situation is that the presence of all of this labour is hidden from the consumer. Partly this is by design – consumers like to think of food as something that is natural. One does not want to think that lawyers have been metaphorically handling one's loaf of bread before it gets to the breakfast table; such a thought is calculated to blunt even the sharpest of appetites. As already identified, advertising plays to this perception, in presenting food as directly linked to the farmer, rather than the reality of a very remote relationship.

This matters to inflation because consumers can be persuaded to 'accept' higher food prices through their failure to understand what actually constitutes food. If wheat prices rise then food producers or food retailers can seek to attribute higher food prices directly to the farmer or the cost of agricultural commodities. The consumer imagines that they are simply subject to the global economic force of international markets, or to the natural forces of weather patterns and climate, and without liking the consequence they can be conditioned to become grudgingly tolerant of food price increases. The illusion allows for increased profit margins along the supply chain, of course, as the price of the finished product is rising more rapidly than is the weighted average of its economic ingredients. Someone is making money from the failure of consumers to understand what it is that they are truly consuming. If consumers reflected on the reality of what they were eating, and the ratio of labour costs to commodity prices, it is unlikely that they would be so accepting of a food producer or retailer blaming price increases on commodities.

Food is perhaps the most extreme instance where this misperception takes place, but it is not alone. The idea that commodity prices dominate inflation is tied to the fact that they are tangible items, and their role in final products is pretty clear. Consumers will be able to more readily grasp the role that commodities play in prices than the role of lawyers, for instance. Consumers are unlikely to comprehend what purpose lawyers serve in bringing bread to their table, or in producing a washing machine, or providing central heating – but of course lawyers are represented in the price of all of these products. Therefore, any product that visibly has a commodity impact – from heating oil to a copper bath – is a product where consumer perceptions of price can be manipulated.

The potential for misunderstanding of what drives prices can increase the pricing power of product suppliers, but it can also foster a sense of frustration on the part of the consumer. The feeling of impotence in the face of larger forces is not something consumers tend to appreciate, and as consumers may also be voters that creates a political problem. Even if the consumer is not a voter, if taken to the extreme, direct political protest may result, creating social instability. Such concerns can lead governments into that most worrisome of developments – the attempt to legislate to control inflation.

Legislating inflation: the economic equivalent of King Canute

The apocryphal tale of the Danish/English King Canute (or King Cnut), setting up his throne on the shoreline to command the tide to retreat, has two interpretations. One version, which seems to be a misinterpretation of the original story, is of an arrogant king deluded as to the force of his own power over nature. The alternative version is that Canute wished to prove his sycophantic advisers to be wrong, and to demonstrate the limits to royal power. These two contrasting stories actually play out relatively well in describing the different motives of those seeking to legislate against inflation.

When consumers feel that prices are rising inexorably, and particularly when they believe that they are subject to global forces, they are likely to turn to the government to do something. There is a demand that governments should take direct control of the causes of inflation, very often against specific items that have particularly provoked the consumers' ire, in an attempt to bring the cost of living under control. The situation arises because consumers either do not understand what is behind the inflation that they are experiencing, or because they believe that the government can in some way influence the components of inflation.

This desire that the authority of government should take on the might of the market through direct intervention has a long tradition. Governments have either legislated price controls in an attempt to pre-empt popular protest, or have responded to public pressure by imposing controls. The second chapter showed the edict of the Emperor Diocletian attempting to fix prices down to the most mundane of objects. Medieval European governments were particularly addicted to passing legislation prescribing set levels of prices of goods, particularly foodstuffs. The English failed harvest of 1314 caused Edward II to impose maximum prices for food items. The protests against price increases of the eighteenth century were protests directed against government as much as the sellers of the offending products, because it was felt that government should intervene to prevent 'greed' (in a world of mob politics 'greed' is often the cause of inflation, as it combines the desirable attributes of blaming someone else for one's loss in living standards with the righteous indignation of occupying the moral high ground against a sin). The French Revolution directed concerns about prices and the cost of living in a direct and ultimately violent fashion against government and the monarchy, and demanded that the government take action. Robespierre's regime in late eighteenth-century revolutionary France imposed price controls, which (from the perspective of the government) was a logical if largely ineffective response to the plethora of complaints that had helped to topple the monarchy.

Nearly a millennium and a half after Diocletian, and President Nixon can be found attempting to do exactly the same thing as his imperial equivalent, personally worrying about the price of hamburger meat while sitting atop an extensive bureaucracy that aimed to control prices and wages.

Early forms of price controls tended to be arbitrary, determining a specific price for a specific product. Nixon's second attempt at price controls in August 1971 (his first being his role in the Roosevelt bureaucracy of the Second World War) was somewhat different. It was not practical to dictate prices in absolute terms when there was not only an enormous number of products, but also regional variation in prices. Instead, Nixon concentrated on limiting price *increases*, initially by freezing prices and wages, and then by requiring government authorisation for any business that sought to change the price of its output or labour.

The problem with trying to legislate prices is that governmental will rarely defeats the force of the market. The retailers' and producers' response to Diocletian's edict was simply not to offer goods for sale, and in reducing supply they inevitably put further upwards pressure on the prices of those goods that were available in the market. The price caps of Edward II in 1314 were defeated by a worse harvest and rising prices in 1315 (when the public complained that it was all the fault of millers and bakers – a refreshing change from blaming investment bankers – and demanded government action). Further poor harvests in 1316 led to reports of cannibalism, and, of course, still the price controls failed. The error of trying to stem inflation with price controls was not entirely without its critics. President Nixon's third involvement with price controls, in the wake of the OPEC oil shock of 1973, led to a shortage of oil and a system that at times seemed to approach rationing.

The futility of trying to control prices when the economic forces that are influencing prices are not affected has long been recognised. In 1316, the forward-thinking Canon of Bridlington boldly declared 'how contrary to reason is an ordinance of prices'.[4] This free-market cleric was right in economic terms, but perhaps a little out of tune with the popular mood of the time. The population felt impotent in the face of rising prices, and concluded that 'something must be done'.

The problem of legislating against inflation is often exacerbated by the failure to distinguish between the two ways of deconstructing inflation that have already been identified. Consumers tend to focus on the more superficial breakdown of inflation, and pass judgement on relative prices. This is natural, as the consumer is conscious of the price of a finished product rising. As the food example has made clear, consumers are generally unaware of the economic components of that finished product. In fourteenth-century England it was bread prices and the profiteering of those that sold bread that were blamed. The twenty-first-century equivalent is perhaps petrol (or gasoline) prices and associated fuel duties that draw fire. Consumers rarely direct their ire against generic but ultimately true causes of inflation by disaggregating price increases into labour costs. This unwillingness to contemplate the primary causes of inflation is understandable as consumers are very often wage earners.

This is not to say that wages are entirely ignored in the legislative process. Wages are very often controlled alongside prices. Nevertheless, the failure to disaggregate inflation properly means that controls tend to focus on prices first and foremost, as the issue that is most likely to raise political pressures. Roman and medieval European wage controls would normally specify an hourly or daily wage rate, but by the time of President Nixon absolute levels were not set but changes to wages were first prescribed, then controlled. In this sense wages were treated in a manner that is not dissimilar to the treatment of prices, and in many cases it was because wages were seen as a price that was being paid in a somewhat less sophisticated economic environment (we would perhaps consider them as being the equivalent of service sector prices today).

Legislating against inflation (be it price inflation, or wage inflation, or both) therefore tends to come from the failure to properly consider the causes of inflation. What is wrong with this as a process? Why not try to hold back the price of rising inflation, if inflation is considered to be economically undesirable? Legislating against inflation has two considerable flaws. The first is that if the legislated prices are set at the wrong level, and the amount supplied at that price under normal market forces is less than the amount demanded at that price, then supply will simply cease to flow to market. Why should one work to produce goods or services if one does not receive what one considers to be an adequate level of compensation? This makes price controls potentially self-defeating; controlling prices reduces supply, creating further upwards pressure on prices. If this cannot manifest itself in the 'official' price (as sanctioned by law) then it will encourage the development of a black market where goods or services will be supplied at the price that truly reflects the supply and demand balance. One very clear example of this pattern comes from the world of foreign exchange. Countries that use legislation and controls to try and fix the price of their domestic currency will create an artificial shortage of foreign currency. A dual exchange rate system then develops. The official exchange rate is used when it cannot be avoided, but otherwise a second market that better reflects the relative value of scarce foreign exchange will spring into being.

The collapse of price controls in the United States in 1946 is another practical example of supply being refused. Meatpackers boycotted the government's attempts to extend the wartime price control process. Very quickly, meat all but disappeared from stores across the United States. Confronted by the loss of hamburgers, the great American consumer rebelled against price controls with an astonishingly decisive shift of opinion. Even a short-term experiment with vegetarianism was a price that was not worth paying for price controls, and so the whole price control process collapsed.

The second problem with legislating to prevent inflation is that it distorts the ability of *relative* prices to adjust. To have governments set prices (or even to constrain the ability of prices to change) presupposes that relative prices will remain static. The ebb and flow of fashion is ignored, and demand patterns are assumed to be static. Over a very short period this may be manageable, but the longer price controls are in place the more likely it is that the relative price will cease to reflect the reality of the relative demand patterns. Just because an apple is assumed to have the same value as an orange today, there is no reason to suppose that it will always have the same value as an orange in the future, but that is exactly what price controls will dictate.

The problems of supply and relative prices apply to wage controls as well as to price controls. This is logical enough: wages are simply another term for the price for labour. Wage controls may lead workers to reduce their effort (if increased effort does not generate increased reward, why should one work harder?). *In extremis*, controls may deter workers from supplying labour at all – if one considers the controlled wage rate to be significantly below one's true worth, why bother working at all? One does not have to go to the extreme of the model Linda Evangelista who famously declared 'we don't wake up for less than ten thousand dollars a day' to see the supply of labour is at least somewhat contingent on compensation.

Similarly, wage controls can keep in place a relative wage hierarchy that is not relevant to the changing supply or demand for the labour of different professions. The Emperor Diocletian ranked a mason, carpenter, cabinet maker and baker as all having the same worth (a maximum pay rate of 50 denarii a day), with a painter and decorator worth 50 per cent more, and a farm labourer 50 per cent less (75 denarii and 25 denarii per day, respectively). Diocletian's edict was not of course adhered to with quite the reverence he doubtless expected. In the US in 2010, the average income of a mason was just over $24 per hour. A carpenter earned 6 per cent less, a cabinet maker 30 per cent less, a baker 44 per cent less. Far from earning 50 per cent more the painter and decorator was paid 24 per cent less than a mason, and a farm labourer 51.5 per cent less. Relative values of labour change over time just as readily as do the relative values of goods (the painting profession must be cursing the introduction of easy-to-apply emulsion paints and the rise of the do it yourself mentality, given its relative fall from grace).

Wage and price controls give rise to two potential distortions, therefore. First, they raise the risk that supply will be constrained and goods or services are not available at the legislated price. Second, they raise the risk that relative prices or wages become distorted as demand patterns change. These reasons create inefficiencies over time which ultimately bring about the demise of controls.

It is worth concluding the section on trying to legislate against prices by observing that there is an important difference between direct legislation of prices, and policies that aim to create an economic environment that is conducive to price stability. Legislating specific prices goes against relative price adjustment by definition, and is trying to tackle the symptoms of higher inflation (the price of specific goods) rather than the causes of the economic disease. Using monetary policy to determine overall economic performance is different. Relative prices can still adjust, and the supply and demand will still be brought into balance at the prevailing market price. However, policymakers seek to adjust supply and demand (by changing the supply of money and influencing the price of credit). This will influence the level of inflation, without interfering directly with the price mechanism.

The price of money

This chapter has been quite mechanical in breaking down inflation, by looking at the importance of the different components in the inflation index – both by examining the formal weightings of finished product, and then perhaps more practically by examining the disaggregation of consumer prices into the different building blocks of inflation like labour and commodity prices. The simplistic idea that inflation can be represented by a single consumer price statistic has already been challenged – by the vexed problem of removing the asset element from housing, and the policy-expedient issue of identifying core and non-core inflation. Disaggregating inflation into its building blocks makes it clear that domestic unit labour costs are the most important components of inflation. This runs counter to the way consumers normally think about inflation because so much of the labour is hidden deep within the finished products that consumers pay for. This failure to connect labour to inflation seems to be exploited from time to time, to get consumers to accept higher inflation than is necessary, or at least to shift the blame for higher prices to causes that do not in fact deserve to feel the heat of the consumer's wrath.

Mistakes in understanding inflation all too often lead to a political reaction that is unhelpful. The consumer, feeling themselves overwhelmed by larger forces in the economy, will often turn to the government to regulate prices (including the price of labour on occasion). The problem is that such regulation does not work – it ossifies relative prices and distorts product or labour markets, and can actually make price or wage inflation pressures worse by deterring supply, if the legislated price level is set too low.

The importance of labour costs to inflation helps to explain the importance of policymakers' credibility, and in particular the credibility of the central bank.

If wage setters' inflation expectations are kept within reasonable bounds then inflation is likely to remain within reasonable bounds. A credible central bank is important to that process – and it is why misperceptions about inflation arising from adjustments to the price index can be so damaging.

The one topic that has not been covered in this chapter is the role of money supply and inflation. It is all very well saying that prices are 60–65 per cent labour costs; as a statement this is perfectly true. It is also true to say that inflation will be driven by the price of money, and therefore the balance of money supply and demand must determine the level of inflation. These statements are not incompatible. The important thing is to understand that it is the balance of money supply and demand that matters to inflation, and not money supply alone. This fascinating topic is the subject of the next chapter.

Notes

1 Gross (2004).
2 Marcet (1817) p 293.
3 The average farm gate price for a litre milk in the UK in 2013 was 31.61 pence. In March 2014, the main supermarkets in the UK were selling four pints (2.27 litres) of milk for a pound. In fact, the milk component of milk is unusually high by historical standards, perhaps reflecting the wish of supermarkets to maintain retail prices at the 'round number' of one pound. Normally, the farmer will receive around half the retail price of milk.
4 Fischer (1996) p 34.

5 Printing money never, ever, ever creates inflation

> Inflation is always and everywhere a monetary phenomenon.
>
> (Milton Friedman, 1963)[1]

The quote from Friedman that heads this chapter is by the standards of the world of economics famous, perhaps infamous. These words, or some half-remembered derivation of these words, are frequently cited in justification of the necessity of controlling money supply at all costs. Variations on the theme of this phrase are used to rouse rabbles and produce panics whenever central banks print money. In one sense Friedman's words are perfectly true. At the same time it is also perfectly true to say that printing money never, ever, ever creates inflation. This chapter is all about reconciling these statements, and identifying why investors need to be careful in interpreting the implications of money printing.

Friedman's assertion is constructed on the solid foundations of the Fisher equation – the accounting identity discussed in the first chapter. The money supply of an economy multiplied by the number of times money changes hands must be equal to the nominal level of economic activity in an economy. It therefore follows that there is a relationship between the money supply of an economy and the prices that contribute to nominal economic activity. Friedman's assertion is also rooted in the logic of supply and demand. If the supply of money increases relative to the supply of goods and services in an economy, then logically the 'price' of money should decline. The quote from Jane Marcet made in 1817 and cited in the second chapter said exactly the same thing. Friedman's thought is not, perhaps, original.

The idea that printing money creates inflation is further supported by the extreme examples of hyperinflation. No one doubts that it was the frenetic pace of printing by the Reichsbank in Weimar Germany that pushed that economy into the spiral of hyperinflation. Similarly, the Zimbabwean inflation of more recent times came about in the wake of a staggering printing of money. Support for the idea of money printing creating inflation also comes from more mundane examples. US President Nixon's obsession with increasing the money supply ahead of the 1972 presidential election and his very explicit bullying of Federal Reserve Chairman Burns to achieve that had a clear role in the accelerating inflation that was experienced (albeit the increased inflation was experienced after the 1972 presidential election – but then that was rather the point).[2]

And yet... despite Weimar Germany, despite the evidence of Zimbabwe, despite the experiences of the 1970s and despite the inescapable logic of the Fisher equation, the world has seen a significant printing of money over the past few years without there being any noticeable pick-up in inflation. Indeed, consumer price inflation since the dramatic printing of money that poured from central banks since 2008 has tended to be lower than it was before the crisis.

The benign nature of inflation in the wake of this money printing is testament to the fact that simply printing money is not the driver of inflation. This is important for investors. The misremembering of Milton Friedman tends to lead to an almost Pavlovian reaction from investors when central banks print money. The belief that money printing leads to inflation is one of the strongest, most pervasive myths of modern economics; even now after a rapid expansion of money and several years of benign inflation many investors still have absolute conviction that the threat of inflation is lurking just around the corner, armed with a sandbag and ready to hit the unwary investor over the head. The false syllogism is that the threat must be there, because 'printing money leads to inflation', and money has undoubtedly been printed, and if inflation has not just happened yet it must just be a temporary delay to lull the financial market investor into a false sense of security. The persistence of this perverse, incorrect logic leads to bad investment decisions.

It is time to correct the false fears of the economic blogosphere. Printing money is not now, and has never been, a source of inflation. It is not printing money that creates inflation, it is printing *too much* money that creates inflation.

That distinction is one of the most important points of monetary economics. The omission of those two italicised words from the relationship of money printing and inflation has the potential to be an extremely costly mistake. To look at money supply in isolation as a guide to inflation is a futile gesture. Investors must consider money supply relative to money demand.

What is money?

Before starting in on the topic of printing money, we should adhere to good economic first principles and define the terms we are using. One of the biggest problems in monetarism is trying to decide what money actually is. Of course, we have the basic and generic definition of it being used as a 'medium of exchange' that was introduced at the start of this book, and that definition rings as true in Chapter 5 as it did in Chapter 1. However, the phrase 'medium of exchange' is a pretty catholic definition for money in a modern economy.

At its most basic money consists of the notes and coins in circulation. Nowadays, however, that is not quite enough – credit cards and debit cards are so widely accepted as to require some broadening out of the definition if we are to encompass everything that serves as a modern medium of exchange. If debit card transactions are considered to be a medium of exchange then bank accounts that can be quickly accessed should be considered money (after all, that is what backs the use of the debit card). But where should economists draw the line? What about bank accounts that can be accessed at 24 hours' notice? Or 48 hours' notice? Or a week's notice? What about a Treasury bill, issued by the government (just like a bank note) and with one month to maturity?

Economists and statisticians have resolved this smorgasbord of monetary options by grading different forms of money according to their level of liquidity. Monetary liquidity basically means how quickly something can be turned into physical cash. Actually, this comes back to that first definition of money as a 'medium of exchange'. Liquidity represents money in a form that can be exchanged for goods or services very, very quickly (preferably with no transaction costs or delay). The more exchangeable the medium of exchange, the more liquid that form of money is considered to be. Bank accounts that can be accessed on demand, money held by banks at the central bank – these are highly liquid forms of money, and are known as 'narrow money'. 'Narrow' in this context refers to the narrowness of the definition that is being used. Narrow money and liquidity are terms that are used interchangeably, and can be thought of as constituting 'cash' or something very like. Narrow money is the medium of exchange that can most readily be exchanged.

'Broad money' fairly obviously constitutes the other end of the spectrum, and incorporates a far broader range of instruments. Broad money will include everything that is in the narrower definitions of money, and then in addition some less liquid forms of money (like bank accounts that take time to access). Broad money can include government bonds, for instance. Although that might seem strange, bear in mind that bonds can generally be converted into liquid form with relatively little effort. It is also worth noting that the earliest forms of paper currency were often interest-bearing securities (in medieval China and revolutionary France, for instance). Bank notes evolved from bonds.

The challenge for trying to assess the relationship between money and inflation is knowing which form of money is most likely to influence inflation. It is all very well saying that inflation is always a monetary problem, but what sort of monetary problem is it? Does inflation respond to narrow money? Or does inflation respond to broad money? The answer to those questions is 'yes'; inflation responds to narrow money and inflation responds to broad money depending on circumstances. This is what makes monetary policy so interesting.

To pile on the complications, there is what economists call 'Goodhart's law', named for the economist Charles Goodhart who suggested the problem in 1975 – although there are older examples of similar concepts. Goodhart's law basically says that as soon as you start targeting something financial it becomes irrelevant, because people will anticipate the effects of the regulation and avoid it. Thus, if the government tries to target narrow money supply, everyone will shift to using broader money supply measures that are not subject to control. What this means is that the precise control of any particular money measure is going to be seeking to control a moving target. The form of money that matters to inflation today may not be the form of money that matters to inflation tomorrow.

Given that the success or failure of targets depends in part on the credibility of those targets, there are grave risks involved if Goodhart's law is in operation. Policy credibility is undermined if money supply targets are hit but the outcome (in inflation terms) is not what is expected. Policy credibility is undermined if targets are continually changed to try to keep up with the shifts in financial fashions and the realities of Goodhart's law. This is why central banks nowadays try to avoid too rigid an adherence to money supply targets – either by not having money supply targets, or by having them in the background as a sort of policy totem that is to be acknowledged with a nod, and then forgotten.

Even if explicit targets tend to be avoided, central banks are still intimately associated with the money supply, or at least they are intimately associated with some forms of the money supply. Central banks tend to have absolute control over the narrowest or most liquid forms of money supply. In almost all instances central banks are the monopoly supplier of physical cash (notes and coins) to an economy, and as such a central bank can ordain what the level of narrow money supply is supposed to be. However, as the definition of money supply broadens out so the central bank has less and less direct control over the level of money supply. For instance, central banks have limited influence over the use of credit cards. Financial regulation gives the central bank a degree of control, but in the main the level of this form of credit is a function of card companies' eagerness to lend, and the consumers' willingness to use credit card debt to finance their lifestyle. A country's cultural attitude to credit can be more important than a central bank's control when it comes to some of the broader monetary measures.

Central banks therefore have a great deal of control over narrow money, but at the same time consumers and companies have the greatest ability to evade restrictions on narrow money indicators. The central bank has to balance control of narrow money with the risk that participants in the economy are scared off by the controls and move to use forms of money over which the central bank has less control.

How do central banks print (narrow) money?

The popular mental image of central banks printing narrow money tends to have a somewhat cartoon-like aspect. The general idea seems to centre on a printing press or photocopier being fired up, and the central bank governor then taking the resulting paper currency and throwing it from the roof of the central bank to flutter into the streets below like confetti. *In extremis*, the effects of narrow money printing are actually not that dissimilar from the cartoon issue – hyperinflation, for instance, tends to be associated with something that is not that far removed from this process. The Reichsbank of Weimar Germany did indeed operate its printing presses twenty-four hours a day, and then ordered more printing presses because the existing capacity of its print works could not cope, and finally started to print the one hundred thousand billion (0.01 quintillion) mark bank note on one side of paper only, in order to save time. There is certainly something Bugs Bunny-esque about such proceedings (even if the humour is noticeably lacking from the consequences of the hyperinflation that ensued).

Away from such extremes, producing narrow money is a little more ordered. Liquidity is rarely if ever just 'created' from thin air. Central banks have balance sheets, just like other corporate entities, and those balance sheets must balance (the hint of that attribute is in the term '*balance* sheet'). So when narrow money is printed some kind of exchange takes place – if liquidity is given out by the central bank, something must be received in exchange.

In simple terms there are two ways that a central bank can print narrow money; or more accurately, there are two sorts of assets that a central bank can receive in exchange for the narrow money that it prints. The first depends, at least somewhat, on external circumstances. If a central bank intervenes in the currency markets to weaken the value of the domestic currency, it can do so by printing the domestic currency (as narrow money) and selling it for foreign currency. The balance sheet balances because domestic cash in circulation increases (the liability for the central bank) and foreign currency reserves increase (the asset for the central bank). The overall size of the central bank balance sheet increases. When foreign exchange intervention is allowed to increase the narrow money in circulation in this way it is known as 'unsterilised' foreign exchange intervention. The alternative option for the central bank is to find some way of taking the cash out of circulation (so the central bank issues domestic narrow money, receives foreign currency, but then finds some way of taking the initial issue of domestic narrow money out of circulation – generally by selling bonds and receiving cash). Fairly obviously that operation is known as 'sterilised' intervention, because the domestic narrow money supply is not 'infected' by the central bank's actions in the foreign exchange market. The concept of sterilisation was introduced in Chapter 2 with the Roman Emperor Constantine, who 'unsterilised' silver and gold by melting down pagan temple ornaments and converting them into coin. It is exactly the same thing – if the money in whatever form is not being used as a medium of exchange, it is sterile. If the money is being used as a medium of exchange then it is unsterilised.

Unsterilised intervention is all very well but it does depend on a willingness to intervene in the foreign exchange market. Intervention is not always an option – there may be objections from other governments about the overt manipulation of the value of one's currency. Senator Schumer of the United States is one of the noted scourges of foreign exchange 'manipulation' (when he perceives governments other than the United States to be engaging in the manipulation), and a government may feel it worthwhile to go to some lengths to avoid attracting the attention of Senator Schumer.

If the central bank is not going to acquire foreign currency to balance the printing of narrow money on its balance sheet, the general alternative asset class that the central bank acquires will be government bonds. Any asset would do, and other assets are sometimes used, although the purchase of bonds and bills (which are just short-term bonds) is the most common way of increasing liquidity or narrow money supply. Indeed, all central banks will engage in this bond buying in the normal operation of their policy. The central bank will buy bonds in the market, and give cash (narrow money) in exchange for those bonds. If the central bank is targeting the level of money supply in the economy with its purchases of bonds and bills then the operation is generally referred to as quantitative policy by economists, and quantitative easing or QE by the media. The media's addiction to the phrase QE was encouraged by the fact that the second wave of US quantitative policy that took place after the global financial crisis could be referred to as QE2 rather than the more correct QP2. The media has these whims, with no regard to how infuriating they may be to economists.

The process is known as quantitative policy because the central bank is seeking to control the quantity of money in the economy. In contrast, monetary policy is about central banks seeking to control the interest rate charged for borrowing money in an economy. Monetary policy (targeting the interest rate) will still require central banks to buy and sell securities, but they are doing so with the objective of controlling the interest rate (the quantity of money in the economy is the independent outcome of that operation). Quantitative policy is buying and selling securities with the objective of controlling the quantity of money supplied to the economy (and the interest rate is the independent outcome of that operation, not the objective of the operation).

It is important to notice that what the central bank is doing when it prints narrow money in exchange for bonds could actually be described as a process of liquefaction. The central bank is purchasing relatively illiquid assets and giving out the highly liquid asset of cash (or its electronic equivalent) by way of exchange. The narrow money supply increases in this instance. Broad money is not automatically increasing in this process. Components of broad money are being exchanged for more liquid instruments. If broad money was (for instance) 20 per cent cash in circulation and 80 per cent other stuff, it might now be 30 per cent cash in circulation and 70 per cent other stuff. The narrow money supply, which is cash in circulation, has increased so that it is now half as much again as it was before the quantitative policy, but the broad money supply total has not changed. All that changes is the composition of broad money.

The process of increasing the amount of narrow money supply is fairly logical if you think about it. The original bond holders will have had to have had liquidity in order to purchase government bonds in the first instance. The government will have received that narrow money and spent it (it is what governments do after all) and the narrow money will have carried on circling around the economy. In the meantime, the bond holders now have bonds in their possession. If the central bank decides to print additional narrow money, then the bond holders sell their bonds to the central bank and receive yet more liquidity in exchange. The narrow money that the bond holders gave to the government is still out there, and now a second quantity of narrow money has been put into the economy – a process that is generally referred to as an 'injection' of liquidity.

Of course this sort of policy operation by the central bank is important to investors. The central bank is buying assets in the financial markets and in doing so will influence the price of those assets. The policy objective of the central bank is to provide liquidity to the wider economy. Whether or not the central bank is receiving an adequate return on the assets that it is purchasing is not likely to be terribly important to the central bank. In other words, quantitative policy will introduce a significant buyer of assets in specific markets, who does not play by the conventional rules of financial investing. This will distort the price of those assets (generally raising the price above the 'market clearing price' of course).

Investors need to be aware that the financial market distortion of quantitative policy will spread beyond the market that is the object of central bank intervention. If the central bank buys government bonds, and raises the price above the market clearing price, that will dissuade government bond investors from buying bonds in that market. These former government bond investors will have to find some home for their money, and if government bonds are unattractively priced they will move into other asset markets (generally markets which are considered to have a higher risk). That will increase demand for assets in other markets, influencing their price. The economic description of this is 'moving out along the risk curve'. The implication of the description is that investors have to accept higher levels of risk to receive the level of return that they desire. So, for investors, quantitative policy is always going to be important when making investment decisions.

There is also a subsector of quantitative policy that needs to be considered, namely monetisation. The mechanisms that a central bank uses to engage in quantitative policy are generally the same (or follow the same broad principle) to the mechanisms that are used in normal times. Central banks will generally need to undertake some form of asset purchases or asset sales to regulate the narrow money supply. The full-blown narrow money printing operations of quantitative policy are just an increase in the scale on which the central bank is operating. Debt monetisation, however, is a little different. For investors the distinction, though subtle, is important. Debt monetisation entails more inflation risk than straightforward quantitative policy.

Debt monetisation is like normal quantitative policy in that the central bank is purchasing bonds and bills. The difference from quantitative policy is that the central bank is purchasing the bonds and bills directly from the government. Conventional quantitative policy does not involve this direct relationship, as the central bank is acting in the market and purchasing assets from investors 'second-hand'. The market mechanism therefore plays a role in setting the price of government debt – it is a distorted role (because investors buy bonds in the knowledge that the central bank is intervening in the market) but some influence is granted to market forces. Moreover, with quantitative policy *someone* other than the central bank must be prepared to purchase government bonds in the first place.

With monetisation, the role of the market and private investors as a collective 'middle man' in the debt-for-cash transaction is entirely removed. In theory, the central bank could decide only to purchase government bonds up to a certain limit and at the market price; this would make the absence of the market in the transaction less of a problem. In reality, if the government is selling bonds direct to the central bank it implies a degree of politicisation. The risk is that the central bank is required to provide liquidity to the government not out of a valid concern to provide liquidity to the wider economy, but as a means of providing cheap finance to the government. In particular, this may be the case if the government is finding it difficult to obtain funding from any other (more conventional) source.

The introduction of politicisation that is associated with debt monetisation means that this form of printing narrow money is typically a hallmark of hyperinflation episodes. Virtually all hyperinflation episodes have been preceded by monetisation. Monetisation is something that investors should worry about; not because it automatically leads to inflation (it does not *have* to), but because it signals a politicisation of monetary policy that is typically associated with inflation. Quantitative policy, which can exist perfectly easily with monetary policy independence, is less of an inflation threat.

Why not cancel the debt?

If the central bank of a country is increasing the money supply by buying government bonds (whether as quantitative policy or as monetisation), a tempting opportunity is often seen to arise – and like most tempting opportunities, it is one that is too good to be true.

The global financial crisis that took hold with a certain authority in 2008 has been marked by two macro policy consequences: government debt levels have generally increased, and central banks have undertaken quantitative policy. As this became evident, a number of media sources gave space to clarion calls that suggested these policy consequences be combined in some kind of 'master solution'. For the most part central banks are owned by the national government (the Swiss National Bank and the Bank of Japan are a couple of notable exceptions). Why should the central bank simply not cancel the bonds that it has acquired for quantitative policy purposes? If one branch of the government (the central bank) owns debt issued by another part of the government (the Treasury/ finance ministry), then does it really matter if the government cancels the debt it owes to itself?

The fact is that it does matter if a central bank cancels government debt that it holds. There are two issues with this sort of policy action. First, as with debt monetisation, such an action introduces an element of politics into the pure world of central banking. If politicians are to sully economics in such a way, the boundaries of monetary policy become blurred. Cancelling government debt is, in this way, not terribly dissimilar from monetisation in terms of the political and reputational risks. The central bank is adapting its policy to accommodate fiscal policy, and this is not generally considered desirable. Economists generally believe that monetary and quantitative policy should work with, but be distinct from, fiscal policy.

More importantly, the main consequence of cancelling government debt held by the central bank would be to permanently increase the money supply and deny the central bank a considerable degree of policy flexibility. Quantitative policy is not, in fact, exclusively about increasing the amount of narrow money in an economy – this is why it is properly known as quantitative policy, and not quantitative easing. Quantitative policy is not a one-way bet: quantitative policy actually means controlling the quantity of money in the economy – which implies controlling the amount of money up *and* down. The central bank giveth, and the central bank can taketh away (blessed be the economists of the central bank). The German Bundesbank, not an institution known for its inflationary tendencies, pursued a quantitative policy for years before it was subsumed into the euro area – and generally its policy was focused on *limiting* the quantity of narrow money in the economy.

If increasing the narrow money supply is no longer necessary, the central bank can reverse course. It is this ability to put quantitative policy into reverse that means that quantitative policy need not be inflationary. Bonds that have been bought can be sold, and the narrow money supply that was printed and issued by the central bank will then be received back into the central bank. Selling bonds would reduce the narrow money supply, and this is an appropriate policy action if high levels of money supply are no longer required.

The problem with cancelling government bonds held by the central bank is that once those bonds have been cancelled, they are no longer available as a quantitative policy tool. If debt is cancelled, then quantitative policy does become a one-way bet. The central bank cannot sell bonds it does not own; that is (generally) considered to be fraud, and fraud is often frowned upon in central banking circles. If the central bank has cancelled government bonds that were purchased in pursuit of quantitative policy, the central bank is permanently, irrevocably increasing the money supply. The very great danger associated with such an action is that changes in the economy may make the increase in the money supply inflationary in the future, if the increase can no longer be reversed. Adequate money supply today can readily become *too much* money supply tomorrow, if money demand changes.

Deciding whether too much or too little liquidity is being produced is a matter of assessing narrow money demand as much as it is assessing narrow money supply. Narrow money demand is a tricky concept to identify, however, and it is worth spending some time considering what it is.

How much is too much? The role of narrow money demand

The importance of narrow money demand in determining the existence or absence of excess narrow money supply goes back to some of the earliest instances of money printing. We saw in the second chapter how successive Chinese regimes regularly used paper money from the ninth century onwards, and how they tended to succumb to inflation or hyperinflation. The spiral into inflation and unchecked money printing may have come about because initial money supply increases tended to have little adverse impact on prices. For instance, from 1160 until at least the first decade of the thirteenth century the Southern Sung dynasty was blithely increasing its paper money supply, to almost four times the original level. Throughout this period, paper money traded at a small discount to copper as the traditional form of money, but that discount (of around 10 per cent) was stable in spite of the increase in money supply. A four-fold increase in the supply of paper money did not lead to any inflation in paper money terms. The reason was obvious enough. As the use of paper money spread, and as the convenience of carrying paper cash rather than the more cumbersome copper was understood, so the demand for paper money increased. People wanted to hold paper currency – they demanded it – because it was perceived as having both utility and value. The government was increasing supply of paper cash, but as long as the supply increase matched the increase in demand, the price of the cash held steady and inflation was zero.

The problem for the Sung, and for countless policymakers ever since, is that they appear to have concluded that because the money supply had been increased in the past with no ill effects, the money supply could be increased indefinitely in the future with similar results. This, as the second chapter has emphasised, is not the case. As soon as the circulation of paper currency reached saturation point, as soon as everyone who wished to use paper currency had sated their demand, any further increase in paper supply would inevitably be a case of printing *too much* money. Printing too much money creates inflation, and so inflation was the result.

We find the same thing time and again throughout history. The British colony of Pennsylvania issued paper currency, and if Benjamin Franklin is to be believed they issued quite a lot of it – taking an initial amount of 15,000 pounds up to 600,000 pounds (face value) over the course of the eighteenth century. Despite the pretty impressive printing of money, the growth of the Pennsylvanian economy ensured a demand for paper currency that kept prices remarkably stable (estimates of Pennsylvanian prices have them rising around 60 per cent in the half century before the colony rebelled against the British).[3] Narrow money demand largely negated the inflation threat of the printing press.

So, what is narrow money demand? In the modern world of sound-bite economics, where the desire is for everything in the world of finance to be reduced to a single graphic, there is an incessant, shrill clamour for a single money demand variable that can be 'tracked' in real time. Such a measure does not exist, and could not exist. Narrow money demand and the related issue of liquidity preference are (with apologies for the economic pun) fluid concepts. There is no one single variable one can look to as the definitive indicator of narrow money demand.

Two basic drivers of narrow money demand can, perhaps, be identified. The first is the demand that occurs in normal times, and which is hinted at in the Fisher equation. Narrow money is demanded because of economic activity. If an economy is growing, then at least some definition of money supply should also grow (if deflation is to be avoided). The innovative use of furs, books and jewellery as 'mobilia' money in the past shows that if the government will not provide the money that a growing economy needs in order to function, the market will find an alternative (a good practical example of Goodhart's law in action).

The money that is demanded to satisfy the needs of a growing economy could be broad money or it could be narrow money, but if there are more transactions or exchanges taking place in an economy, and money is the medium of exchange, then more money will be demanded. At least some part of that demand is likely to be for narrow money, all things being equal. The fatal flaw of the gold standard is that current levels of economic activity mean that the demand for money will grow faster than the supply of gold can accommodate, hence the deflationary bias of the gold standard.

Superficially, therefore, the level of demand for narrow money can be assumed to be the same as the level of nominal economic activity in the economy. Indeed, if absolutely forced to come up with a proxy for narrow money demand in normal times, this is what most economists would suggest (at least as a short-term expedient). Nevertheless, this is too crude an indicator to be reliable. Technology and financial sophistication mean that the use of narrow money changes. The fact that roughly 12 per cent of British retail sales today take place via the internet, and therefore require electronic money in some form, is an instance of technological change. The growth of credit and debit cards over the past forty years is another instance of technology adjusting the demand for liquidity. Monitoring the narrowest form of money supply (notes and coins in circulation) against nominal economic activity as a proxy for total money demand is no use in this situation. The changing pattern of consumption changes the sort of money that is demanded; one would expect a decline in narrower money in relative terms, and very possibly in absolute terms in this situation.

There is one important point that investors should take from this form of money demand: if an economy is growing, then all things being equal the money supply of that economy (in some form) should also be growing. It may not be narrow money supply that grows, but some form of money supply should be increasing. The amount of money in circulation today may be appropriate for economic circumstances now, but it will almost certainly not be appropriate for economic circumstances in the future. The fact that economic activity levels change means that on some broad definition money demand changes, and money supply must change to prevent either inflation or deflation from occurring. This is why monetary policy can never be static.

The second stream of narrow money demand occurs at times of crisis, and is often characterised by the phrase 'liquidity preference'. The broader forms of money generally require some degree of trust. A bank deposit that requires a week's notice before the money is withdrawn requires the depositor to trust that the bank will remain solvent and in business for another week. A bank account of any description requires the depositor to trust that the bank will remain solvent and in business for at least the length of time it takes for a depositor to withdraw their money. If that trust is shaken in any way then depositors will seek to move their money into more liquid forms. *In extremis*, this may take the form of cash under the mattress. In 1933, the US citizenry followed just such a course and to quote a contemporary economist 'depositors developed a most inconsiderate and unpatriotic desire to have their money in their own hands'.[4]

This form of narrow money demand is what dominated central bank policy in the aftermath of the global financial credit crunch. The queues of investors lining up outside the British bank Northern Rock in 2008 were queuing because they feared that they would not be able to get their money back before the bank

---

Box 5.1 Money demand in hyperinflation

The demand for narrow money is generally tied to economic activity. However, hyperinflation episodes are an exception to this. A hyperinflation episode is an extreme perversion of liquidity preference, whereby liquidity is so profligate that illiquidity ends up being preferred instead.

What happens in a hyperinflation episode is that consumers do not want to hold onto narrow money (cash) for a moment longer than is necessary, for fear that the inflation level will render the paper money worthless. Instances of this abound – at the peak of the German hyperinflation, train tickets could only be purchased for a limited part of the journey, as it was assumed that hyperinflation would have raised the price by the end of the trip. In Hungary's hyperinflation in 1946 money could lose its value in a matter of hours.

When this occurs consumers are desperate to get rid of their money as quickly as possible – in other words the demand for narrow money collapses. Instead, investors want to hold durable goods (not a very liquid form of cash) that are of practical and therefore real value. Canned food is one example of the sort of product that will be sought in a hyperinflation period.

Of course, the collapse in the demand for money means that the growth of *excess* narrow money ends up being determined by both the growth of narrow money supply and a collapse in narrow money demand.

---

failed. In most instances the fear was irrational (as the government guaranteed the majority of depositors at the bank), but the fear was enough. People wanted cash, the most liquid form of money that they could get.

In fact, the increase in demand for liquidity that followed in the wake of the financial credit crunch was multifaceted. Consumers demanded liquid (narrow) forms of money because they were unsure of the security of their banks. Some consumers had to demand liquid forms of money because their credit lines were cut – if one cannot get a credit card or extend one's credit card limit, one cannot use a credit card for purchases, and that means of course that all purchases must be made with cash. Listed companies suddenly felt the need to demonstrate to their shareholders that they had enough liquidity to ride out the tough times ahead, and that meant that they wanted to hold cash. The smaller companies that dominate economic activity in almost every developed economy were hit by two financial credit crunches; banks reduced their lines of credit, and inter-company credit imploded (inter-company credit means companies lending to other companies, typically by allowing customers to settle invoices for goods some period of time after they received the goods – inter-company credit is the single most important form of credit for small businesses, far more important than bank credit). Smaller businesses that wanted to receive goods were asked to pay for those goods with cash, and sometimes with cash in advance of delivery. That again increased the demand for liquidity.

What the financial credit crunch has meant, in simple terms, is that economies have become more cash based than they were before the financial crisis. What the financial credit crunch has meant, in economic geek terms, is that the velocity of circulation of narrow money has declined relative to the level before the financial crisis. It does not matter how one chooses to express the phenomenon, for the outcome is the same. The demand for liquidity or narrow money increased in nearly every major economy as a result of the global financial credit crunch.

In the United States, the amount of narrow money known as M1 increased by $1.38 trillion from the end of 2006 until the end of the first quarter of 2014. That is a relatively sizeable increase in the narrow money supply. However, the amount of cash held by US households and companies (as spare change) increased by $0.93 trillion over the same period. Fully two-thirds of all of the money printed by the Fed wound up gathering dust in the checking accounts of US consumers and on the balance sheets of Google, Apple and their ilk. The money was supplied because it was demanded. This is hardly a new development – Sparling, writing of President Roosevelt's increase of US narrow money supply in 1933, declared (quite correctly) 'little of the two billion dollars of new money printed in Washington has been put into circulation'.[5] What he meant by that was that the money had left the Federal Reserve System, but that the increase in supply was simply satiating the increase in demand.

In the wake of the global financial crisis of 2008, the increase in narrow money supply that has taken place in most industrialised economies has met an increase in narrow money demand; to date, there is absolutely no evidence that the increase in narrow money supply has exceeded the increase in narrow money demand. There is no evidence that too much money has been printed.

Japan has experienced exactly the same phenomenon, but over a far longer time horizon (over two decades, indeed). The Bank of Japan has increased the narrow money supply of the Japanese economy time and time again, and yet inflation has remained extremely low and periodically fallen into deflation. Why is this? Because the increase in narrow money was demanded; hoarded by banks, hoarded by companies and hoarded by consumers. If monetary inflation is the phenomenon of 'too much money chasing too few goods', then Japan's problem was that the yen refused to chase anything and instead stayed at home (hiding under the futon and declaring 'shan't' whenever the Bank of Japan tried to coax it out of the shadows and into the harsh light of the real economy).

Here, then, is the rebuttal to the idea that 'all that money' that has been printed since 2008 must inevitably lead to inflation. Money supply has been adequate rather than excessive. The behaviour of inflation to date is entirely to be expected in this environment.

As the global financial crisis becomes part of economic history, the important question that central banks need to consider is what will happen to liquidity preference. Printing too much money is conventionally thought of as being a result of central banks increasing the money supply too rapidly – that is what has historically created inflation. Today, however, too much money can be created by a decline in liquidity preference and thus narrow money demand, without any further increase in money supply. Liquidity preference does not have to revert to pre-crisis levels to create an inflation threat; such was the scale of money printing required to slake the thirst for liquidity in the crisis that even a modest decline in liquidity preference against the backdrop of current money supply could prove to be inflationary. The importance of measuring money demand has suddenly increased.

What should investors look for to determine money demand?

The absence of a single, stable indicator for narrow money demand is an annoying problem for investors, but that does not mean that they must grope blindly in the darkness in assessing whether money supply is sufficient, excessive or inadequate. As ever, economists can offer a beacon of illumination. There are several things that can be looked to as indicating trends in narrow money demand.

The first indicator, somewhat perversely, is the behaviour of money supply. If broad money supply is not growing particularly strongly, but narrow money supply is growing strongly, that is at least suggestive of shifting liquidity preference. If narrow and broad money supply are both growing, then that suggests that there has been no major change in liquidity preference (and that the central bank may therefore be risking excess money supply through its policies). Remember that central banks have less and less control over money supply as the definition of money supply moves from narrow to broad.

The second indicator is the level of bank credit creation in an economy. Credit growth is, naturally, dependent on the willingness of banks to supply credit, and the willingness of creditors to borrow credit. If there is a willingness to use credit, that suggests that an economy is becoming less cash based and therefore demand for narrow forms of money will decline. Most economies publish credit numbers which give real-time indications of the state of bank credit growth, but this is not a terribly forward-looking indicator. Investors have other resources, however. Several countries publish what are known as 'senior loan officer' surveys, which are basically questionnaires that ask commercial banks about what they intend to do with lending. Some surveys of consumers and companies ask either about the availability of credit directly, or about related matters (for instance, the willingness of consumers to buy 'big ticket' items like cars and household appliances).

Surveys of corporate access to credit need to be treated with a little caution. As already mentioned, the most important form of corporate credit for small businesses (which are the most important part of the economy) tends to come from inter-company credit and not bank credit. Companies may therefore be reporting on inter-company credit conditions and not necessarily on bank credit conditions. Policymakers need to be sensitive to this – it would be inappropriate to implement policies that target bank credit creation if the problem lies mainly with inter-company credit.

Inter-company credit demand is more difficult to pull out of the economic data. Anecdotal evidence from surveys is one possibility. Data known as trade payables and trade receivables is another indicator of inter-company credit, but this is not very timely. Finally, there is the evidence of cash holdings by corporates which (particularly when expressed as a proportion of GDP) can give some indication of trends in narrow money demand relative to economic activity.

It should be clear from this section that the calculation and presentation of money demand is not a precise science. Economics itself is not a precise science, so this should not occasion much surprise. There is no magic indicator for money demand. Instead, a variety of measures need to be looked to if the investor is to gauge where narrow money demand is heading.

What is also clear, however, is that if there is a general sense that narrow money demand is weakening, and narrow money supply is high and expanding, then there is a risk of inflation. The demand for and supply of narrow money needs to be maintained in balance, and this is a dynamic and not a static process. The massive printing of narrow money that followed from the global financial crisis was not initially inflationary because it initially met narrow money demand. That does not mean that those levels of narrow money supply will always be appropriate, or that the current narrow money supply will always be absorbed by narrow money demand. As economic circumstances change, the inflation risks around existing money supply will also change.

The future for money supply and demand management

So far there has been a pretty strong assertion that the money printed in the wake of the global financial crisis need not create inflation, because it is not excess liquidity. Nevertheless, it is also true that money supply and demand are not static concepts. As the sense of crisis fades, at least some of the liquidity preference should fade in industrialised economies. Consumers will wish to use credit again. Banks, once they have adapted to the new regulatory regime, will wish to lend money (this is, after all, a way by which banks can generate profits and banks prefer to generate profits if they can). There is therefore a very real possibility that the demand for liquidity will decline. Obviously, this is not specific to the current situation; in the wake of any crisis-induced increase in liquidity, inflation may result if the central bank does not manage money supply and demand to keep them in balance.

A central bank has four options if it believes that the demand for liquidity or narrow money in an economy is fading. Assuming that the central bank does not wish to see higher inflation, the objective of the central bank must be to make adjustments that keep money supply and money demand in balance.

The first option sounds somewhat peculiar; the central bank can do nothing. Masterful inactivity on the part of a central bank does not sound like a terribly good prescription for preventing excess money being created, but under the right circumstances it can work. The central bank has to gamble on the idea that the economy will continue to grow, and that therefore the decline in narrow money demand associated with reduced liquidity preference will be offset by an increase in narrow money demand as a result of increased economic transactions. This might be considered the 'organic' solution to the risk of excess narrow money supply.

The concept of an economy growing its way out of an excess money supply threat is the least threatening to investors, if it works. The central bank is not disrupting financial markets or the banking sector with such a policy – the status quo is maintained, and the status quo is always relatively easy for investors to understand. The investment risk with this strategy is that it is a relatively slow process of bringing narrow money supply and narrow money demand into equilibrium. Either the decline in liquidity preference must be relatively slow or the increase in narrow money supply would need to be relatively modest for the whole of the adjustment process to be managed through this organic process.

The second option is also a relatively natural process. If a central bank has purchased bonds and bills to increase the narrow money supply, it obviously has a portfolio of fixed-income assets. Of course, bills and nearly all bonds will mature in time. The government must repay the face value of the bill or bond, and surrender cash (narrow money) in payment as the bill or bond matures. The central bank then has a choice as a bond matures: it can either reinvest the money it receives (keeping the narrow money supply unchanged), or it can choose not to purchase any further bonds and take the narrow money out of circulation. If the central bank chooses not to reinvest the proceeds of a maturing bond, then the narrow money supply will fall.

For investors this is also a relatively natural way of reducing narrow money supply. The central bank is not selling assets as such; it is just choosing not to purchase new assets as the old assets mature. The government is forced to sell bonds into the market without the distortion of the central bank as a buyer. The advantage of this method is that the only official seller of government bonds is the government; the central bank is not adding to the 'official' supply of government paper. The problem for investors is that this method of managing narrow money supply is relatively 'lumpy'. Unless all of the narrow money supply increase was engineered through the purchase of short-term bills, the central bank has very little short-term control over the money supply. Money supply can only be reduced when bonds and bills that are held by the central bank mature. Bonds and bills held by the central bank are extremely unlikely to mature with a nice, regular, smooth profile. Instead, maturing assets are likely to fall due in clusters or 'lumps', with potentially long intervals in between episodes of maturity. If the central bank wishes to reduce the narrow money supply today but none of the central bank asset portfolio is scheduled to mature, then it is tough luck for the central bank.

The third option for the central bank is the option that most investors assume will be followed – sell the bonds. This has an elegant balance in its simplicity. If narrow money supply increased as a result of purchasing bonds, and narrow money supply now needs to decrease, then surely the appropriate policy response is for the central bank to reverse what went before and sell bonds into the market?

Despite the simplicity of this method, this is the process of narrow money supply control that investors have most reason to fear. When a central bank purchases bonds, the act will distort bond markets and other financial assets. Similarly, if a central bank reverses the process then there will be an additional distortion in asset prices. Bond yields will likely rise, because in addition to the government selling bonds in the normal course of financing its debt, there is now the additional 'official' supply of the central bank gradually divesting itself of its bond and bill portfolio. This rise in bond yields may be unwelcome, because there are economic consequences from that distortion, and those consequences are not necessarily predictable. If bond yields rise for government debt, bond yields may rise for corporate debt. If bond yields rise for corporate debt, investment may slow. If investment slows that may change economic growth, employment and ultimately inflation. There is no way of being able to predict the extent of this chain reaction, and therefore the distortion of the central bank selling bonds must add an additional element of uncertainty into the calculations of financial market investors.

The fourth option for the central bank is to try and control not narrow money supply but narrow money demand. The idea of printing too much money does, after all, depend on the interaction of supply and demand for money, and there is no reason for the central bank to concentrate all of its attention on one side of the balance.

Controlling money demand is, inevitably, less precise than controlling money supply. The central bank has monopoly power as a supplier of narrow money. It does not have quite the same authority when it comes to money demand. Nevertheless, the central bank is not entirely impotent in influencing the levels of demand for narrow money, in particular. Most central banks are also regulators of the financial system. Even the European Central Bank is belatedly being given regulatory powers – still too little, and definitely very late in the process of building a monetary union, but it is finally starting to look a little like a grown-up central bank. The ability to regulate the financial system does give a central bank some control over liquidity preference. This is because the central bank can order banks to hold more or less narrow money under the guise of 'prudential regulation'.

One of the oldest forms of prudential regulation is the reserve requirement ratio that is applied to the banking system. The reserve requirement ratio represents the proportion of a bank's deposit base that must be held in highly liquid forms of money (instead of being lent out into the wider economy). The level of these reserves is designed to meet the normal demands for narrow money that a bank is likely to be subjected to. If the demand for narrow money exceeds the reserves held by the bank, then there is a problem (think of the character of George Bailey in the 1946 film *It's a Wonderful Life* desperately pleading with the citizens of Bedford Falls not to withdraw their money because one person's deposit was their neighbour's mortgage).

If a central bank has printed money because there was a sudden surge in liquidity preference, and that liquidity preference has then abated, then one option is to seek to 'artificially' raise liquidity demand once again by requiring banks to hold a higher proportion of liquid assets as part of their reserves (it would be liquidity *demand* rather than liquidity *preference*, because banks would doubtless prefer not to hold more liquidity). With bank regulation very much in vogue in the aftermath of the global financial crisis this has to be considered a realistic option. Investors have been conditioned by the years of laissez-faire economics that marked the 1990s onwards to assume that central banks will not use regulation to achieve non-prudential policy objectives. Nonetheless, the use of reserve requirements and regulation has a long history as a mechanism for containing excess liquidity in many economies, and some element of this may well return.

Printing money and investing

Printing money does not create inflation – if nothing else that is the one message investors should take from this chapter. Roosevelt's printing of money in 1933 did not create inflation, because it was absorbed by a demand for narrow money on the part of the American public of the day. Japan's prolific production of cash over the past quarter century has not created any meaningful inflation, as much of the cash that has been printed has been tucked away under the metaphorical futon. Similarly, six years after central banks embarked on a significant increase in narrow money supply across the industrialised world, an increase in money that aimed to avoid repeating the depression-inducing errors of the 1930s, inflation has yet to appear because that liquidity has been absorbed by demand. As long as the increased money supply is gathering dust under the mattress, or sitting idle on corporate balance sheets, the increase in money supply presents no significant inflation threat.

Investors need to have two concerns when it comes to money printing. The first is largely unconnected to inflation, and it is that the action of printing money will generally create some distortion in financial markets as the central bank purchases assets in a liquefaction process. This will generally mean that more risk has to be taken by investors if they wish to achieve a specific rate of return.

The second concern is inflation related. Investors need not worry about the inflationary consequences of printing narrow money, but they do need to be aware of the inflationary consequences of printing narrow money relative to the fluctuating levels of narrow money demand. Money demand is not simply identified, and the difficulty of pinpointing the level of money demand is one reason why central banks may periodically make mistakes and allow inflation or deflation episodes to arise.

The final point to make when considering money printing and inflation is around the independence of central banks. Political interference in the conduct of central banks is almost a necessary requirement for too much money to be printed. From medieval China via Weimar Germany to Zimbabwe, political addiction to the ease of printing money means that political interference all too often equates to too much money being printed. An independent central bank can make mistakes in its estimation of the levels of narrow money demand, and that may cause a temporary inflation surprise, but an independent central bank has measures it can take to reverse the excess money problem (either by reducing narrow money supply or artificially increasing narrow money demand).

Perhaps the best rule of thumb for investors is that printing money with a politically compromised central bank is likely to lead to inflation. If the central bank is politically independent, run by economists, then investors can afford to relax a little about the inflation consequences of any money printing that is undertaken.

Notes

1 Friedman (1963).
2 See, for instance, Abrams (2006) and Bowles (2005).
3 Paarlberg (1993) p 32.
4 Sparling (1933) p 3.
5 Sparling (1933) p 4.

6   Inflation numbers 'aren't true'

> Long before I took charge of the Bureau of Labor Statistics I had become very
> suspicious of the Bureau's index numbers, especially its retail price index.
> (Royal Meeker, Commissioner of the Bureau of Labor Statistics,
> speech made in 1915)[1]

Up until now the arguments put forward have attempted to undermine some of
the nonsensical assertions of the economic blogosphere and destroy the more
pervasive myths of sound-bite economics. Now, however, it is time to tackle one
of the issues that is likely to become increasingly important in the coming years
– the belief that whatever drives inflation, the consumer price inflation data is in
some way untrue.

Before diving into this topic, readers needs to take a deep, cleansing breath and
remind themselves of what it is that consumer price inflation is trying to measure.
Consumer prices are an attempt to measure the evolution of the cost of living in an
economy. That fact is a lifeboat of sanity that investors should seek to cling to in
the maelstrom of invective that surrounds consumer price debates much of the time.

Having reminded the reader of that fact, this chapter will attempt to point
out that some of the mistrust of consumer price inflation numbers is not valid.
The next chapter will then go on to point out the ways in which consumer price
inflation data is misleading as a guide to the cost of living, and why that is so
important to investing.

There are two particular reasons why inflation data is mistrusted. The first is a
simple problem of any individual's behaviour, which is a widespread difficulty;
consumers rely on their instincts rather than impartial analysis to shape their
perceptions of inflation and the instinct of the average consumer is likely to be
wrong. The second reason is more complex, and it is a problem that is more
generally discussed amongst the inflation cognoscenti they meet: inflation data is
adjusted to encompass the impact of changes in quality and in spending patterns.

Inflation and the great tragedy of civilisation

One origin of the distrust that clouds consumer price inflation data like a miasma
wells up from what is undoubtedly one of the great tragedies of human civilisation:

simply put, there are not enough economists in the world. If only this single problem could be remedied, much angst and misunderstanding could be avoided. Sadly, in the absence of universal economic education, we must recognise that nirvana is beyond the reach of humanity and non-economists will walk among us.

The paucity of economists means that rational economic theory will not always guide consumer behaviour, nor will it always determine investor decision-making. Irrational behaviour plays a far greater role in economic and investment decisions than is healthy. Nowhere is this irrationality more evident than in popular perceptions around prices. Consumers forever believe that governments' consumer price data is failing to capture inflation properly. This is because consumers fail to consider inflation in a rational, economist-like manner.

The construction of the consumer price basket for a modern developed economy is a genuine attempt to capture the average (mean) experience of the consumer in that economy. This means that the prices of a myriad of goods and services will be aggregated together under some kind of weighting system to come up with a single figure representing the average movement of consumer prices. Consumer prices are normally published on a monthly basis (some, like those of Australia, are quarterly). Self-evidently, everything that is purchased by a consumer on a monthly basis should be included in the data, as changes in the price level of such items will demonstrably affect the standard of living of the consumer. Food is normally purchased several times a month. Fuel for the car and for the home (including things like electricity) should obviously be included in the index. Public transport, telephone charges, internet connections – all these things are monthly purchases and should obviously be included in a monthly calculation of the cost of living.

The first consumer price indices of the nineteenth century were content to leave things at that. The earliest consumer price indices were mainly aimed at measuring the cost of living for the urban poor, and so food and fuel were the main items the typical household would consume. However, to just focus on monthly purchases is to miss much of the modern cost of living. What about the purchase of a car? In an advanced industrialised economy, households will often own a car, although this ownership is not likely to be the result of a monthly purchase. What about the purchase of consumer durable goods, like washing machines, televisions and computers? These are products that (as their categorisation implies) are built to endure. The consumer does not expect to purchase such goods frequently, but they do expect to purchase them occasionally. Moreover, the purchase and consumption (or use) of such goods contributes to the standard of living that the consumer experiences. This being so, the cost of such goods should somehow be included in the cost of living that the consumer price index attempts to discover.

Modern calculations of the consumer price basket will seek to include all of this in their indices. Crudely put, if a product is purchased once every three years, then one thirty-sixth of the product will be assumed to be purchased in any given month. By applying such a weighting to the value of the product, the cost of living will capture the price of smartphones, sports utility vehicles, computer game consoles, dishwashers and all the other trappings of modern civilisation.

Calculating the US consumer price index entails the capture of some 80,000 different prices every month across cities of the United States (rural areas are still ignored in calculating US consumer price inflation).[2]

Unfortunately, the consumer, denied the clear-sightedness that is handed out with every economics degree certificate, does not generally tend to think along these lines. When the consumer considers what inflation is, they will instead tend to consider only the price of goods and services that are immediately before them. The price of a chocolate bar purchased from a vending machine is remembered; the price of the television purchased last year is lost in the mists of time (and any comparison of the price of the television purchased last year to the price of its predecessor five years before that is apparently beyond the scope of human memory). In the mind of the non-economist, chocolate is extremely important to inflation, while the price of the television will barely register. In fact, the bar of chocolate is not noticeably more important than the television: candy bars and chewing gum had a weight of 0.183 per cent in the US consumer price index in 2014, while televisions carried a weight of 0.161 per cent.

Consumers' perceptions of inflation are therefore strongly influenced by the price of things that they buy frequently. What exactly it is that consumers buy frequently will vary from consumer to consumer depending on their lifestyle (a fact of critical importance to the next chapter), but some generalisations can be made. Food is obviously a frequent purchase, and something that punches far above its weight class when it comes to shaping consumers' inflation perceptions. Depending on the pattern of consumption this may be individual product prices, or it may be the sum total represented by the price of the standardised weekly food basket – either way consumers will tend to be very sensitive to the price. Fuel, particularly fuel for the car (petrol or gasoline, or diesel), is another high-frequency purchase. With the price of fuel prominently displayed at point of sale, even pedestrians are continually reminded of its cost.

Perceptions of consumer prices can also be influenced by somewhat less frequent purchases if there is a regularity to the purchase and a standardisation to the good or service – for certain groups in society, private school fees are an object of constant price comparison, because it is a standard product that is regularly purchased (three times a year as a rule), and it is a price that the purchaser is likely to remember. However, the overwhelming majority of people in practically any industrialised economy do not pay private school fees, and thus rising school fees may simply be a relative price shift without giving any indication of general inflation tendencies – whatever the parents may choose to believe.

Basically, consumers will be aware of the prices of goods or services that meet three criteria:

- The goods or services are homogenous (the same article, basket of articles or service is purchased over time, facilitating an easy comparison).
- The goods or services are purchased frequently enough that the last price paid can be recollected (although it should be noted, the previous price paid is often misremembered).

- The price of the goods or services is visible – a train ticket (even a season ticket) is a visible price that consumers will remember. However, putting random amounts of money on a travel card ('topping up') that is used to pay for a series of journeys renders the consumer far less sensitive to the price of travel – because the journeys are paid for *ad hoc*, and comparing the price of one journey with another is more difficult.

The reality of this misperception of inflation can be shown with some effort. Several economies publish data that surveys consumer perceptions of inflation. Unfortunately, for the most part, the surveys generate relatively imprecise answers; for example, characterising prices as having risen 'a lot', 'moderately', 'a little'. That lack of precision leaves economists silently banging their heads against the wall while mentally cursing the surveyors (Eurostat in this specific instance – anyone who has spent any time navigating Eurostat's website in search of information will readily appreciate that a quiet, desperate sense of despair is the default state of any Eurostat user).

Nonetheless, some surveys can be helpful. Figures 6.1 and 6.2 are drawn from the Bank of England's quarterly survey of inflation attitudes. Here the proportion of the population who believe inflation exceeded 5 per cent is compared to the consumer price index excluding food and energy prices, and then to an index of just food and energy prices. Food and energy inflation, which is taken as a proxy for the inflation rate for high-frequency purchases, is clearly better correlated with high inflation perceptions. It should be noted that overall headline inflation only

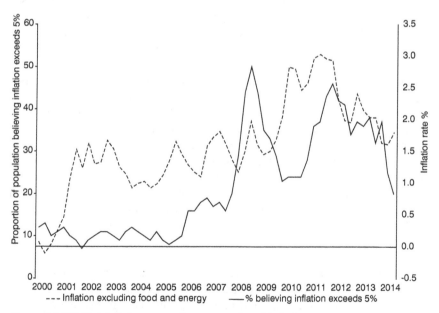

Figure 6.1 UK high inflation perceptions versus 'core' inflation

Source: Data adapted from Haver Analytics.

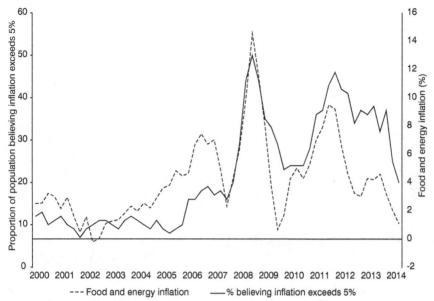

Figure 6.2 UK high inflation perceptions versus food and energy prices

Source: Data adapted from Haver Analytics.

exceeded 5 per cent for two months of the period covered by the figures. The proportion of the population believing inflation to have exceeded 5 per cent was nearly always wrong, therefore.

A cursory comparison of food and energy inflation with core inflation shows that relative price shifts are a quite common occurrence. There are several periods when food and energy prices are changing significantly, not just in absolute terms but relative to other prices in the economy. This means that it would be unwise to use food and energy prices as a representative example of overall inflation – but that is what the consumer, mesmerised by their high-frequency purchases, is inclined to do.

If consumer perceptions of inflation are strongly influenced by high-frequency purchases, and if the price of high-frequency purchases is not representative of overall inflation, then consumer perceptions of inflation will generally be wrong. In the case of the US, where consumer durable goods price inflation (low-frequency purchases) has been less than consumer non-durable goods price inflation (high-frequency purchases) for most of the past twenty years, this bias towards high-frequency purchases means that inflation perceptions are not only always wrong, they are nearly always wrong in one direction (too high). Indeed, consumer durable goods have tended to be falling in price (outright deflation) since 1997 (Figure 6.3). Ignoring deflation is only going to add to the perception problems.

One of the most celebrated instances of inflation misperceptions came from the introduction of the glittering wonder that is the euro. The single European

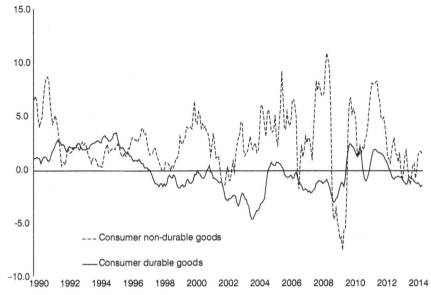

Figure 6.3 US consumer price inflation for durable goods and non-durable goods

Source: Bureau of Labor Statistics.

currency was introduced in two stages – first in a virtual sense, which had only a limited impact in the real world, and then in a physical sense (the reason being that it was not physically possible to produce all the required notes and coins to meet the first deadline for the creation of the euro). This process meant that the introduction of physical notes and coins required prices to be redenominated from the legacy national currencies into the new euro. The conversion created an opportunity for goods prices to be revised, because of course retailers tend to like to sell their items in 'round numbers'. Selling something for one euro and ninety cents is a whole lot less convenient to the retailer than is selling something for two euros. When prices were converted from round number national currency amounts into the superficially random euro amount equivalent, the practice was (as a general rule) to round up the euro amount to the nearest whole number.

Of course, the rounding up of prices would be most noticeable where prices were fairly small in the first place. Rounding from one euro and ninety cents to two euros is obviously a relatively visible five per cent increase in the price. Rounding from nine euros seventy to ten euros is proportionately far less, and thus far less impactful to consumer perceptions. Moreover, because high-frequency purchases tend to be lower-priced items like food, the impact of that five per cent increase in the smaller price is further magnified in the mind of the buyer. The change in the cost of an espresso coffee in Rome was often cited as being incontrovertible proof that the consumer price inflation data of the euro was wrong, when of course it was no proof at all. The change in the price of an espresso in Rome was accurately captured in the consumer price calculations of the time. Even Italians have a finite capacity for concentrated caffeinated beverages, and this means that the price of an espresso is not as important to an Italian consumer's standard of living as the Italian consumer might believe.

The extent to which consumers were mistaken was astonishingly large. Evidence from Italy suggests consumers were railing against 18 per cent inflation in 2002 (in the wake of the introduction of the physical euro notes and coins). Actual inflation was 2 per cent.[3] Lest this be thought to be a peculiarly Italian condition, perhaps brought about by some kind of caffeine-induced hallucination, it should be pointed out that the pattern of misperceiving inflation was repeated across the euro area around this time.

There is a further complication to the perception of inflation, and one which seems to have been especially vigorous around the introduction of the euro. We turn again to our old friend, that most versatile of economic concepts 'loss aversion', which was introduced back in the first chapter. Inflation is clearly a form of loss – it represents a loss to the value of one's real standard of living. Non-economists dislike losing something more than they like gaining the equivalent. That suggests that a 10 per cent price increase of one item and a 10 per cent price reduction of a similar item do not balance each other out in the mind of the consumer. Instead, the net effect in the mind of the consumer will be that they have suffered a real loss. Because a loss in real living standards is perceived as being more important than a gain in real living standards, when it comes to price changes consumers seem to have brains that are hardwired to remember price increases but to forget (or at the very least downplay) price reductions.

Remembering price increases and forgetting price reductions is always going to lead to a skew to inflation, and it means consumers will tend to think inflation is higher than it actually is. Thus, not only is inflation perception generally going to be wrong, it is more likely to be wrong and higher rather than wrong and lower. This was a particular problem with the introduction of the euro, because so many prices were changing all at the same time. In one sense, at least, the price of everything changed. If consumers were predisposed to remember the price increases and dismiss the price reductions, it was perhaps inevitable that their perceptions of inflation deviated so far from reality.

In theory, consumers could train themselves to look through the noise and become truly impartial in their observations of inflation. A test that examined high-frequency inflation expectations of central bankers, academics and students[4] showed that the economists of a central bank were best able to filter out the noise of high-frequency purchases and concentrate on the reality of the cost of living. As a result, their inflation perceptions were noticeably less volatile. We are back to the tragedy of there being not enough trained economists in this world. Others in the survey would change their perceptions of inflation with alarming frequency – every week, roughly a third of those surveyed changed their forecast of the inflation rate that they expected in the future. Inflation forces do not change with that sort of frequency in the real world, and the perception is a great deal more volatile than the reality.

The consequence of too few economists

The misperception of inflation that is created by the disproportionate influence of the price of high-frequency purchases, and by the skew to forgetting when prices fall, is an important problem for investors. Investment decisions may be skewed by a belief that inflation is higher or lower than is the case in reality. If the perception of inflation is higher than the reality, then consumers may unfairly discriminate against certain forms of investment – fixed-income assets like government bonds, for instance. If the perception of inflation is lower than the reality, then consumers will find that their returns do not satisfy their needs – their real investment income will be lower than they expect.

Theoretically, handing one's investments over to a professional fund manager could avoid the perception problem, and it should certainly mitigate the risk. However, professional managers may well still be influenced by their own personal perceptions of inflation. The phrase 'I don't believe the inflation statistics' is heard too often in the investment community to be able to give much comfort to those who entrust their money to the professional ministrations of others. The seeming importance of anecdotal evidence in the professional or institutional investment process is quite terrifying.

There is one additional consequence from the misperception of inflation on the part of the consumer, which is that a misperception of inflation may create inflation in reality. The consumer's perception of inflation is flawed, no doubt, but if the consumer is also a worker (as many consumers are) and if the consumer has some degree of influence in pay bargaining, then the misperception of inflation may lead to higher pay claims which may then lead to higher inflation.

Clearly, the chain that links inflation misperceptions to wage cost pressures on prices is only going to exist if the labour market is relatively tight; that is to say, if there are not many workers available to take up job offers. In such a situation workers are in a position to bargain for higher wages. If the labour market has high unemployment and spare capacity (the two concepts are not always the same thing) then it is unlikely that workers will have enough pay bargaining power to create the problem. But what this does mean is that the investor would be wise to consider inflation perceptions and high-frequency goods price inflation as being an important input into the investment process at times when unemployment is low.

Investors therefore need to have some self-awareness about what inflation actually is, and put their faith in the official figures and not in the anecdotal evidence of their weekly forays to the local supermarket. But this then brings up the second problem. Even if investors succeed in breaking free from the inflation illusion, can the official figures be trusted?

Never mind the price, feel the quality

The issue of high-frequency purchases creates doubt about inflation because consumers are not measuring their own price experiences accurately. The second criticism of inflation arises not from misperception, but from the correct perception that the officials responsible for creating inflation data will adjust the numbers. Inflation, at least in the form of consumer price inflation, does not simply measure visible price changes.

Again, it is worth remembering that what consumer price inflation data is trying to capture is how prices impact the standard of living. Simple, published price changes may not actually be the best way of reflecting this. The two big adjustments that cause so much controversy are quality adjustment, and adjusting for changes in consumer spending patterns. The two adjustments are sometimes known, not always accurately, as hedonic adjustment and chain weighting respectively. In fact, hedonic adjustment and chain weighting are very specific forms of quality adjustment and spending pattern adjustment. The mathematical nature of the former and the variable nature of the latter means that they tend to attract more attention than other forms of quality and spending pattern adjustment, and the terms are sometimes misapplied as generic terms. Examining these adjustment mechanisms in turn reveals that they are not a deliberate attempt to manipulate the statistics and delude the consumer, but instead are a process of valid adjustments that the investor should not fear.

Some areas of quality adjustment are obvious, easily calculated, and generally applauded by the consumer – but actually are not popularly considered to be quality adjustments. The standard example that is given is that of a bar of chocolate. This is actually used with good reason, because the confectionery industry is particularly inclined to use this particular method of 'quality' adjustment. Economists have written academic papers about it (economists get to write papers about really weird things from time to time).[5] The quality adjustment is really a quantity adjustment – if a bar of chocolate shrinks in weight by 10 per cent, but the price does not change, then the inflation rate should rise, and will rise, to reflect the reduction in quantity. The consumer is getting less for their money; were the consumer to pay to consume the same amount of chocolate in quantity terms as in previous months, it would cost the consumer more money. It does not matter whether the size of the packaging is unchanged or not; if the contents are less, then quality adjustment will make sure that the consumer price index goes up.

There are those in the blogosphere who claim that quantity and size adjustment allow stealth inflation and go unrecorded in the consumer price inflation statistics.[6] Nothing could be further from the truth. Indeed, not only are changes in quantity and size factored into the consumer price basket, but the British Office for National Statistics went so far as to specifically mention that chocolate bars were getting smaller in size in its October 2012 Statistical Bulletin – and to highlight that this was behind the rise in food price inflation as calculated in the statistics. The British Office for National Statistics clearly takes its chocolate bars very, very seriously indeed. Mess with the size of a bar of 'Fruit and Nut' and the full wrath of the statistical profession will descend on the confectioners of the country.

Reducing the size of a bar of chocolate is a pretty obvious change. However, there may be other 'quality' changes. The United States adjusts for shifts in housing quality when comparing rents. What if the old rent included utility bills (like electricity) but the new rent does not? Is it fair to say that this is a direct comparison? Clearly not – the renter today is getting less for their money than the renter last month was getting, and the US inflation data will capture the fact that they are getting less. Similarly, if one is comparing the rent of a one bedroom apartment today, equipped with the latest kitchen equipment and air conditioning with the rent on a garret single bedroom apartment with none of the modern luxuries, the difference in what the renter actually receives for their money needs to be accounted for.

Products and services like chocolate and rent that change in size or quantity are all very easy to adjust for. The changes in the nature of the product or service are easily and objectively measured – the chocolate bar can be weighed, and the value of having air conditioning can be isolated from rental payments without too much fancy adjustment. Sometimes investors complain about these forms of adjustment, but for the most part these changes actually raise the cost of living. Because of the principle of loss aversion, investors tend not to be critical of a process that raises the officially reported inflation – it is when inflation is lowered by adjustment that investors feel that they might be losing out.

Where things start to get tricky is when the whole product or service is changing, and a direct comparison is no longer possible. This is when a specific form of quality adjustment has to be used – the process known as hedonic adjustment, which has already been mentioned. Really, hedonic adjustment is just a pretentious way of saying quality adjustment – statisticians like to dress up their craft with fancy language, no doubt feeling it enhances their academic credentials and sets them above their peers in the world of accountancy. However, hedonic adjustment differs from other methods of measuring quality changes because it has to rely on mathematical techniques to tease out the quality change in the good or service. This is generally because the product has changed so much over time.

The classic example that is always brought out on these occasions is the computer. A computer today has more power and can do many more things than a computer of ten years ago, and much, much more than a computer of twenty or thirty years ago. Indeed, the computing power of a modern mobile phone (or cell phone, to translate from proper English for the benefit of Americans) outclasses a home computer from the early part of the 1980s, like a ZX Spectrum or an Acorn Electron. Yet the nominal price of a modern smartphone today is very roughly the same as the nominal price charged for one of those archaic home computers back in the mists of time. The Acorn Electron sold for £199 in the heady excitement of its launch in 1983. The Apple iPhone 4 currently sells for £218 for the basic handset in 2014.

Does this mean that the price of computing has been unchanged over three decades? It hardly seems a fair comparison – the smartphone is home computer, internet device, mobile phone, video camera, potentially a video phone, pager and much more besides. To even attempt to replicate all those applications thirty years ago would have cost much, much more than the price of a computer alone. Of course, thirty years ago some of the applications of a modern smartphone would not even have been possible. The concept of updating one's Facebook status on an Acorn Electron is so far beyond the reality of what such a machine could accomplish, it would have melted the magnetic tape cassette deck that initially served as that computer's main storage device. The consumer today is getting far more for their money.

So, what does this mean? It means that the consumer price index should try to adjust for changes in quality when calculating inflation. If the consumer is getting more for their money, then their standard of living is rising. (It is true that this presupposes that the additional functionality of a smartphone raises the user's quality of life, which may be a moot point, but let us work with the assumption.)

Quality adjustment is particularly important for those products that are frequently upgraded – because it is difficult to do an apples to apples comparison in the world of smartphones if last year's smartphone model cannot be purchased anywhere except for an antique shop. To take another example – and one that is often unfairly ridiculed – the United States hedonically adjusts educational textbooks. This modest tome on inflation will be subject to hedonic price adjustment should it ever enter into US consumer price index calculations. Hedonic adjustment is necessary because, with a publication date of 2015, it is not possible to compare the price of *The Truth About Inflation* in 2015 with the price of *The Truth About Inflation* in 2014, because the book did not exist in 2014. What the American statisticians will do is take the price of another economics book in 2014 and compare it with the price of *The Truth About Inflation*. (Modesty should forbid my suggesting what book would serve as a suitable comparison, but being an economist I have no modesty. Keynes's *General Theory* might do, or anything from a recent Nobel Laureate.) There is not a direct comparison going on. The whole hedonic adjustment issue became important with the advances of technology. What if one of the textbooks in the comparison comes with a DVD or a CD ROM of additional data as part of the book, and the other book is just good old-fashioned paper? The consumer is getting more than a book bundled up in one purchase, but just getting a book with the other purchase. The additional features that are bundled together need to be teased apart to try and get a fair sense of what is happening to inflation.

Hedonic adjustment is relatively expensive to undertake, and for this reason it is not widely used – certainly not for products that have relatively long life cycles, with little quality change. As a result, the amount of consumer price inflation that is adjusted for quality using hedonic adjustment is relatively small – in the United Kingdom 0.5 per cent of the consumer price basket is adjusted in this way. A further part of the basket will be affected by changes in size and quantity, mainly in the food category, but that is not where the controversy lies. It is also notable that the United Kingdom has reduced the number of products that are hedonically adjusted for quality changes (as of March 2014), as it felt that some of the products concerned – mobile phones and digital cameras – were no longer changing in quality at a rapid enough pace as to warrant the move.

As Table 6.1 demonstrates, hedonic adjustment is hardly an overwhelming feature of any country's price process. The number of goods affected tends to be very narrow – the US, admittedly, is more enamoured of the practice than most

Table 6.1 Selected economies' hedonic adjustments

Country	Items subject to hedonic adjustment	Weight in basket	Notes
Australia	PCs	Below 1.56%	Australia published the weight for computers and audio-visual equipment combined, hedonic adjustment being applied to a subset of that
Canada	PCs, laptops, printers, monitors, internet services	1.3%	2013 weight
Germany	Used car, PCs, laptops, tablets	1.1%	Weight from 2004 ECB paper
New Zealand	Used cars	2.0%	2014 weight
Sweden	Clothing and footwear	Below 5.2%	June 2014 weight. Only specific apparel items are hedonically adjusted, and the weighting is for the entire category. Used cars are quality adjusted using a panel of experts, rather than hedonics. Their weight is just under 0.1%
Switzerland	PCs and laptops	0.5%	June 2014 weight
United Kingdom	PCs, tablets, smartphones	0.5%	2013 weights for these categories. Digital cameras and smartphones were no longer subject to hedonic adjustment from March 2014
United States	Clothing, footwear, refrigerators, washing machines and dryers, ranges, cooktops, microwave ovens, televisions, DVD players	2.9%	July 2014 weight. Computers were adjusted from January 1998 to September 2003

Source: Data adapted from Ahnert and Kenny (2004); Wells and Restieaux (2014); US Bureau of Labor Statistics; Statistics Canada; Eurostat; UK Office for National Statistics; Haver Analytics.

other economies, but even here the adjustment amounts to a mere 2.9 per cent of the basket of goods. Even if hedonic adjustment were to correct prices by 10 per cent – an absurdly high change – it would impact headline consumer price inflation to the tune of some 0.3 per cent in the US.

One of the interesting issues around quality adjustment and inflation is that the argument has not all been one way. The wartime economy of the United States in the early 1940s was gripped by arguments over the role of quality in inflation

– but the argument in favour of quality adjustment arose because it was felt that the *deterioration* in quality was being under-reported. Consumer price statistics in the 1940s were not adjusted for quality, which was felt to be unfair. Inflation was popularly supposed to be considerably higher than was reported (in the absence of quality adjustment) because one was paying the same price as before but receiving inferior goods in exchange. Ford Hinrichs, the Commissioner of the US Bureau of Labor Statistics, actually took to the airwaves in 1943: a government-sponsored radio programme entitled 'Housewife versus Economist' starred Hinrichs alongside his own wife in debating quality adjustments to the consumer price inflation measure. One can only lament that such highly educational broadcasts have disappeared from the world of modern media, crowded out by makeover shows and reality television. Think how much better modern home entertainment would be if debates between economists and their partners formed the core of the evening's television programme schedule.

Part of the problem during the war years was the emergence of a common problem that bedevils economists to this day – the use of single anecdotes as antidotes to a wealth of valid data. Members of the trade union movement were aggressive in their attempts to demonstrate that inflation was being under-reported, because in a world of pay and price controls wage increases were dependent on the level of inflation. Reports packed full of anecdotes, which appealed to the public, were used in defence of the union position. One report lamented that Pittsburgh restaurants had stopped giving free bread and butter with meals. This is a legitimate cause for complaint on the grounds of quality adjustment, but the loss of free bread and butter in one city, while no doubt traumatic for the diners concerned, does not necessarily constitute certain proof that rampant inflation is stalking an economy.

The arguments about quality adjustment lingered on after the war. In 1951, the United Electrical, Radio and Machine Workers of America described the consumer price index as a 'fraud against labour', a comment which was picked up by the Soviet Union and used as proof that the capitalists of the United States were exploiting labour to further US military ambitions.[7] It is worth pausing for just a moment to reflect that this passion and international high diplomacy is being caused by a debate about the quality adjustment of the components of consumer price data.

Quality adjustment is not necessarily a major part of the consumer price index; in some countries, beyond adjusting for quantity and size changes, it does not take place at all. Despite this, quality adjustment, and specifically the mathematical hedonic quality adjustment, seems to arouse considerable passion from consumers and investors. However, intuitively, if consumer price inflation is supposed to be measuring changes in the standard of living, some account must be taken of quality change. Why then does quality adjustment cause so much angst? There are two problems: alternatives, and what quality adjustment tends to do to the data.

The first problem is that the consumer may well argue that they are paying for additional features that they do not actually want. Modern products and services are very often bundles of features. As life has become more complex, so the complexity of what we purchase has increased. The consumer who does not want the quality improvement still has to pay for the quality improvement. If they are not using the quality improvement – if they use a smartphone as a phone, and regard the camera, video phone and other applications as a waste of money – then there is some validity in the complaint that the quality adjustment of the consumer price index is artificially reducing their inflation rate. Those who subscribe to cable television packages and receive a whole series of channels that they never watch often feel the same way about bundling and the unnecessary complexity of product the consumer is forced to purchase.

This is a valid criticism of quality adjustment, but it must be assumed to apply to a relatively small section of the population. The consumer may not want or use the additional processing power on their newly purchased computer, and lament the older and simpler times, but for the most part purchasers of the computer will find the faster speed, better memory or higher-quality graphics to be something that enhances the value of the product to them. The 'I don't want the additional quality' crowd must be assumed to be a somewhat curmudgeonly minority. Consumer price inflation is something of a 'one size fits all' statistic, and some small group is always going to feel misrepresented.

The second problem is that in modern times, *hedonic* quality adjustment for products will tend to reduce inflation rates rather than raise them. Quality adjustment has not always been a disinflationary force, as the vociferous complaints of the 1940s demonstrate, but nowadays there tends to be an incremental improvement in product quality. Moreover, because innovative, new products will often have lots of upgrades in the early years of their lives, these goods are both more likely to be subject to hedonic quality adjustment in the consumer price index and at the same time more likely to be an object of interest for consumers. It is a bit like the high-frequency purchases issue mentioned earlier – if one is constantly checking the price of the latest computer, one is likely to be sensitive to the headline price of that computer.

The exception to the incremental improvement in quality leading to a lower recorded inflation rate is the quality adjustment for housing and for clothing which takes place in the United States. Adjusting the price of housing for quality (which is not a mathematical hedonic adjustment, but a more straightforward comparison) has led to an increase in the price of housing – the inflation statistics recognise a deterioration in housing quality. The price of clothing (which is a hedonic adjustment – clothing fashions rarely last from one year to another) is adjusted up and down according to quality changes – quality is variable here, but with a bias to the adjustment raising the price of clothing; clothing is assumed to be of lower quality today than was the case in the past.

For non-clothing hedonic quality adjustment, and in particular for technology products, the hedonic quality adjustment process will tend to lower prices. The old, lingering fear of loss aversion can then come into play once again. If inflation would be higher without the hedonic quality adjustments, this may give rise to the mistaken belief that all forms of quality adjustment are just part of a conspiracy by the government to delude consumers or investors into believing that inflation is lower than it really is. If an investor takes hold of the idea that the government is adjusting the inflation data with the deliberate aim of reducing it, it is only a matter of time before they will start calling into radio talk shows and trawling the blogosphere to bond with like-minded individuals. That only a tiny proportion of the prices in the consumer price basket are affected by the hedonic quality adjustment process is not normally taken into account by a typical conspiracy theorist. A logical assessment of factual evidence is rarely ever taken into account by a typical conspiracy theorist.

The eagerness with which governments have embraced quality-adjusted consumer price inflation does not, perhaps, help the cause terribly much. Part of the problem (which will be discussed in more detail in Chapter 9) is that a lot of government spending nowadays is in some way tied to the level of consumer price inflation. The original idea was to index-link government spending on items like benefits in order to depoliticise increases in spending. If the principle was established that benefit payments or pensions should rise automatically to 'keep pace' with the cost of living, then the potential for political disagreement over such spending should melt away. What actually happened, of course, was that the process of index-linking spending made the calculation of consumer price inflation a political football. If the idea of index-linked payments has been firmly established, the only way such payments can be reduced is to target the calculation of the consumer price index itself. This politicisation of inflation becomes a problem for the recipient of inflation-linked income – and by the mid-1970s roughly half the population of the United States had some part of their income linked to the consumer price index.

This came to a head in the United States with the report of the Boskin Commission into consumer prices, published in 1996. The report led to the more widespread use of quality adjustment in the US consumer price data. Unfortunately, one prominent argument, given emphasis by the politics of the time, was that the introduction of quality adjustment could lower the government deficit through cutting index-linked government spending. It was claimed that by 2006 (i.e. within a decade) the miscalculation of consumer price inflation would be the fourth largest form of 'government spending', as a consequence of the indexation of benefits and other forms of government spending. As a point of fact the relationship between the consumer price inflation rate and government spending was true, and it does not undermine the legitimacy of the adjustment process. Unfortunately, this aspect of the debate seems to have stuck in the minds of investors, who now instinctively associate quality adjustments with an attempt to 'cook the books' and that they serve to meet the nefarious intentions of politicians.

Private sector arguments in favour of quality adjustment have also tended to be loudest when there is an element of self-interest. The auto sector was keen to claim that quality improvements meant car prices were falling in 1939. IBM advocated quality adjusting the prices of its computers as part of an anti-trust case it was fighting. Again this is not to deny the validity of these claims, or the need to adjust consumer price inflation to take account of quality changes – but it is easy to see why quality adjustment has acquired something of a bad reputation amongst some investors.

Inflation data is trying to measure changes in the cost of a living standard. That does mean that where the quality of a good or service changes, and thus the standard of living changes, the inflation data should be able to distinguish that change. Those who argue that quality changes should not affect inflation need to remember the shrinking chocolate bars of the UK in 2012; few would contest the idea that a smaller bar of chocolate sold at an unchanged price is effectively a price increase.

The hedonic adjustments for technology, or occasionally for clothing and cars, are the same principle as the adjustment for the bar of chocolate. The difference is that these adjustments are a little more complicated to calculate. The cost of compiling hedonically adjusted statistics is sufficiently high as to ensure that they remain a very limited part of the overall consumer basket, as Table 6.1 suggested. Consumers should not fear quality adjustments to the consumer price index – it is a very small but very necessary adjustment to understanding when inflation is taking place.

Consumption patterns

The other adjustment that is made to inflation data is to adjust the weights applied to each component of the shopping basket. To the well-ordered mind, this is the logical consequence of the fickleness of fashion. There is no point in trying to assess the standards of living today using the spending habits of yesteryear. Therefore, the cost of living should adjust to keep pace with what is in and out of the typical shopping basket.

The conspiracy theorist may not have a well-ordered mind. Instead, their fevered imagination sees dark, Machiavellian forces conspiring against the humble investor, deliberately tweaking the data so as to disguise the extent to which inflation is rampaging out of control. The rallying cry for this group tends to go something along the lines of, 'If inflation was calculated the same way as it was twenty years ago, it would be x per cent higher than the government *claims* it is today.' (The sarcastic emphasis of italicisation is added.) To be fair, this rallying cry can also encompass some of the inflation that has been lost due to the introduction of quality adjustment methods, but as quality adjustment is so small a part of the inflation calculation the bulk of this cry of protest must be attributed to shifts in the weighting of the basket.

For an economist, this anguished protest seems to be almost too conservative. Why fret about the changing calculation of inflation over the past twenty years? Why not worry about the changing composition of inflation over the past century? If this is to be a conspiracy, let us make it a big conspiracy. Why should we not use the consumer price methods of the past, if adjusting them is just manipulating the data?

Figure 6.4 is a rough approximation of the impact of changes. There is a US consumer price index (a level, rather than the inflation rate) as calculated with

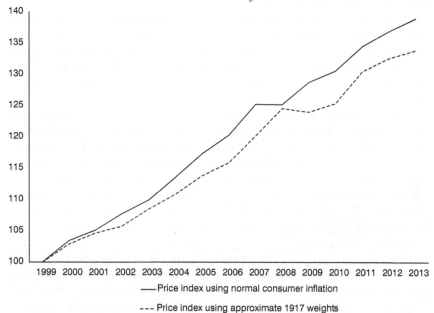

Figure 6.4 Consumer price indices in recent times according to modern weightings, and approximating the weightings of the 1917 index[8]

Source: Bureau of Labor Statistics, National Industrial Conference Board (1926), Rees (1961), author's calculations.

such painstaking attention to modern detail by the Bureau of Labor Statistics today. There is also an approximation of consumer price index judged using the relative importance of the categories contained in an earlier consumer price index – specifically the consumer price index of 1917. Why use the 1917 index as the basis for the calculation? Because this was before the corruption of changing weights was introduced into the calculation of the basket.

The results are pretty clear. The conspiracy theorist is proved partly right by this data. Today's inflation calculated with the same weightings as it was in the past is very different to the reported inflation today. Unfortunately, for the conspiracy theorist, today's inflation is higher. The reason for this owes much to the treatment of housing, which was weighted far lower in 1917 than it is today.

Of course this whole graphic is an absurdity. Back in 1917 the Bureau of Labor Statistics in the US calculated inflation with nearly 40 per cent of the weight being food. Alcohol was not included at all (and pretty much the entire economics profession will testify to the importance of alcohol in determining the standard of living of a modern economist). There were no consumer electronics in 1917, no entertainment measures beyond the cinema, and pretty much no services aside from medical and barbering services. Even within the eternal components like clothing, weightings have changed: detachable celluloid collars for men's shirts formed 0.06 per cent of the consumer basket of 1917. Detachable celluloid collars are no longer worn with quite so much enthusiasm, and indeed such is the fickleness of fashion that they no longer appear at all in the modern consumer price basket. To a rational and style-conscious economist, taking the weighting of detachable celluloid collars from 0.06 per cent to 0 per cent seems a right and proper adjustment, though of course the conspiracy theorist is free to disagree.

It is also worth noting that, remarkable though it is to contemplate, the consumer price inflation of 1917 was an overtly *racist* statistic. In calculating typical spending habits, the US authorities specifically excluded the spending patterns of African-American households, along with the spending patterns of any household that did not speak English (which effectively excluded Hispanic-American households). Their spending patterns were not considered important enough to policy decision-making. The spending of 12,096 explicitly white families in 92 towns formed the basis of the weighting for the consumer price basket.

The conspiracy theorist might complain that this is an unfair comparison, that obviously spending patterns have changed over so long a period of time. Yet spending patterns are in a continual state of flux, and what mattered to the cost of living yesterday is not what matters to the cost of living today. President Nixon's obsessive worrying about the price of hamburger meat (uncooked) in the early 1970s is incomprehensible to a modern generation who only recognise hamburger meat when presented beneath a golden arched logo. The price of a black and white portable television was of supreme importance to the author as a teenager, as I can recollect saving for months to purchase a television of my own. Not only is it impossible to buy a new black and white television today, but the modern teenager is far more likely to access their entertainment via an iPad, on demand, than using the near century-old communication method that even a flat screen, high definition, colour television represents.

Judging today's standard of living by the consumption pattern of our grandparents, parents or even our early youth seems absurd. What we want changes, and what we want forms the standard of living we want. Therefore, we must periodically adjust the weights of the components of the basket of goods and services that makes up the inflation rate – unless we are to be reduced to wearing detachable celluloid collars while watching 'Big Brother' on bulbous black and white television screens.

The next problem is how best to adjust for changing weights in consumer spending. There are essentially two options available. One is to simply 'rebase' the index – periodically adjust the weights that are applied at arbitrary intervals. Thus, one could calculate inflation based on the 2000 consumption weights, and then later on use the 2005 consumption weights, and so forth. This is how most consumer price indices are calculated. It does allow a certain imprecision to creep in. If consumption patterns have shifted in the interval since weights were last calculated, then for specific products there may be a slight distortion in the consumer price inflation calculation. However, this is a very different order of magnitude from the change that would be wrought if we were to calculate consumer price inflation in the way that we did twenty years ago. Periodic rebasing has to be considered an acceptable way of tracking the changes of consumption spending.

The advantage of adjusting the composition of inflation by picking a base year is that it is relatively simple to calculate, and relatively simple to comprehend. But the world of consumption is not quite as simple as this process suggests, and this has given rise to the alternative of chain weighting. Chain weighting is a process that continually updates the composition of the consumer price basket according to monthly changes in the spending habits of consumers. The process of chain weighting is not generally used for consumer price inflation, which relies on the periodic reassessment of changing base years. It is, however, used for the calculation of prices for GDP and it is also used for some other price metrics (the US personal consumer expenditure deflator for instance). The US has also started to publish a chain-weighted consumer price index, although the base year weighted index is still the principle consumer price inflation measure.

The process of chain weighting takes into account an important part of consumer behaviour, known as the substitution effect. This takes place when consumers substitute one good for another (hence the name – economists are good at coming up with names for things like this). This does mean that chain weighting will impact inflation, but is also impacted by inflation. An example should make this clear. If the price of pork rises relative to other meats, then consumers are quite likely to switch to another form of meat. Why pay more for pork if beef is not rising in price so much? Calculate inflation with a base year of weights, and this substitution will not be captured. The price index will rise, even though most consumers are not in fact paying the higher price (because they have eschewed the more expensive pork).

Under the chain weighting process, however, the higher price of pork reduces the weighting of pork in the aggregate price calculation, because consumers have reduced their consumption of pork. Consumers have chosen to substitute beef for pork, and so beef is more important in the basket and pork is less important. Of course this means that the increased price of pork will reduce a chain-weighted measure of inflation because consumers react to the inflation by substituting other goods. Chain weighting prices is almost guaranteed to create lower inflation statistics than using a base year, because consumers will tend to favour cheaper goods over more expensive near substitutes.

The chain weighting process is controversial in part because it is structured to create a lower inflation rate. The fact that it more accurately reflects the spending patterns of the consumer is not normally considered.

In inflation we trust

Investors should not fear the adjustment process that accounts for quality shifts, nor the changes that reweight the inflation rate according to changes in fashion. Inflation is supposed to reflect the price of enjoying the consumption patterns of today's consumer, not the consumption patterns of our grandparent, or even of ourselves a decade ago. Times change, and economists must change with the times.

The process of adjusting for quality and spending patterns is not perfect in any price index. This is inevitable when considering the complexity of the modern economy. However, the adjustment processes will generally produce a more accurate assessment of the changes in the cost of living than would an unadjusted price index.

US bank notes are, somewhat controversially, printed with the motto 'In God we trust'. For investors it is not trust in any deity that is the problem, but trust in statistics. The belief that inflation numbers are somehow manipulated is remarkably pervasive, but generally perverse. The failure to believe that the official inflation statistics accurately represent price changes can lead investors to make poor investment decisions – eschewing certain investments in the mistaken belief that they will not be compensated for inflation, for instance. Mistrust of official inflation data may also add uncertainty to an investor's view of assets – and that uncertainty will increase the risk premium demanded; a risk premium which is economically damaging.

The first thing any rational investor must do is learn not to trust their instincts. Their instincts on inflation are almost certainly wrong. Human nature being what it is, only the most meticulous of record keepers is likely to be able to compare the prices of everything that they consume. Recollecting the price paid a couple of years ago, even for relatively major purchases, is beyond the scope of most human memories. The bias to focusing on high-frequency purchases is not helpful. Further, the insidious nature of loss aversion in infiltrating human psychology is such that we are all inclined to forget the good news of things becoming cheaper, and remember only the bad news of price rises.

The second thing any rational investor must do is to steel themselves to have some faith that statisticians know what they are doing. Anything which gives a consumer more, or less, for their money must be accounted for in an inflation measure. The methods that statisticians use to account for this are valid mechanisms of adjustment. The method is, on occasion, complex but that is because the world is a more complex place than it was in the past. Adjustments for quality may not be perfect, but they create a more accurate measure of inflation than any index that fails to adjust for quality change.

Finally, there must be acceptance of a need to change the weightings of the inflation basket relatively frequently. Indeed, as society has become more and more consumer driven, the need to keep pace with quantity changes in consumption patterns has become more and more important.

Part of the problem is that inflation statistics as they are currently compiled almost certainly overstate inflation per se. Inflation numbers capture price changes, but they will also capture quality changes. Inflation in the form of consumer price inflation will not adjust for the fickleness of fashion with the same speed that the consumer adjusts. Inflation today is inflation, plus other things. What this means is that any improvement in the quality of inflation data is also likely to lead to a lowering of inflation. Such is the esteem with which we view politicians, any improvement in the quality of inflation statistics is likely to be considered as being part of some dark, sinister attempt by politicians to defraud the general public. It has to be admitted that politicians themselves do not help the process by advocating changes to inflation numbers as a means of lowering government deficits and controlling inflation-linked spending. US President Obama's advocacy of a chain-weighted consumer price index as being something that would help reduce government spending on benefits is a case in point. That such moves may be economically valid does nothing to dispel the perception of statistical change motivated by political self-interest. This mistrust of the data goes back to the 1940s, and it is not going to go away any time soon.

Technology and changes in retail spending patterns mean that we will potentially have a lot more information about prices in the future than we have today. Capturing price data from the internet or from checkout scanners reduces the risk of human error, and increases the potential sources of information. It allows statisticians more scope to adjust consumer price inflation in the future.

Investors need to recognise that consumer price inflation generally does what it sets out to do – it provides an aggregate measure of inflation in an economy, without too many distortions. The casual comments of the blogosphere need to be treated with the contempt they deserve. Changing sizes and quality are accounted for, shifts in spending patterns should be considered. We are not all sitting around wearing celluloid collars, watching black and white television sets. If the chocolate bar we are eating shrinks in size, then the price of that bar rises. Inflation data comes reasonably close to doing what it says it does. Inflation data accurately captures an aggregate measure of the change in the cost of living.

The problem is, inflation data is almost certainly not accurately capturing the cost of living of any individual investor. It does not set out to do so. And that is the problem that is examined in the next chapter.

Notes

1 Cited in Stapleford (2009) p 87.
2 Cage *et al.* (2003) p 8.
3 Del Giovane *et al.* (2008) p 3.
4 Galati *et al.* (2011).
5 David Slawson analysed chocolate bars in the United States, although this being America he called them candy bars. He found that candy bars rose in price in five cent increments from five cents to thirty-five cents from the 1950s until 1983. With each price increase the bar would become larger (heavier). This was because the bar shrank progressively in between price increases – so the consumer was getting less chocolate (or candy) for their cash, even though the price was not changing. The example is cited in Fischer (1996) based on Slawson's book *The New Inflation*.
6 See *What's up with Inflation* at http://www.zerohedge.com/news/2013-07-25/whats-inflation (last retrieved 2 December 2014). If you really must. I do not recommend reading the article, but it does demonstrate the range of inaccuracies that the blogosphere can blithely assert with seemingly complete ignorance of reality.
7 Cited in Stapleford (2009) p 287.

8 The 1917 index weights the current consumer price subcomponents as follows: food consumed at home (no beverages) 38.2 per cent, private sector rent 13.4 per cent, male clothing 6.1 per cent, female clothing 4.6 per cent, infants clothing 6.1 per cent, fuel for the home 5.3 per cent, furniture 5.1 per cent, medical care 8.5 per cent, personal care products 3.6 per cent, public transport 4.5 per cent, recreation 4.5 per cent. The last three items' weights are the author's estimates based on the available historical information; these goods formed part of the general classification of 'miscellaneous goods' and the weights were not spelled out as percentages in the original documentation.

7 Inflation numbers really aren't true

It's the same the whole world over; it's the poor what gets the blame; it's the rich what gets the pleasure; ain't it all a bloomin' shame.
(*She was poor but she was honest*, British nineteenth century music hall song, traditional)

The last chapter highlighted that some of the more common criticisms of inflation inaccuracy are not true. Inflation data today, adjustments and all, largely achieves what inflation data sets out to do. However, inflation does *not* set out to determine an individual's experience of the cost of living. Inflation sets out to determine the *average* cost of living. The average cost of living does not help investors a great deal.

The average nature of inflation leads to a significant problem with how inflation statistics are used and interpreted – a problem that has grown over the past two decades. In calculating the average (mean) inflation rate, inflation statistics will tend to be plutocratic not democratic statistics. That is to say, the composition of an inflation basket is *not* weighted on the principle of one person generating one vote. The composition of an inflation basket is weighted on the principle of one dollar (or one euro, or one pound) generating one vote. The influence of the rich consumer over the composition of the consumer price basket is therefore considerably greater than is the influence of the poor consumer over the composition of the consumer price basket. When it comes to calculating inflation – at least modern-day inflation – it is the consumption habits, fashions and tastes of the rich that matter. The poor consumer has very little significance.

If the sort of things that rich consumers purchase were rising in price at the same pace as the sort of things that poor consumers purchase, this would not make a meaningful difference to the use of inflation data. However, the past thirty years have witnessed three trends (which are not unrelated):

- Income inequality has risen.
- Consumer spending patterns for rich and poor consumers have become increasingly divergent.
- The price of labour-intensive goods has tended to rise less than the price of commodity-intensive goods over a relatively long period of time.

The combination of these three trends has given rise to the phenomenon of not just income inequality but inflation inequality. The past two to three decades have seen inflation rates for lower-income groups in society rise faster than inflation rates for higher-income people. Put simply, it is cheaper to be rich than it is to be poor.

The statement that higher-income inflation rates have risen less than lower-income inflation rates will generally be met with profound cries of anguish from the upper echelons of society. The top 1 per cent will doubtless be spluttering incoherently over their morning champagne with a sense of rage, while summoning their valet to horsewhip the economist who has dared to make such a suggestion. A couple of points of clarification therefore need to be made about this statement.

The first point to acknowledge is that luxury price indices like *Forbes Magazine*'s 'cost of living extremely well' price index do often show significant price changes. The problem with these indices is that they do not show inflation. Indeed, these indices do not show anything that really needs to be taken seriously by economists or investors. These indices do not purport to be inflation indices in the sense of a cost of living index. Instead, these indices set out to measure the price of luxury goods: a food basket of chateaubriand, champagne and caviar, for instance, with no thought to the more mundane but still purchased items like milk or eggs. There is no sensible attempt at weighting the components, nor is there any attempt to replicate the broad range of goods and services that rich consumers will purchase.

The pertinent issue here is that the luxury goods that are randomly piled into these indices are, by definition, luxurious. They cover a tiny subset of the goods and services that a higher-income group will consume. The fact that these indices rise in price tells us that some aspects of a higher-income consumer's cost of living will be rising in price – they do not tell us anything constructive about the overall cost of living for a higher-income consumer. These are an instance of high-end relative price changes and relative price changes are not inflation, as we established way back in Chapter 1. Indeed, a cynic might suggest that the items in these indices were selected by dint of the fact that they have a history of having risen in price; 'luxury goods rise in price at the same rate as other goods' is not really a magazine-selling headline, after all. Basically, luxury price indices are cheap tricks (pun intended); they are media devices that are of no real use to anyone – with the possible exception of the equity analysts who cover the stocks of luxury goods companies.

The second point of clarification comes back to asset prices. The cost of buying high-end housing in London or the price of a Corot at Sotheby's has gone up by more than the headline rate of consumer price inflation. The problem with citing this as a source of high inflation for high-income groups in society is that these are asset prices. Asset prices, as has been mentioned before (Chapter 4), do not represent the cost of living – they represent a future potential source of income. This is why assets are not included in the cost of living. The cost of *occupying* high-end housing is included in consumer prices with an appropriate weighting as to the running costs of owning a home. In some price statistics, like those of the US (but not Europe), implied rent will be added to the inflation number in order to further capture the cost of occupying a high-end home. Even the standard of living aspect of high-end artwork is sort of captured in consumer inflation calculations; consumer price inflation includes some category for home decoration, as a rule. This is not quite the same as purchasing original artwork, but that is because the original artwork has an asset value as well as aesthetic value, and the asset component has no place in calculating inflation. The fact that asset prices are rising says nothing about the cost of living on a day to day basis.

Dismissing luxury goods aggregations and asset values as frivolous distractions from the task at hand, and smartly evading the horsewhip-wielding top 1 per cent, we can get a sense about the relative inflation rates of high-income and low-income groups by rather crudely reweighting the price changes of the disparate parts of the consumer price basket according to the spending patterns of different income groups. Many industrialised economies periodically survey the patterns of different consumer groups in society, and it is quite common to break down consumer spending into income quintiles of the population (that is to say, divide the population into five income tranches according to the levels of household income). By applying these weights to the broad consumer price categories, an economist can recreate inflation patterns for each income quintile.

Figure 7.1 shows how the price level has changed between the start of 1997 and the start of 2014 for the top and bottom quintiles (20 per cent bands) – the richest

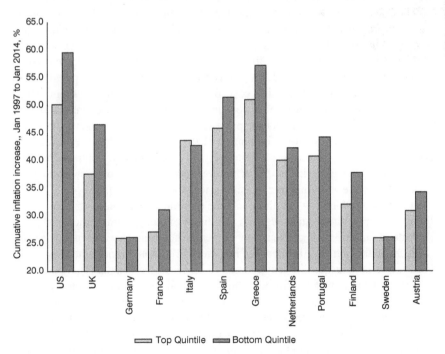

Figure 7.1 The cumulative change in prices for the poorest 20 per cent and richest 20 per cent in society, for selected economies, 1997 to 2014

Source: Author's calculations.

and poorest in some key industrial economies. The poorest band is generally referred to as being in the 0 per cent to 20 per cent of income distribution (if quintiles are talked of) or the 0 per cent to 10 per cent of income distribution (if deciles or tenths are employed). Obviously, then, the top quintile band is in the 80 per cent to 100 per cent range of income distribution.

As Figure 7.1 shows, over the best part of the past two decades the trend has been for divergent inflation to become the norm. This was not always the case; inflation inequality has been a relatively new phenomenon. In the 1960s and 1970s, inflation divergence between different income groups would occasionally emerge, but it would tend to trend revert over time – that is to say, if one group experienced a period of above-average inflation, it would eventually give way to an offsetting period of below-average inflation. However, since 1997, the richest in America have experienced a cumulative inflation rate that is 9.4 per cent less than the cumulative inflation rate of the poorest in America. The 9.4 per cent widening of the gap between the real living standards of the rich and the poor that can be attributed to inflation inequality is an important factor in considering social inequalities. Only Italy has bucked this trend. Although not shown here, even Japan has seen income inequality grow over this period – in the case of Japan this is because higher-income groups have more deflation in their consumer basket, whereas the lowest-income groups have a tiny amount of positive inflation.

There are caveats to these statistics (the economics profession lives for caveats – caveats are what allow economists to be infallible with the benefit of hindsight). Because the reweighting process is calculated using actual consumer spending derived from consumer expenditure surveys, the imputed rent element for a country like the US is ignored. As discussed in the last chapter, imputed rent is an attempt to calculate a housing cost, but it is not actual money spent. Thus, imputed rent does not appear in the consumer spending data for countries like the United States. This US data does capture mortgage interest payments, however. This means that the 'shelter' component of the US income-specific reweighted consumer price measure is less significant than is the 'shelter' component in the official consumer price index. Other costs associated with home ownership are included in the reweighting of consumer prices for the US and Europe.

It is also worth noting that these income quintile-based inflation statistics are, themselves, plutocratic statistics. The weighting of the consumer price basket for the bottom quintile will not accurately reflect the goods and services purchased by someone in the bottom 10 per cent of income distribution, because the weightings used in the bottom quintile will be skewed closer to the consumption pattern of someone at the top of the 20 per cent range than to the consumption patterns of someone at the bottom of the 20 per cent range. Even within these bands, the relatively rich carry more weight than the relatively poor. These statistics are therefore inaccurate – it is just that they are less inaccurate than are the headline statistics when considering the inflation rate faced by different income groups in society.

Inflation inequality matters in a social sense because, of course, it exaggerates the existence of income inequality. Humans are rather materialistic creatures –

as a species we do not care about income, so much as what we can buy with the income we have. This is why it is real income inequality and not nominal income inequality that matters. It also shows remarkably good economic sense. Money has no intrinsic value (as Chapter 3 indicated). Money only has a value to people for the useful goods or services it can purchase.

Real disposable income inequality has grown more than nominal disposable income inequality in recent years in the developed economies of the world. The importance of this is perhaps heightened by the somewhat insidious nature by which real income inequality is exaggerated by inflation in an economy. It is very, very rare indeed that governments or even social organisations will use real income statistics that even attempt to reflect the existence of inflation inequality, even when calculated. The UK government makes no use of the pensioners' price index that it calculates (capturing low-income, elderly people's inflation), not even for determining the indexation of the state pension. The index is strictly ornamental. The aggregate inflation index is resorted to: charitably, inflation calculated using a plutocratic aggregate is used for convenience, or out of ignorance as to the disparities of inflation inequality; less charitably, inflation calculated using a plutocratic aggregate is used because such an inflation rate will generally lessen the appearance of politically awkward inequalities in real living standards.

It is important that investors understand how this has come about, because this inflation inequality has a powerful role to play in investment decisions.

Origins of inflation inequality

The starting point for inflation inequality is income inequality. Inflation inequality is more prevalent in societies that start out with a relatively high level of income inequality in the first place. The United States has seen some of the most divergent inflation experiences across its income spectrum, because in the developed world at least, the United States is a relatively unequal society. Some European economies have been less prone to inflation inequality, as they start out as more equitable societies in income terms. Figure 7.2 demonstrates this loose relationship, showing the gap in the cumulative inflation of the highest and lowest-income groups in different societies over the past sixteen years, and the widely used if somewhat simplistic income inequality measure known as the Gini coefficient (the higher the Gini coefficient the higher the income inequality). The Gini measure used here looks at nominal disposable income, after taxes and social security payments have been taken into account, because it is that income that is most likely to influence consumer spending and therefore the sense of economic well-being. What Figure 7.2 is showing is that countries that are less equal in their income distribution are also likely to be less equal in their inflation distribution.

Why does this trend emerge? Logically enough, the more unequal the distribution of nominal disposable income, the greater the difference in the sorts of goods different consumers are likely to purchase. If there is a gaping chasm separating the income levels of rich and poor, then the types of goods and services that the rich in society can purchase are likely to be significantly different from

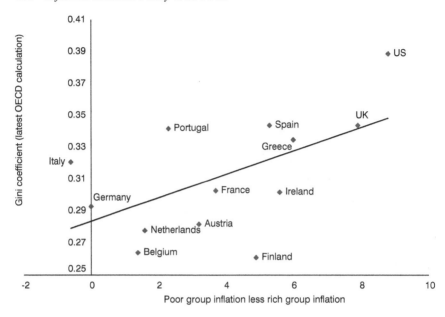

Figure 7.2 The level of income inequality compared to the difference between rich and poor peoples' inflation, 1997 to 2013

Source: Organisation for Economic Co-operation and Development, author's calculations.

the types of goods and services purchased by the poor in society. The different consumption baskets are all captured in the aggregate consumer basket, but the consumption basket of the rich will tend to dominate the aggregation process. The high weighting given to the consumer spending of the higher-income groups, and the process of averaging consumer spending patterns across society as a whole means that lower-income groups are assumed to have a portion of caviar in their weekly shopping basket – metaphorically, at least. In a more equitable society, of course, the consumption baskets of rich and poor are likely to be more homogeneous, though differences will still occur. That means there is less caviar and more bread and cheese in the consumer basket of a more equitable society, with bread and cheese being consumed by all.

The difference in the composition of the consumption basket is significant. It is not just the case that the rich consume more of everything – if that were the case there would be less risk of inflation inequality. If it were just a case of consuming larger quantities across the board, a relative price shift between two types of goods would affect the rich and the poor in broadly the same proportion. The issue is that the rich consume a lot more of some things, and proportionately less of other things. This then brings us to the third component of inflation inequality – relative price shifts. If the price of one part of the basket of goods that consumers purchase shifts relative to the price of other parts of the basket, the combination of that relative price shift will impact the relative inflation rates of different income groups.

Thus, for instance, lower-income groups spend more of their income on food than do higher-income groups (in the UK, the bottom 20 per cent spend 11.8 per cent of their total spending on food, while the top 20 per cent spend 7.0 per cent). If the price of food rises relative to the price of other goods and services, then the cost of living for lower-income members of society will rise faster than it will for higher-income groups. Similarly, if the price of purchasing leisure products (home entertainment, for instance) falls relative to other products, then the chances are that the inflation rate for higher-income groups will decline relative to the inflation rate for lower-income groups (in the UK, the bottom 20 per cent spend 8.9 per cent of their total consumption on the purchase of leisure products, while the top 20 per cent spend 13.4 per cent).

Remember Figure 6.3 in the last chapter, which compared the inflation rate of consumer durable goods with consumer non-durable goods in the United States? Consumer durable goods price inflation has been notably lower than consumer non-durable goods price inflation. In Chapter 6 this was being used to illustrate the issues of high-frequency and low-frequency purchases, but it equally applies to high-income consumer and low-income consumer purchases. High-income consumers are more likely to purchase consumer durable goods than are low-income consumers. Inevitably, given the trends that were evidenced in the last chapter, this means that high-income consumers are more likely to benefit from subdued consumer durable goods price inflation than are low-income consumers.

In fact, this is an illustration of the third factor behind inflation inequality; labour-intensive goods and services have tended to rise in price by less than commodity-intensive goods and services. This can be shown very simply by comparing commodity prices with overall consumer prices. Commodity prices are volatile, of course, but the trend of the past couple of decades has been obvious (the US is used in this example to avoid the complication of comparing different currencies: commodity prices are quoted in dollars, as of course is US consumer price inflation). The level of commodity prices has far outstripped the overall level of consumer prices. Labour remains the most important component of consumer prices, but what Figure 7.3 indicates is that the price of any good that is more commodity intensive is more likely to rise above the average price in the economy.

The shrewd reader will have spotted one important consequence of inflation inequality. If the average inflation rate is a plutocratic statistic, and if there is a bias to higher-income groups having lower inflation rates than the inflation rate experienced by lower-income groups, then it logically follows that *a majority of the population will personally experience an inflation rate that is higher than the aggregate reported inflation rate*. This is a pretty powerful statement. What we are saying here is that the official inflation rate is almost certainly wrong, and in recent years is almost certainly too low, when set against the inflation experiences of a majority of the population. In fact, for a country like the United States, the official consumer price inflation rate reflects the spending patterns of someone around the seventy-fifth percentile of income distribution (the upper quarter of the population).

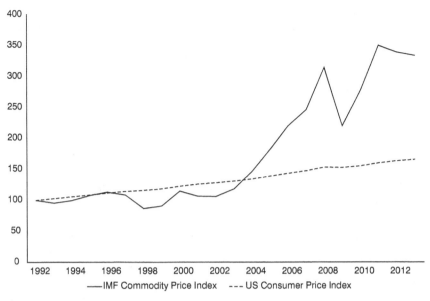

Figure 7.3 The IMF commodity price level compared with the US consumer price level
Source: Derived from data from Haver Analytics.

This sounds like the assertions of the previous chapter are being revoked – but that is not the case. The inflation rate is calculated in a perfectly accurate manner, with all appropriate adjustment. The official inflation rate of most economies does exactly what it purports to, and estimates a cost of living measure for a plutocratic average of society. The problem is not with the statistics or their calculation per se – the problem is the tendency of investors, policymakers and even some economists to treat inflation as if it reflects a universal cost of living that can be applied equitably to all. Investors are trying to torture inflation data into representing something it was never designed to represent.

There is official recognition of these different inflation rates. The UK's BBC has an inflation calculator that allows the public to define their own inflation rate (according to fairly broad parameters, but it is better than nothing).[1] The UK Retail Price Index (a specific consumer inflation measure which differs in composition from consumer price inflation) deliberately excludes the top 4 per cent of income distribution from its calculations on the grounds that 'the rich are different from you and me' – or more formally that the consumption patterns of the rich do not reflect the consumption patterns of the country at large. By makeweight, poor pensioners are excluded from the same index. In Australia, alongside the official headline inflation rate, there are a series of inflation rates created to specifically mimic the spending patterns of certain household structures and income levels. The problem is, in a world of sound-bite economics, no one ever pays attention to these thoughtfully provided subsidiary measures. It is all about the one 'headline' number, the single-line chart on the television screen, the sensationalist tabloid title, and then the media moves on. Investors are not well served by this barely cursory glance at the data, and investors run the risk of making bad decisions on the back of what amounts to economic misrepresentation.

If the inflation numbers investors are using are wrong, it is worth considering why this problem has arisen. Once investors know why inflation inequality has become a feature of our economies, investors can better understand what the risks around inflation inequality are in the future. With that understanding, investors can then think about how to manage their money so as to properly guard against the risks of future inflation – not in the meaningless, generic sense, but in a sense that matters to them as investors and to the investment objectives that they hold. The questions of 'Why?' and 'What to do about it?' will occupy the rest of this chapter, and probably form the most important part of this book. The reader may want to grab a cup of coffee and hitch up their mental faculties for the rest of this story, because this is where things start to get serious.

Why has inflation inequality become more prevalent?

Inflation inequality was not so much of a problem forty or fifty years ago as it is today. Part of the issue now is the persistence of inflation inequality over time – in the past a period of high inflation for one group would eventually give way to a period of low inflation. The process might take a few years, but eventually things would sort themselves out. Things have been different in recent years. In spite of the turmoil of the global financial crisis – arguably the biggest and potentially most disruptive economic shock to hit the global economy in eighty years – the persistence of inflation inequality has clung on. The balancing process of trend reversion of past years has ceased. Why is this?

Partly, the process is because the distribution of income within individual economies has tended to be more unequal than in the past. This is a highly controversial topic, at least as it pertains to the precise levels of income inequality. Income distribution has been compared with the 'robber baron' era of the late nineteenth century, or even with feudal societies. These comparisons may or may not be sensationalist, but for the purposes of explaining inflation inequality the absolute degrees of income inequality are largely irrelevant hyperbole. What matters is that income inequality has grown relative to the past. Few, if any, economists would dispute that relative income distribution is less equitable today than it was in the 1960s and 1970s within most if not all industrialised economies. The precise degree of inequality, and whether the inequality has allowed a higher overall standard of living or not, is not germane to the issue. Greater income inequality to any degree will tend to make inflation inequality more likely, because of the impact on consumption patterns that has already been explained.

Alongside this shift in the distribution of income, there has been a second global development. As already alluded to, the prices of labour-intensive products and services have generally risen by less than the prices of goods that are commodity intensive. Consumer durable goods prices have fallen (or risen by very little) when food prices have gone up, for instance. Because low-income consumers tend to buy proportionately more goods and proportionately fewer services than do high-income consumers, their consumption basket is less labour intensive. Because low-income consumers tend to buy proportionately more commodity-intensive goods within their goods basket than do high-income consumers, their consumption basket is more commodity intensive.

The consequences of a more globalised economy in recent years has meant two things. First, and most obviously, the supply of labour has risen globally. The integration of many economies (including most notably China) into the global capitalist economy has contributed to a lower cost of labour in some parts of the world. The increase in global trade levels as a function of improved technology, more efficient transport, and deregulation of trade barriers has been phenomenal. In the past twenty-five years, the global trade share of the world economy (a shorthand for measuring 'trade globalisation') has doubled.

The good news in this process is that this has led to a more efficient economy – and greater efficiency has led to lower prices, as greater efficiency normally does. This is generally considered beneficial, as it has allowed more people to raise their standards of living by purchasing products that would previously have been beyond their means. Alongside that, to the extent that higher-income groups purchase more labour-intensive things, the more efficient use of labour in the world economy has benefited higher-income groups more than it has benefited lower-income groups (though both groups have benefited).

The second consequence of a more globalised economy is that the world economy has generated a possibly unprecedented degree of income *equality*. This seems to fly in the face of all the earlier discussion, but there is an important caveat. Hitherto the discussions of income inequality and inflation inequality have focused on the rise of inequalities *within* economies. Inequality when comparing Briton and Briton, American and American, or Mexican and Mexican has risen. However, the disparity of living standards between nations has moderated. From 1990 to 2010, seven hundred million people left the category of 'extreme poverty' (using the World Bank definition), and this at a time when the world population continued to grow. The proportion of the world classified as being in extreme poverty fell from 43 per cent to 21 per cent over the two decades. The phrase 'the emerging middle class' is often overused and too imprecise as to parameters to serve anything other than as a rallying cry for the worst kind of tabloid financial journalism. Nonetheless, the absolute rise in living standards of huge swathes of the global population has been a remarkable feature of the recent past.

What does this global improvement in living standards suggest? It suggests that there will be an increase in demand for the things that make higher living standards possible. That implies increased demand for food, increased demand for better-quality housing, and ultimately improvements in infrastructure. These, at least, are the first instincts of people emerging from extreme poverty. People emerging from extreme poverty rarely prioritise services or luxury goods. It will be noted that these desires are generally commodity intensive. This increase in demand for commodity-intensive product will raise the price of such products. What this means is that improving the standard of living of some of the lowest-income groups in the world will also raise the cost of living of some of the lowest-income groups in developed economies.

Another way of thinking about this is to say that the middle-income groups of emerging markets, who are benefiting from the rise in their countries' standard of living, will tend to have the same sort of income levels as the lowest-income groups in developed economies. A household in the bottom 10 per cent of the United States in 2012 would have had the same income level in US dollar terms (on average) as a household around the 50 per cent income mark in China (i.e. a household that could be considered to be middle class by Chinese standards).[2] In both cases the disposable household income level would have been around US$9,000, converted using purchasing power parity data (which may exaggerate China's income).

Because the US has quite extreme income inequality, the role of middle income groups becomes even more apparent at the next decile – the second poorest group in the US (between 10 per cent and 20 per cent of income distribution) have a disposable income level that is somewhat richer than the 80 per cent level in China with a disposable income of over US$20,000. We can therefore say that someone in the bottom fifth of the US population has the income of someone in the top fifth of the Chinese population, if we are a little cavalier with the presentation of the figures. It is hardly surprising that the upper middle class in China and the lowest-income groups in the United States are seeking to consume similar sorts of goods today, at least to some extent. This is a relatively new phenomenon; twenty years ago the Chinese upper middle class did not exist, at least not in any recognisable and internationally comparable sense, and there was no prospect of them pursuing and bidding up the price for the sort of goods that low-income Americans were seeking to consume.

Globalisation is therefore something that both raises and lowers prices. This is something that will be discussed in fascinating detail in the next chapter, but for now it is enough to acknowledge that globalisation is not a one-way pressure on prices. We also need to maintain a sense of proportion. As will be discussed in Chapter 8 the impact of globalisation on prices is *not* as significant as is popularly supposed. The problem from the perspective of inflation inequality is that globalisation has encouraged a relative price change, because it has tended to consistently raise the prices of some categories of goods, and simultaneously has consistently tended to lower the prices of other categories of goods.

To grossly overgeneralise, low-income households in developed economies tend to spend most of their income on three things: food, energy and housing. What has tended to go up most in price in the course of the past twenty years? Food, energy and housing. What are commodity-intensive products? Food, energy and, depending on circumstance, housing. If the trends that have produced this pattern of inflation continue in the future (and they probably will, albeit perhaps in a more muted way than hitherto) then inflation inequality will continue and may even become more unequal.

Other divisions

So far we have considered inflation from the perspective of different income groups. Income-specific inflation rates are the most obvious, and generally the most controversial aspect of social problems with inflation, because income-specific inflation rates are directly linked to the plutocratic nature of the inflation statistic. Ultimately, income-based inflation inequality will aggravate the plutocratic distortions of a society by actually furthering real disposable income inequality. The structure of income-based inflation inequality in recent years has also meant that a majority of the population experience an inflation rate that is above the published, plutocratic average. Given the loss aversion humanity is prone to, the fact that most people have an inflation rate above the reported rate is bound to make income-based inflation inequality particularly controversial. However, rethinking inflation based on income is not the only distinction that can be made when breaking down inflation data. Once the principle of average inflation as an inappropriate statistic has been grasped, all sorts of groups can be identified. Because everyone has a unique consumption basket, and because many different groups in society have different trends in spending, we can consider specialised inflation rates that are more than just income specific.

One pertinent way of breaking down inflation in many modern economies is to consider inflation not by income group but by age group. There will inevitably be some overlap with income-related inflation rates, but considering inflation by age will also add in other factors. The importance of age-related inflation rates arises because many people will seek to save in order to finance their retirement. If the cost of being old is rising more rapidly than the aggregated consumer price inflation index, then prospective pensioners may need to save more than they think to meet the costs of old age care. Investors may be seduced into thinking that their future standard of living is assured because their investment returns exceed the published consumer price inflation. If old age inflation is in fact higher than average inflation, then the investor will have a nasty shock when they retire, and their hopes of even maintaining (far less improving) their standards of living are likely to be dashed. With demographic trends increasing the numbers of the elderly in many societies – developed and emerging – this is a problem that is only going to grow in importance.

When considering age profiles and inflation there are obvious differences in the consumer basket that have to be considered. Consumers who have retired are unlikely to have a standard of living that is significantly affected by the cost of children's clothing, or of spending on education. On the other hand, the elderly population are likely to be heavy consumers of healthcare. Any shift in the relative cost of healthcare is going to weigh on the inflation rate of the elderly quite noticeably.

Healthcare costs are likely to be one of the big concerns as a society ages – even in societies that are still relatively young overall. The United States is ageing less significantly than Europe, but owing to a peculiarly inefficient healthcare system the cost of being ill or being old in the United States is particularly high. That high

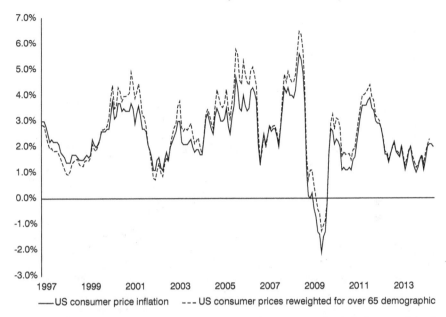

Figure 7.4 Overall US consumer price inflation and consumer price inflation reweighted for spending by the elderly

Source: Author's calculations.

absolute cost of US healthcare is compounded by the fact that the inflation of US healthcare costs has tended to be higher than overall inflation of the consumer price basket.

Economists can apply a crude weighting method to age cohorts in the same way that we did to income cohorts, to calculate age-specific inflation rates. The US example shown in Figure 7.4, demonstrates (again) that average inflation is not necessarily terribly helpful as a guide to the cost of living of the elderly. This chart mimics the method of calculating inflation that was used for income groups in Figure 7.1, and it clearly shows the American elderly tend to face a higher rate of inflation than does US society as a whole.

The peculiar importance of this for investment is something that will be discussed in the next section of this chapter. For now, the reader just needs to remember that inflation tends to be higher the older one is. The UK is the exception to this rule, somewhat ironically as the UK Office for National Statistics goes to the trouble of producing two retail price indices for the low-income elderly. The reason for the UK exception is the very low personal spending on healthcare (as healthcare is government provided). However, even if not directly relevant to the UK, the importance of healthcare to inflation for the elderly makes the warning given by the British politician Neil Kinnock in 1983 apposite: 'I warn you not to fall ill. I warn you not to grow old.'[3] In modern society it is not just political ideology and fiscal policy that present the

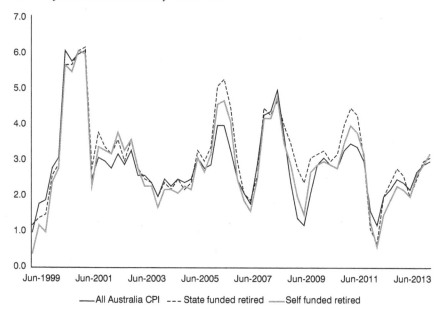

Figure 7.5 Australian inflation rates – average, lower-income elderly and higher-income elderly

Source: Australian Bureau of Statistics.

challenge; we need to warn against the distortions of relative price shifts and what that means for the reality of inflation.

Australia brings together the two issues of inflation inequality by officially calculating the inflation faced by the older generation, but dividing that age cohort into those who receive state benefits, which are means tested, and those who finance their own retirement and who can be assumed to be higher income (Figure 7.5). Both groups of elderly Australians tend to face a higher inflation rate than does the population as a whole, but those receiving state benefits are more likely to face higher inflation than those of independent means..

We can go on and on in the disaggregation of inflation. The inflation rate faced by a university endowment will be different from that of average inflation. The inflation rate of a charity focusing on the environment will be different from that of average inflation. The inflation rate of people with no children will be different from that of average inflation. It is the economic equivalent of the multiple world theory – multiple inflation rates exist simultaneously in our world, the existence of each inflation rate generally a mystery to those around it.

What the last quarter century has done is create a situation where the average inflation rate reported by consumer price statistics and other plutocratic aggregations is not especially relevant to a majority of any economy's population. Moreover, the plutocratic consumer price average is likely to become less relevant in the future. Unfortunately, society has become enslaved to the plutocratic average inflation rate as a totem of prices. Investors, politicians and consumers all blindly accept that their cost of living is the reported average cost of living, and they behave accordingly. Government spending and social benefits are inflation linked – but inflation that is linked proportionately far more to the cost of living of the rich even if (as with social security payments) they are trying to assist with the cost of living of the poor. Wage bargains are struck with both sides referencing the plutocratic inflation rate. Pension fund managers congratulate themselves on having made a positive real return, even if the inflation rate they use to discount their performance is lower than the inflation rate that their pensioners face. There is an irony in that society has become mesmerised by aggregate statistics as the divergence within society has increased. Judging one's standard of living against the metric of published inflation is wrong. The trends that have emerged in *relative* prices in recent years mean that the only thing one can really say about average inflation is that it is irrelevant to nearly everyone in the population.

The ultimate conclusion from this is a rather sobering one for a middle-aged economist. Basically, in order to experience a relatively low cost of living, one should strive to be as young and as rich as one possibly can. Economists rarely fall into either classification.

The conclusions about the myriad inflation rates that a single society experiences are not properly appreciated in modern investing. As inflation inequality continues, however, investors need to pay more attention to these trends. Disastrous investment decisions can be made by failing to consider what it is that investors really wish to achieve with their investment portfolios.

The implications of inflation inequality for investors

To start with the most basic points, if investors want to invest wisely they need to generally ignore aggregate inflation numbers (other than as a very, very crude guide), and they need to understand what they are investing for. Investors buy assets in order to receive money in the future, so that investors can spend money in the future. What assets should investors be buying if they want to pay for retirement? What assets should a healthcare insurer be buying if it wants to meet future healthcare costs? What assets should an Oxford college be buying if it wants to provide for the education of future generations? The portfolios of each investor will necessarily be very different. Indeed, the narrower the basket of goods and services that the investor wishes to purchase, the less likely it is that generic inflation will serve the investor's needs. A healthcare insurer necessarily has a very narrow price basket, and persistent relative price shifts could create very significant diversion between healthcare inflation and headline inflation.

Let us start by rejecting a couple of ideas. The first concept that needs to be treated with extreme caution is the idea that buying inflation-linked securities (index-linked gilts in the UK, or TIPS – Treasury Inflation Protected Securities – in the United States) will provide a *perfect* insurance for investors who are seeking to guarantee their investments against their future inflation risk. Such instruments will offer *some* protection – they do hedge against a portion of inflation risk. Even in an environment of inflation inequality, inflation rates for different subcategories do tend to be correlated; if inflation for poor consumers is rising, inflation for rich consumers is also likely to be rising, as is aggregate inflation. If aggregate inflation is rising then the return on inflation-linked instruments will go up in line with the aggregate consumer price basket. However, in normal circumstances, if one's personal experience of inflation is higher than the reported average inflation over a number of years, buying inflation-linked instruments is simply guaranteeing a lower-than-expected real income in the future. Going back to Figure 7.1, a US investor buying TIPS inflation-linked securities to provide a retirement income will be 9.4 per cent worse off in 'real' (in the sense of 'true') real terms than they think. Guaranteeing future losses is not really a good idea for most investors.

Remember, in recent years the plutocratic nature of inflation has meant that a majority of people in an economy have experienced an inflation rate that is higher than the reported average. This means that inflation-linked securities will earn a lower real (income-specific inflation-adjusted) rate of return than the security advertises, for the majority of the population.

Second, beating the investment return that is generated by a generic 'benchmark' is not necessarily desirable as an investment objective. A lot of funds reference benchmarks as a simple way of measuring investment performance. Benchmarks can be anything – a model portfolio, the local equity market index – anything generic. The problem with benchmarks is that they often dominate an investor's view of the world, and beating the benchmark (that is to say, exceeding the return of the benchmark) becomes everything. To say 'my portfolio rose 2 per cent more than the US S&P 500 Equity Index' allows a certain amount of bragging rights, albeit slightly vulgar bragging rights. However, that is nothing to be proud of if the inflation rate the investor is trying to offset rose by 4 per cent more than the US S&P 500 Equity Index. In fact, the investment strategy here should be considered a failure.

Benchmarking is a concept that is beloved by the fund management industry because it allows the fund managers to demonstrate their performance in a simple manner; as a marketing device, benchmarks are very popular. But if rational investors reject generic inflation rates as not fit for purpose, they should similarly reject generic benchmarks.

In fact, if investors are to consider what sensible investment strategies might look like, they may have to consider the idea that underperforming a generic benchmark could be a good thing. Why should an investor revel in the performance of a portfolio that has returned less than (say) the average performance of the equity market? Why should an investor delight in having an outright negative return on their portfolio? The answer is relatively simple, if only the investor thinks in the right real terms.

If we go right back to basics, the point about saving is that an investor is giving up consumption now in order to be able to consume in the future. The point about managing inflation risk is to make sure that an investor can consume at least as much in the future as the same investor can consume today, and preferably a bit more than the investor can consume today. The way that this is achieved is through investing to receive a rate of return, but that rate of return needs to be compared against what we want to consume in the future. If the *specific* inflation rate experienced by an investor is falling, or is lower than the average, then all the investor should care about is whether *their* inflation rate is being beaten. If healthcare cost inflation in the future is -2 per cent (which is unlikely, but let us work with the assumption), then a healthcare insurer should delight in a -1 per cent rate of return on their investments. The delight of the healthcare insurer should not be tempered even if the overall equity market has returned a positive 2 per cent return.

Of course what matters is how this return is being created. If the healthcare insurer in the hypothetical example above has a portfolio that mimics healthcare costs, then in the event that healthcare inflation suddenly soars by 12 per cent the healthcare insurer should also expect their portfolio to return at least 12 per cent. The specific inflation rate of the healthcare insurer has become the benchmark against which it should consider its investment performance. The prudent investor will seek a portfolio that will benefit when the price of the goods and services that they buy goes up, and they should not worry so much if that same portfolio suffers as the price of the goods and services that they buy goes down.

This approach to investing sounds very simple, and it is very simple. It is also a little impractical. It is time to drag the workhorse of an economic theory out of the stables once again, for loss aversion plays a role. It is all very well thinking philosophically that a decline in the value of a portfolio is justified by the falling inflation rate that is specific to the investor's needs; in reality a loss is a loss, and investors are averse to losses. Being told that one's specific cost of living is falling is a very chilly comfort when one has suffered an absolute loss – and, what is worse, when one has suffered an absolute loss at a time when others are making profits (and therefore the absolute loss is also a relative loss). As humans we should take joy in the good fortune of others, when they fare better than we do; as a general rule, in the world of investing, we do not tend to follow this admirably altruistic maxim. If our neighbour's portfolio performs better than our own investments, we tend to be inclined to glare malevolently across the garden fence and mutter resentful imprecations in a bitter undertone.

Another problem with seeking to insure one's investments against a personal rather than a generic inflation rate is that it may be difficult to find assets that closely shadow the components of a personal inflation rate. A pension fund can buy assets that benefit when pensioners spend money – but will it mimic the living costs of high- and low-income pensioners at the same time? A healthcare company can invest in pharmaceutical equities, but what asset tracks the wage costs of a hospital? What about an Oxford college, the main costs of which are likely to be academic salaries? What sort of an asset mimics academic salaries? None do, of course, and so imperfect substitutes will have to be found.

Taking to the barricades – radical economics in the face of inflation inequality

The existence of inflation inequality does not mean that inflation statistics are 'wrong'. That sort of naïve assertion is worthy of the blogosphere, but not of serious analysis. The existence of inflation inequality means that plutocratic inflation statistics are perfectly correct, but that investors, charities, politicians and others are interpreting the perfectly correct inflation statistics in a perfectly incorrect manner.

Back in the first chapter, there was a clear declaration that this book is not about predicting inflation – and it is not. However, it is possible to predict with some certainty that divergent inflation experiences are likely to continue in the future, whether average inflation is higher or lower than it is today. Inflation inequality has come about because of relative price changes. Relative price changes have come about because demand for certain products has increased, and supply of other 'products' (specifically labour) has increased. This is a relatively welcome development when viewed from a global perspective, reducing the instance of global poverty. At the same time it is going to present a challenge to investors in developed markets.

Protests about income inequality are likely to be fuelled by inflation inequality. Unless sales of this book significantly outperform the publisher's projections (one can dream) and there is some sort of Damascene enlightenment across the mass of the population, the popular awareness of inflation inequality is not likely to be either precise or articulated. The closest we have come to awareness of this problem is the campaign for a 'living wage' – and that is a campaign that focuses primarily on raising wages above the minimum wage, albeit spurred by awareness about the cost of living in certain areas. It seems, for example, relatively unlikely that social security payments will be linked to income-specific inflation rates, or that pay settlements will take account of the precise spending patterns of the workforce. It would be fantasy to suggest that pension fund managers will start using an inflation rate specific to the elderly when considering the returns on their portfolio, excepting maybe in the very unlikely instance that old age inflation rates fall below average inflation.

This failure to recognise inflation inequality, but awareness of the ultimate consequences for living standards, will likely breed a festering sense of injustice and resentment. Inflation inequality will remain not entirely hidden, but lurking beneath the surface of many investors' portfolios.

The hidden nature of inflation inequality is dangerous. It may manifest itself in unjustified attacks on legitimate aspects of inflation (hedonic adjustment, for example). One of the subjects of those unjustified attacks is the subject of the next chapter, for foreigners will often be blamed when consumers have an undefined sense that they are somehow being treated unfairly. The hidden nature of inflation inequality may also cause policy to be misdirected, or further misdirected than it already is (for example, in implementing price controls). The fact that most people legitimately experience an inflation rate that is higher than the plutocratic average used to calculate the published consumer price index only serves to fuel conspiracy theories about the manipulation of statistics. And, above all else, inflation inequality can create an inflation illusion for investors, who will suddenly find that the returns on their portfolio are unexpectedly insufficient to meet their future needs.

It is this last aspect of inflation inequality that is most troubling in the current investment climate. It seems reasonable to conclude that the world economy has embarked on a period of lower nominal investment returns than has been experienced in the past two or three decades. There are myriad reasons for this – regulation, the end of falling risk premiums, home country bias and the partial unwinding of the globalisation of capital. The point is that if the world *has* embarked on a lower nominal return episode, then the importance of using the right inflation rate becomes more and more important in generating genuinely positive real returns. Of course, some investors (because of regulatory constraints) may not have the option of generating positive real returns, but for those who have the freedom to invest as they choose, getting inflation right becomes of paramount importance.

Ain't it all a bloomin' shame?

The critical point from this chapter is to make clear that aggregate inflation indicators are but an imprecise barometer for all investors. The convenient shorthand of the aggregate statistic has become universal, and in doing so it has stretched the use of inflation beyond reasonable bounds. Aggregate inflation is treated as a universal proxy for the impact of price on *everyone's* standard of living. This is not what aggregate inflation is, this is not what aggregate inflation has ever pretended to be, and it is increasingly unlikely that this is what aggregate inflation will be in the future.

Investment is all about achieving a future real standard of living. Modern investors need to consider what *their* needs are in the future, not what the needs of a plutocratic aggregate are going to be. If those needs are going to be satisfied by a future investment income, then investment strategies will need to be devised that at least come close to mimicking the specific costs of the future standard of living. Those costs may differ from the cost associated with today's standard of living – saving for retirement should be more sensitive to medical expenses than is the current cost of living, as a rather obvious example.

For policymakers, inflation inequality should suggest a more sophisticated approach to how spending and taxation are treated. The ubiquitous nature of headline consumer price indices as a form of automatically adjusting spending, social security and other aspects of government life dates back to the late 1960s and US President Nixon – who ironically thought he was reducing the politicisation of key aspects of the government's work. In an era of more equitable inflation, this was relevant. In an era of significant relevant price adjustments, creating a turbulent undercurrent beneath the seemingly calm surface of the headline inflation figures, governments that genuinely wish to influence the well-being of their citizens through their social policies must become more sophisticated – just as the economy has become more sophisticated.

The good news is that the era of big data and computer power allows for far more sophistication in the capture and the calculation of our economic statistics. The bad news is that the world's official statistical agencies seem unwilling or unable to harness this data, in this particular field at least.

The twenty-first-century global economy has changed. From a humanitarian perspective, viewed from the economic high ground that is morally above the borders of countries, this change is for the better. The numbers of people in absolute poverty have fallen, and living standards on almost any metric have improved for large swathes of the population. From a holistic, global economic perspective things are better. Within countries, however, inflation inequality has compounded income inequality. Inflation experiences now fracture by income, by age and by a myriad of other factors. Headline inflation rates are not fit for purpose for anyone – investor or policymaker – who wishes to protect future spending power and standards of living.

Notes

1 http://www.bbc.com/news/business-22523612 for how to calculate personal inflation (last retrieved 2 December 2014).
2 The comparison is derived from data published by the Euromonitor Group in its publication *World Consumer Income and Expenditure Patterns 2014*, Table 10.13.
3 Speech in Bridgend, Glamorgan, 8 June 1983, http://www.youtube.com/watch?v=-QPhMVbleU0, retrieved 3 August 2014.

8   It is all the fault of the foreigner

And Florentynes to bere here golde sone
Overe the see into Flaundres ageyne;
And thus they lyve in Flaundres, sothe to sayne,
And in London wyth suche chevesaunce
That men call usure to oure losse and hinderaunce.

(*Libelle of Englyshe Polycye*, 1436 – this extract
roughly translates as 'You can't trust Italians')

The last chapter demonstrated that ordinary citizens may be subjected to a higher inflation rate than the reported, aggregate, headline consumer price inflation. In such circumstances, particularly when the damage to living standards is not properly understood, there is often a desire to focus anger onto a single point – whether that point is the cause or not. Having a single scapegoat simplifies things, which allows political rhetoric to condense into political propaganda and, if desired, political hysteria. In most economies the most suitable scapegoat for economic ills is obvious: whatever is wrong with the economy it must all be the fault of foreigners.

Blaming foreigners is always easy to do. Foreigners must be the cause of all the problems in the domestic economy, simply because they are foreign and therefore not 'like us'. It is a long-established trait, as the opening quote demonstrates (the *Libelle* is a jingoistic, mercantilist poem of the fifteenth century – an era when the economics of trade was considered a suitable subject for popular poetry; a golden age for English literature, clearly). From a political perspective, the desirability of treating foreigners as the scapegoat for domestic ills is made ever more attractive by the wonderful fact that foreigners do not have the vote. Politicians can be as unpleasant as they like about foreigners, and it will not harm their prospects of re-election. To the extent that xenophobic economic policies can be presented as 'patriotism', being nasty to foreigners may well win votes.

In spite of countless economic works dating back to David Ricardo and the early nineteenth century, demonstrating that free trade is mutually beneficial, trade protectionism is still resorted to in times of crisis. Why? Politicians always seem to advocate protectionism with an appeal to the noblest of reasons. Protection is needed not to boost the competitiveness of domestic industry – certainly not. To suggest that domestic industry is in some way uncompetitive could be construed as an unpatriotic thought. No, protection is needed because foreigners are taking unfair advantage, and it is therefore necessary to 'level the playing field' in a phrase so beloved of the self-righteous (the US Senate recently held hearings specifically entitled 'Levelling the playing field'). Protectionism is needed because foreigners are cheating. It is all the fault of the foreigner.

The example of trade protectionism is relevant in part because it is a good example of the general principle of scapegoating foreigners for economic ills. It is also relevant because issues of competitiveness and the role of foreigners in the domestic economy often come down to issues of price. However, trade is just one aspect of the way in which foreigners are scapegoated for inflation issues. In reality, there are three big issues that tie, or attempt to tie, foreigners to domestic inflation: exporting monetary policy; global supply and demand; and exchange rate policy and trade. Examining these in turn we find that in fact foreigners play far less of a role in influencing domestic inflation than is popularly supposed.

Global monetary policy

In September 2012 the Brazilian finance minister, Guido Mantega, launched an attack on the United States for what he considered to be protectionism.[1] The protectionism had nothing to do with tariffs or quotas being imposed by the United States. Instead, the protectionism cited by Mantega was the decision by the US Federal Reserve to engage in another round of quantitative policy, purchasing bonds to increase the domestic money supply of the United States. This, he declared, was the start of a global currency war. If this were indeed a war, then the United States lost – the dollar strengthened against the real during the subsequent period of US quantitative policy.

It should be noted in passing that the decision to describe US monetary policy as 'protectionist' was probably not coincidence, as Brazil had been criticised for engaging in measures of a more conventional trade protectionism in advance of these remarks.

Underlying Mantega's comments is a belief, pervasive throughout the centuries, that the monetary policy of one country can have direct and lasting implications for the inflation of another country. This belief received additional succour during the years after the global financial crisis when quantitative policy – the printing of quantities of money – became the new fashion of the world's central banks. If inflation rose in China, then surely it was directly the result of the Federal Reserve's reckless money printing operations? Since 2007 the United States had printed so much money, amounting to the equivalent of over 16 per cent of US GDP, and around 4 per cent of global GDP, that instinctively foreign politicians felt that it must have an impact. In truth, any impact from the Federal Reserve's policy on inflation rates outside the borders of the United States was indirect, limited and ultimately more determined by domestic policies. Brazilian inflation is infinitely more sensitive to the actions of the Brazilian finance minister than it is sensitive to the actions of the US Federal Reserve, whatever the political desirability of claiming otherwise.

The absolutely central point to remember is that a currency is a claim on the goods and services of the country that issues that currency. This means that in the first instance an increase in the money supply of a country needs to be considered against the goods and services of that country – and as was eloquently explained in Chapter 5, it is not enough to say that 'money is printed, therefore it creates inflation'. Printing *too much* money is what creates inflation, not the printing of money per se. Most of the money that was printed by the US Federal Reserve, as we have seen in Chapter 5, stayed in the United States. If the US dollars printed by the central bank are sitting on the balance sheet of General Motors or Google, then those US dollars are not really terribly relevant when it comes to considering Brazilian inflation, or German asset prices.

Furthermore, as long as a country has a currency of its own, then the money supply of another country cannot be relevant to domestic prices in the domestic currency. Try paying for a taxi in Munich using pounds sterling – the response is likely to be fairly terse, possibly even brusque. No matter how much an economist might insist that the pound sterling is a perfectly respectable currency – and that black cab drivers in London (who are the most discerning individuals in the world) will readily accept it – the German taxi driver will not want it. It does not matter how much or how little sterling the Bank of England has printed, sterling has no claim on the goods or services of Germany (and a ride in a Munich taxi cab most definitely counts as a German service – a relatively high-priced service, one might add).

It is true that if the dollars printed by the United States had escaped the geographic confines of that country, they might have had an impact on the dollar price of globally traded commodities. Commodities are priced in dollars, and if more dollars are pursuing a fixed or relatively fixed supply of commodities then dollar commodity prices may rise. However, the relevance of this to a country's domestic inflation depends on what it does with its currency. The price of commodities is rising relative to the price of the US dollar in such circumstances. There is no need for the price of commodities to rise relative to any other currency, or relative to other prices (like labour, for instance) in such circumstances. As it happens, the point has been moot in recent years, as the increased dollar money supply did not head out in pursuit of commodities.

The only way monetary policy is really likely to have an impact beyond its currency area is through the impact on risk appetite, sometimes known as 'animal spirits'. This was mentioned in Chapter 5, on the topic of printing money. If a central bank, through offering a more accommodative monetary policy, changes perceptions about risk and its economy, there might be a global implication from that; policy accommodation from the Federal Reserve might lead to optimism about the growth prospects of the US, which might lead to an increased desire to take risk on the part of German banks, which might lead to German credit expansion, which is a real-world easing of German monetary policy, which might lead to inflation pressures increasing in Germany. There are five uses of the word 'might' in that last sentence. It is not, perhaps, a terribly direct mechanism for one country to influence the inflation rate of another.

Of course, one country can choose to fix its monetary policy to that of another. Dollarisation or Euroisation are examples of this, where the currency of one country circulates as the legal tender of another country. Similarly, pegging a currency to that of another country, as Hong Kong does with its US dollar currency board, also fixes the monetary policy of that country to another. It is sometimes claimed that (for instance) the monetary policy decisions of the United States Federal Reserve are thus exported to Hong Kong. In fact, it would be fairer to say that Hong Kong has chosen to import the monetary policy decisions of the US Federal Reserve into the region. It is the policy of Hong Kong that has led to this arrangement, not the policy of the Federal Reserve. If the Hong Kong Monetary Authority wished to change the monetary conditions prevalent in the region it could do so by the simple expedient of abandoning its ties to the US dollar.

To talk about global inflation consequences from one country's monetary policy is therefore a rather dramatic overstatement. The monetary policy of one country is only going to escape the borders of its currency area via sentiment, risk appetite or animal spirits. For the most part this is a fairly tenuous link to inflation pressures elsewhere in the world, although it can never be entirely ignored. It also does not have to be a large country that changes risk appetite, as the relatively small economy of Iceland was able to demonstrate during the recent global financial crisis.

Risk appetite aside, monetary policy in one country may change the economic performance of that country. That is, after all, the general idea behind monetary policy in the first place. But in changing the economic performance of a country, the demand for global goods and services and potentially the supply of global goods and services from that country may shift and that may then have an implication for global prices. It is time to turn, therefore, to the role of supply and demand.

Supply and demand

A more valid concern about foreign influences on domestic inflation than fears of monetary policy contagion comes from the role of economies in driving global supply and demand. This was something briefly alluded to in the last chapter, when the discussion of trends in relative prices was raised. In the twenty-first century it is China that has attracted most attention for its role in influencing this aspect of inflation. The views around China's role as a source of change in global inflation rates seem to depend on a somewhat perverse position, because China has been simultaneously accused of creating inflationary forces *and* deflationary forces in the global economy. In actual fact, China *has* simultaneously created inflationary and if not deflationary, at least, disinflationary forces in the world economy. In the world of economics such things are possible and not in any way contradictory.

China's critics, ever keen to conjure up the image of the Middle Kingdom as an all-devouring dragon of global economics, tend to side with one side of the argument or the other. What China's critics fail to notice, or choose not to notice, is the balance that occurs when both opinions are considered together as complementary forces (which is how these opinions should be considered). The scale of China's economy and its development over the past quarter century means that China serves as an ideal example to illustrate the complex way in which one country can influence inflation rates elsewhere in the world through global supply and demand.

The supply-side argument about China and global inflation is a simple one. China is now the workshop of the world, so the argument goes. The popular belief is that the Chinese population labour for very low wages, with little regard to welfare or environmental concerns, and this popular belief has in turn fuelled the idea that China has been able to increase its market share by providing cheap exports to the rest of the world through the simple expedient of undercutting the prices of its international competitors. The prevalence of this idea means that the playing field is not 'level' in the minds of non-Chinese politicians; for some of them the playing field is an economic Everest of distortions working to impede domestic industry. The belief of an unfair competitive environment rests on the criticism of the different regulations that govern Chinese industry – companies operating in China do not have to pay for the welfare of their workers, for instance, in the way that companies operating in the United States have to pay for the welfare of their workers. Different costs mean different cost pressures on pricing, hence the deflationary or at least disinflationary impulse of China to the rest of the world.

Strictly speaking what is being argued here is that China has increased the global supply of labour by adding its domestic pool of workers to the world economy. Global trade has meant that Chinese labour now has a global dimension and a global impact. This is not a particularly novel concern. In 1867 Leone Levi was writing 'There is a material difference... in the cost of maintenance of a British labourer who eats daily wheaten bread and butcher's meat, and of a Chinaman who lives exclusively on rice.'[2] It is something of a statement of the obvious, but a recurring concern over the centuries nonetheless.

A further coincidence gives comfort to those that want to attribute global disinflation pressures to China's supply of goods to the rest of the world. China's emergence as a global economic power is correlated with a definite reduction in global inflation pressures. China's economy hovered around 2 per cent of the world economy in 1990, putting it in line with Brazil, India and Russia. Over the past quarter century nothing much has changed for the other three economies. Of these three economies only Brazil exceeds 3 per cent of global GDP today, and that just barely. (The whole concept of the so-called BRICs (*Brazil, Russia, India and China*) as a dynamic bloc of economies is mythical, rather like an economic version of unicorns; oft claimed, but remarkably elusive to prove in reality.) For China, however, things are very definitely different. By 2014, China is comfortably over 10 per cent of the world economy, if we accept the foreign exchange conversion rates used by the World Bank and others in comparing economy sizes.[3] China joined the World Trade Organization in 2001, which helped to increase its share of global trade. And while all this was going on, the developed economies of the world enjoyed extremely low inflation rates. In the minds of the conspiracy theorists, such correlation must prove that China caused global inflation rates to weaken.

Wearily, economists must once again repeat the mantra that 'correlation does not mean causation' – correlation could just mean coincidence. Quite a lot of other things that were relevant to global inflation were happening at the same time as trade globalisation and China's economic emergence. Central banks became more independent. The power of organised labour diminished in many economies. Inflation expectations, which had been ratcheting down since the inflation shocks of the 1970s, were finally brought within normal bounds. There was a lot more going on than China and international trade. It is time to turn to hard facts to pick apart the arguments about supply and inflation. These matter in assessing factors that drive global inflation rates, and they matter specifically as the globalisation of trade seems set to slow in the years ahead.

The starting point should be to consider China's exports relative to the world economy. The headline number is that Chinese exports accounted for over 11 per cent of world trade in 2012, if we just look at goods and ignore services. China does not export much by way of services. That amounts to 2.8 per cent of global GDP. For those that criticise the latter number as being too low, remember that global trade is only roughly a quarter of the world economy. For all the much vaunted nature of globalisation, the vast majority of the economic activity that matters to a country's inflation rate is home-grown economic activity.

Still, 2.8 per cent of global GDP is a significant number, and it is a number that has risen. China's exports accounted for just 0.3 per cent of global GDP in 1990. Partly that increase is because China has gained market share as an exporter, and partly that increase is because the global trade share of the world economy grew from 1990 onwards (it doubled, broadly speaking).

Surely the increased role of Chinese exports in the global economy has an impact on global inflation? Well, it does, but not to the extent that the raw export data itself would suggest. Chinese exports may hover around 3 per cent of the world economy, but Chinese exports are not all Chinese. Consider the Apple iPad. The iPad is purportedly 'Made in China'; it says so on the box. In fact a lot of the components come from outside China. In 2010 the materials which came from outside China accounted for almost a third of the total price. Korean components made up nearly 7 per cent of the price, and Taiwanese components 1.4 per cent. Chinese cost pressures do not affect the price of the Korean or Taiwanese technology that goes into the Apple iPad. Chinese costs do not affect the price of the American intellectual property that goes into the Apple iPad, nor the marketing of the product – and those elements accounted for almost a third of the price. If we want to get an understanding of how Chinese costs may impact global inflation for iPads, we need to discover not the value of China's exports of iPads, which include in the box all the Korean and Taiwanese and American inputs. What the rational economist must focus on is the value of *China's contribution* to the value of the iPad. In fact, China's contribution to a 'Made in China' iPad was one of the least important parts in the iPad manufacturing and retail process. In 2010, a 'Made in China' iPad was 1.6 per cent Chinese labour. The rest came from outside China.[4]

The Apple iPad is something of an extreme example. However, as global supply chains have become more and more complex, understanding the contribution of individual links in the chain has become more and more important in the world of economics. This has prompted the World Trade Organization and the Organisation of Economic Co-operation and Development to calculate statistics known as 'Trade in Value Added'. These are sometimes presented under the happy acronym of 'TiVA'. This identifies the actual contribution of an economy to what is exported – so in the case of an iPad, China gets the 1.6 per cent of the value of the product that can be chalked up to its efforts.

So what does TiVA tell us? It tells us that in 2008, before the global financial credit crunch completely took hold, China contributed the equivalent of 1.6 per cent of global GDP through the effort it put into making its exports. The similarity to its contribution to an iPad is coincidence. This was up from 0.4 per cent of global GDP in 1995, and 1.1 per cent of global GDP in 2005 when China was beginning to enjoy the fruits of having joined the World Trade Organization. This is the number that matters. What this tells us is that if Chinese production costs fell 10 per cent a year (which is a pretty significant decline in production costs), and if all that production cost decline was passed on to the end consumer, then China's falling costs would reduce global inflation by around 0.16 per cent.

A reduction in global economic inflation of 0.16 per cent is the sort of change that an economist would refer to, with characteristic precision, as a 'rounding error'. One would have to have far greater faith in the abilities of statisticians than most economists possess to get worked up by a 0.16 per cent inflation change in global inflation. Global inflation statistics are not as reliable as all that.

It is worth noting in passing that China's production costs have generally not fallen by 10 per cent a year. That was an extreme example. It is an example that matters, because what applied in the past also applies in the future. If Chinese production costs were to rise in the future, then they would impact the global inflation rate (directly) in proportion to the importance of Chinese economic endeavour to the rest of the global economy. Back in 2008 the importance of Chinese economic endeavour to the rest of the global economy was a factor of 1.6 per cent. The importance of Chinese economic endeavour fell in 2009, but that is not really a fair comparison because the global financial crisis was particularly devastating to global trade in that year.

The discussion so far has concerned the dynamic aspect of pricing – if Chinese costs rise more slowly than foreign costs rise, year after year, then there is a direct impact on global inflation. That direct impact is felt year after year, but on a relatively muted scale given the relatively low weight Chinese exports have relative to global GDP. However, we also have to consider the possibility of a one-off change in inflation coming from foreign supply. If goods were produced in one country at a cost of $10, and are now produced in China (sticking with China as our example) at a cost of $5, then there will be a one-off but direct reduction in inflation (assuming that these cost savings are passed on to the global consumer). There is no denying the reality of this. Again, we must consider the relative importance of China to the world economy. Chinese endeavours were 1.6 per cent of the global economy in 2008; they were 0.4 per cent in 1995. Over thirteen years, therefore, the importance of Chinese economic endeavour to the rest of the world grew by 1.2 per cent of global economic activity. Putting it another way, shifting production to China accounted for perhaps 0.1 per cent of global economic activity each year.

Even if we assume quite monumental cost savings in any production shift, the cost savings from a production shift would have to be multiplied by a factor of 0.1 per cent in any given year to get an idea of the impact on global inflation. Multiply any cost saving you like by a factor of 0.1 per cent, and the chances are that you end up with a rounding error.

So, the direct impact of China on global inflation rates, in spite of the significant shifts that have taken place over the past quarter century, is still fairly muted. For the individual manufacturer the cost savings of changing production can be significant, but the manufacturer is just one part of a lengthy supply chain. That supply chain makes the cost savings associated with manufacturing a relatively small part of the overall price of the goods that are purchased by global consumers. It is worth reiterating the point that a high proportion of the price that the consumer pays for any goods will end up going to the various stages of the *domestic* supply chain – transport, advertising, retail and the like. The manufacturer does not necessarily get that much of the money; generally less than half.

Having put the role of international supply into its proper context there is a subsidiary supply issue that is worth stressing. If modern media magnifies the possibility that jobs will be moved overseas to cheaper competitors (the inelegantly named 'offshoring' process) then this may very well influence the behaviour of workers in the domestic economy. It should be noted that offshoring is different from outsourcing. Outsourcing is simply 'buying in' goods or services from outside the company. The location of that external provider is not considered. When offshoring is perceived as a viable option a worker is perhaps more likely to temper their demands for pay increases; they believe that their job could disappear entirely to a cheaper foreign location, and if they wish to keep their job they should not widen the pay differential with the cheaper foreign location. Economically there is evidence to back this up in the realms of both service sector and manufacturing sector employment.

This, then, is international trade working on inflation not in a direct and real way, but through an often unsubstantiated fear. Politicians or the media may sensationalise the threat of offshoring for their own ends – to win votes or readers or viewers – but the sensationalism still has real-world consequences. Certainly, the perception of offshoring has tended to be exaggerated relative to the reality; offshoring occurs on a far smaller scale than is popularly supposed. The perception is not helped by all the 'Made in China' (or 'India' or 'Vietnam') stickers that adorn the products that are purchased in developed economies. In fact, at least some of these goods are 'assembled' rather than 'made' in these countries, but that 'Made in' sticker becomes stuck in the memory.

Foreign influences on inflation can be discerned through the supply side via trading patterns (a direct impact) and via developed economy wages under the threat, real or imagined, of offshoring (an indirect impact). But what of the demand side? China's share of the world economy grew roughly five-fold over twenty-five years, at a time when the global economy itself was growing with remarkable persistence. Surely this demand must have an impact on global prices?

The answer of course is that such a shift in global living standards will have an impact on prices, primarily of raw materials. The appearance of markets emerging out of poverty – for as we saw in the last chapter the reduction in extreme poverty is not just a China story but one of the great *global* success stories of economics in the past twenty-five years – will necessarily mean an increase in demand for 'stuff'. To use China as the example once again, because its changes are so dramatic, in 1992 Chinese net imports accounted for less than 5 per cent of world trade in metals and energy. By 2010, Chinese net imports accounted for over 5 per cent of world energy trade. Net imports of metals were around 30 per cent of world trade. Net imports of iron ore were a rather noticeable 60 per cent of world trade. This is a meaningful change.

By 2010, Chinese consumption of non-renewable energy was 20 per cent of global consumption (note that this is not quite the same thing as net imports as a proportion of trade). Just under a quarter of global agricultural crops were consumed in China, and base metal consumption was 40 per cent of world consumption. Remember that China is just over 10 per cent of the world economy, and that figure is derived by using the World Bank definition which flatters China's significance, so China's growth has led to commodity consumption that is out of proportion to its economic size.[5]

This means that China has a bearing on international commodity prices. International Monetary Fund analysis in 2012 suggested that growth shocks from China would have a discernible impact on commodity prices, and in particular the price of copper and the price of oil. China's impact on global commodity prices is exaggerated by the fact that its commodity consumption is out of proportion to the size and stage of development of its economy. This is not just an emerging market story: in terms of consumption per person, both Korea and Brazil consumed proportionately fewer commodities than does China, when Korea and Brazil were at the stage of economic development that China is at today.

The interesting thing is why China consumes more commodities than its stage of economic development would suggest. One reason is that China has invested relatively heavily in big infrastructure projects – think of the Three Gorges Dam, or the various ring roads around Beijing that seem to be constantly crumbling, or the new plans for railway expansion. These projects do tend to be commodity intensive. But the other area of commodity-intensive economic growth in China is nothing to do with the domestic part of the economy: China is commodity intensive because its international trade tends to be commodity intensive. The energy and raw materials that China is demanding end up being exported once again, packaged up in all those iPads and other consumer products.

This comes back to the issue of relative prices that was highlighted in the last chapter. China has contributed in some way to reducing the price of manufactured products in the world – either directly or indirectly. At the same time, and in part as a function of its role as a global manufacturer, China has also contributed to the relative increase in commodity prices in the world economy. The inflation inequality issues that were highlighted in Chapter 7 can be considered to be partially the 'fault of foreigners', to the extent that foreigners have contributed to this relative price shift.

The relationship between economic growth and commodity prices is complex. China is a major commodity consumer, but in part this is because it is an inefficient commodity consumer. Were China to improve consumer efficiency (as happened a few years ago with its steel production, which became meaningfully more energy efficient), then its demand for commodities would decline. Chinese economic growth still has less of an impact on global commodity prices than US economic growth because China remains relatively less integrated into the global economy. A boost to US GDP will reverberate around the global economy (economists call this 'spillover effects'). A boost to Chinese growth is felt elsewhere in the world, but not to the same degree. If China and the US experienced the same growth shock, the impact of the US on global commodity prices is estimated at four or five times the scale of the impact of China on global commodity prices. The US economy is double the size of that of China, but it is also more commodity efficient. What drives the bigger impact of the US is the fact that if the US grows then Europe grows, and Asia grows, and Latin America grows. As these regions grow so their demand for commodities grows, and thus commodity prices rise.

So where does that leave the supply and demand relationship between foreigners and inflation rates? Considering aggregate inflation rates, a country like China has not made much of a difference over the past thirty years. On balance, most economists would come down on the side of China having been marginally inflationary for the rest of the world. To a very limited extent 'foreigners' (other countries) have caused global price pressures to rise through increased demand. This should not be considered too surprising given that China and other economies have seen their living standards and overall levels of demand in the world economy rise. This is compounded in the case of some economies, like China, that remain relatively inefficient consumers of commodities.

What China has done is change relative prices, and that is where foreign influences are most likely to be felt. Foreign supply and foreign demand patterns are likely to differ from domestic demand patterns – this is, after all, what drives global trade. If everyone demanded and supplied identical product at identical cost, there would be no economic advantage to global trade. The increase in global trade from 1990 has not had a very direct impact on aggregate inflation. It has had some indirect impact on inflation through scaring workers into subdued wage claims. But the real impact of global supply and demand shifts has been on relative price adjustment.

Of course we are not finished with the impact of foreigners on inflation. Supply and demand and monetary policy are all very well, but they are not the principal political focus. The principal political focus for foreigners and pricing is the very specific price of the foreign exchange markets. Nothing gets a protectionist politician animated like the issue of 'fair' exchange rates.

Exchange rate policy and import and export prices (and domestic components)

Foreign exchange markets are one of the most visible aspects of the way in which foreign pricing could potentially impact domestic inflation – a foreign exchange rate is, in some sense, a manifestation of a foreign country's worth redenominated into domestic currency terms. There is therefore a strong interest in the relationship of foreign exchange rates and inflation, and a strong suspicion in some quarters that foreigners are trying to manipulate currencies in order to manage the price of their exports.

The relationship between currencies and inflation should be simple. In fact it is the misleading, superficial simplicity of the foreign exchange–inflation relationship that is a big part of the problem economists have in explaining the true nature of the behaviour of foreign exchange, competitiveness and domestic inflation. The theories that abound around the topic of floating exchange rates are simple – but deceptively so. Politicians have a tendency to latch onto these simple theories, ignore the progress of almost fifty years of economic thought, and present the relationship between prices and foreign exchange as if it were a truism: currency appreciation bad, currency depreciation good (if it is the politician's own currency that is under discussion); currency appreciation means export prices up, currency depreciation means export prices down. It is all very Orwellian, in an *Animal Farm* sort of a way.

The critical issue in the relationship between foreign exchange markets and inflation is how companies have adapted to the world of floating exchange rates. As this is an evolutionary tale, it is probably best to start with the move to floating exchange rates and explain what they were *supposed* to achieve in terms of domestic and international inflation shifts. From that starting point, the course the global economy takes towards the modern relationship can be plotted.

The collapse of the dollar standard that had kept foreign exchange rates more or less rigid in the aftermath of 1945 was something of a shock to the global capitalist trading system. It is worth pointing out that the standard, conventionally known as the Bretton Woods system, was far more rigid than at least some of its architects had intended. Lord Keynes, heading the British delegation at Bretton Woods, had assumed more frequent changes in foreign exchange values than the very rare and always tortuous adjustments that did take place. Nonetheless, for good or ill, the relatively rigid system had stood in place until August 1971 when President Nixon abandoned the fixed dollar price for gold, aided by an import surcharge that was illegal under the General Agreement on Tariffs and Trade and indeed of dubious domestic legality. The courts allowed the authority on the rather tenuous grounds that the president as commander in chief had the power under the terms of the Trading With The Enemy Act, a piece of legislation that had been left lying around on the statute books after the First World War.

The dying days of Bretton Woods had been marked by current account imbalances, and in particular current account imbalances in the United States – the very country that was supposed to stand at the centre of the system. The result was a drain on the gold reserves of the United States (they fell every year bar two over the period from 1958 to 1972). The Bretton Woods system had also tended to put the burden of correcting current account imbalances on the debtor nations (which were required to spend less) and not the surplus nations (where spending more would potentially resolve the problem). This, like the foreign exchange rigidity that became a feature of the system, was not supposed to be the case. A more equitable solution of imbalance resolution had originally been envisaged. With the burden of correction disproportionately placed on current account deficit countries, Bretton Woods acquired a growth-deflating bias. Floating exchange rates were supposed to provide the magic solution to these problems with a wave of the free-market wand.

The economic theory that dealt with the move away from fixed exchange rates was simple and elegant. It also did not actually work that well, but this is a technicality. There are those in the economics profession who are less concerned about practical functionality as long as the idea can be expressed in a mathematical equation. What was supposed to happen is that a current account surplus country would have a currency that appreciated. The appreciation of the currency would lower the price of imports (in local currency terms) and raise the price of exports (in foreign currency terms). As a result, foreign consumers would reduce their demand for domestic goods, and domestic consumers would clamour to consume cheaper foreign goods (when priced in domestic currency terms). The balance of payments would miraculously swing back into balance without politicians having to do anything. Any economic policy that requires politicians to do nothing is generally recognised as being a policy worth pursuing.

Floating exchange rate theory sort of worked initially, and that 'sort of worked' period is what has embedded itself in the collective mind of the world's politicians. In the 1970s, as the world dealt with the convulsions of the ending of fixed exchange rates and then the disruptions of the oil price shocks, currencies moved quite significantly. The movements of currencies led to shifts in import and export prices – not necessarily immediately, it is true, but after a period when importers and exporters had time to adjust. And thus we have a relationship emerging between foreigners and inflation. If foreigners weaken their currency, domestic inflation will fall. If the domestic currency weakens, domestic inflation will rise. If foreigners change their currency level, then import prices will change in the domestic economy, which means that domestic inflation will change – a direct chain reaction.

The theory that underpins all of this is the law of one price. This is not actually a law, unless one subscribes to the adage that laws are meant to be broken, but what it suggests is that a company should expect to get the same price in one

---

Box 8.1 Price and floating exchange rate theory

Why are import and export prices supposed to change with moves in foreign exchange markets? Imagine a British producer is exporting a good to America (for the sake of argument, let us use the standard good of economic textbooks and imagine that there is a thriving Anglo-American trade in 'widgets'). It costs £9 to make a widget in Britain, and the British producer wishes to make an additional £1 profit. The widget is therefore sold for £10. At the same time an American rival is producing American widgets at a cost of $9. Coincidentally, the American widget manufacturer is also keen to make an 11 per cent profit margin, is looking for a profit of $1, and so charges $10 per widget sold.

If the pound sterling is worth two American dollars, then obviously one American dollar is worth fifty pence in Britain. If the British exporter wants to receive £10 for its product, then it will have to charge $20 when selling its widget in the United States to get the desired amount in sterling terms. With the American-made product being so much cheaper, there are unlikely to be too many British exports to the United States. On the other hand the American exporter is perfectly happy to sell American widgets to Britain for £5 – because the American exporter will get the desired $10 price by doing so. As a result, the British market is flooded with cheap American imports.

Now let us assume that the pound sterling weakens – and is worth less. If a pound is now worth not two but just one American dollar, then obviously a dollar is worth a pound. The pound has halved in value. But see what this does to the prices of the exports. The British widget exporter is now perfectly happy to receive $10 when selling its widgets in the United States, because that translates back into £10 when converted at the new, weaker value of the pound. At the same time, the American widget exporter will not take less than £10 for its widgets, because anything less would yield the American exporter a sum below $10 when translated into the US currency.

Thus the weakening of the value of the pound sterling *in theory* leads to a higher import price into the United Kingdom, and a lower export price from the United Kingdom (lower import price into the United States).

---

market as it gets in another market, when those prices are converted into a common currency. This is essentially what Box 8.1 is explaining – the widget manufacturer wants to receive the same amount of money from the export market as from the home market. It is also the concept that underpins the pure version of purchasing power parity, which generates non-market based foreign exchange rates.

So, the traditional interpretation of floating exchange rates gives foreigners quite a lot of influence over inflation, at least for traded goods, through the way exchange rates move. If foreigners allow their currencies to strengthen (for example, as happened with the US dollar in the early years of President Reagan's time at the White House) then domestic inflation pressures (inflation outside the United States in the early 1980s) should build with the rising cost of imports. Conversely, a weaker foreign currency (the dollar after 1985 for instance) should reduce inflation pressures in the domestic economy. It is all very logical. So why is it that this theory no longer works, and the relationship between foreign exchange markets and inflation has broken down?

The reason for the breakdown is not macroeconomic, but microeconomic. Firms have changed the way that they behave. The first reason for this is that the structure of firms has evolved since the early 1970s. The second reason for this is that corporate chief executives have a longer-term view of the world than many foreign exchange traders.

The law of one price sort of worked in the 1970s, in a large part because trade was still quite 'imperial' in its structure. Manufacturing economies would import raw materials, convert them into manufactured goods, and then export the finished product. This echoed the practices of the late nineteenth century, when commodity trade was worth 70 per cent more than manufactured goods trade.[6] It was nice and simple. But then, in the 1980s and especially in the 1990s, things started to get a little more complicated. Supply chains became more involved, and the 'raw materials in, finished product out' model became less relevant.

In particular, over the past forty or so years, companies have become global in their production. As capital controls were lifted from the 1980s onwards more overseas subsidiaries could be set up – sometimes leading to the offshoring process that has already been mentioned. As a result of this companies began to trade goods between their different subsidiaries as the components of the final product moved up the supply chain (the politically correct name for these global behemoths is 'transnational corporations' or TNCs). This process has continued to evolve so that today it is estimated that around a third of global trade is conducted intra-firm – that is to say, inside the same company.[7] Clearly, if a company is moving goods from subsidiary to subsidiary it has less and less interest in reacting to every exchange rate fluctuation when setting its prices. It is all internal anyway, and foreign exchange rates are not terribly relevant if a company is just 'selling' product to itself. This sort of intra-company trade is very unlikely to experience changing prices in the face of foreign exchange fluctuations. The imperial model of importing raw materials from the rest of the world in order to export finished product has gone the way of the Dutch and British Empires that spawned it. There may be a few outposts that are still dependent on the model but for the most part things have moved on.

So, the emergence of transnational companies means that at least a third of global trade should be largely independent of foreign exchange market fluctuations. But that still leaves a good proportion of global trade that should be influenced by currency moves. What has happened here?

The answer is that a theory known as 'pricing to market' has taken over as a stronger force for a great deal of global trade. Let us get the caveats out of the way first, for there are two caveats to dispense with. The first caveat is absolutely critical: pricing to market does not apply to commodities. Commodities are generally relatively homogenous products that trade in international markets, and are almost universally priced in dollars. If a currency moves in value against the US dollar then the price of imported commodities will shift. There is a direct translation (in part because in so standard a product, which is universally sought after and sold in bulk, traders would at once take advantage of any difference in price that were to emerge in the wake of a foreign exchange market move). Commodity import price inflation will be dependent on the movement of foreign exchange markets, and commodity import price inflation will have a bearing on domestic inflation in proportion to the intensity of commodity consumption within the domestic economy.

The second caveat is that pricing to market strategies *may* not apply to the imports of small economies. Certainly, pricing to market is a strategy that holds sway in the larger economies of the world, and an exporter from a small economy will almost certainly follow pricing to market. Pricing to market is less likely for a small country's imports because the market will generally be less important for exporting companies.

So, what is this pricing to market strategy of which we hear so much? Pricing to market occurs when a company sets the price of its product according to local market conditions, and not according to the fluctuations of the foreign exchange market. So a European car exporter like BMW is unlikely to change the price of its cars exported and sold in the United States just because the euro–dollar exchange rate has shifted by 10 per cent (up or down). BMW does not behave like the widget manufacturer in Box 8.1, and in fact rejects the behaviour of the widget manufacturer entirely. However, if a US competitor to BMW changes the price of its cars sold in the United States, then BMW may change its prices.

There are several ways we can see this process in action. With the increased computing power available to economists nowadays it is possible to process a lot more data and identify trends. Two economists, Baxter and Landry,[8] analysed the price action of the Dutch-registered furniture store IKEA over seventeen years. In examining the pricing behaviour of companies, IKEA is the sort of firm that economists dream about. IKEA is the world's thirtieth largest retailer. IKEA sources products from fifty-five countries around the world. IKEA tends to produce its products in single locations, that is, one product, wherever it is sold in the world, will have been made in one country. It has stores all over the world. Above all else, its products are in the nicest possible way homogenised. The IKEA 'Billy' bookcase has infiltrated homes across the planet, and it is the same product in Paris as it is in Abu Dhabi or Chicago. Just following the law of large numbers, in the event of there ever being a global apocalypse there has to be a reasonable chance that a Billy bookcase will survive the conflagration as a lasting memorial to the achievements of the human race. If ever there was a company that was going to apply one price across its product range, surely that company is IKEA.

IKEA does not follow the law of one price. In fact, IKEA does not really adjust prices at all when exchange rates change. Depending on the circumstances, only 14 per cent to 30 per cent of an exchange rate fluctuation over the course of a year is passed through to the consumer in the form of a price move. The only time the exchange rate seems to be a factor in determining product prices is when a new item is introduced – the law of one price seems to be more applicable in those circumstances, although it is still not applied rigidly. This makes sense, as it is an initial price that is being determined. Subsequent *changes* to that initial price are contingent on local market conditions and not on the fluctuations of the foreign exchange market.

IKEA's pricing strategy is one example of pricing to market, and we must be careful not to extrapolate too much from a single company. However, the macroeconomic data support the idea that most companies do not change the price of their product when foreign exchange markets move. In the years since the global financial crisis there have been two relatively big exchange rate moves, which allow us to examine the behaviour of firms from a macroeconomic perspective. The British pound sterling, which was (in the view of most economists) significantly overvalued prior to the crisis, weakened by some 25 per cent in late 2008 and early 2009. Meanwhile, the Japanese yen, the valuation of which is more controversial, weakened in the wake of yet more printing of money by the Bank of Japan; the yen weakened over 30 per cent from the latter part of 2012.

From the British data we can see what happened in Figure 8.1. The value of sterling weakened, shown by the move in the trade-weighted exchange rate (the line for this is inverted, so a rise in the line means a weaker sterling). Under the old theory, a weaker sterling should mean lower export prices. However, as soon as exporters had time to gather their thoughts, export prices rose (which

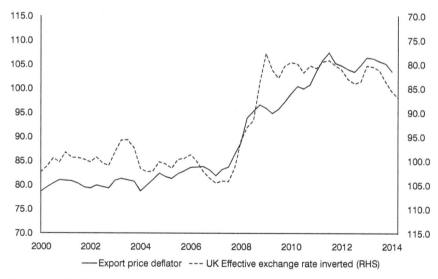

Figure 8.1 British exporters raise sterling prices and hold foreign prices unchanged when the pound weakens

Source: Derived from data from Haver Analytics.

is what the export price deflator is showing – this is a broad measure of export prices drawn from the GDP calculations, and in Figure 8.1 it is shown as an index level, not an inflation rate). The key point to remember here is that the export price level shown in this figure is the price of British exports when converted into *pounds sterling*. British exporters are choosing to hold their foreign currency prices constant, and de facto increase their sterling price and thus their sterling profit margins. The weakness of sterling has no impact on the overseas price of UK products, in spite of the really very significant fall in the value of sterling at this time. Pricing to market.

The Japanese are even more obliging. Japan publishes statistics for various measures of all its export prices. One of these statistical sets measures the price of all Japanese exports in yen terms. A second statistical set measures the price of all Japanese exports in contracting currency terms – that is to say, the currency Japanese companies are actually paid in. Figure 8.2 shows what happened to the export price inflation rates of the two indices. The period of particular yen weakness has been highlighted, though frankly the behaviour of the yen export prices makes it obvious. In foreign currency terms Japanese prices barely moved in the wake of the weaker yen. Contracting currency export prices fell a little, but remember that most of Japan's overseas competitors were cutting prices at this time. Japan was just matching its export prices in foreign currency terms to the pricing strategies of its competitors, which is consistent with the dictates of pricing to market strategies. In yen terms the inflation rate of Japanese exports

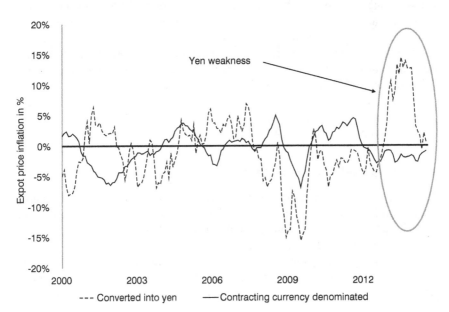

Figure 8.2 Japanese export price inflation rates in invoice currency terms, and converted into yen

Source: Derived from data from Haver Analytics

soared, basically matching the depreciation of the yen. What Japanese companies chose to do was hold their foreign currency prices broadly constant and increase their profit margin in yen terms. Pricing to market.

Why do companies follow pricing to market strategies? Because it makes sense, basically. A company that has spent time and money building up a customer base in a foreign market will have sunk a lot of costs in that process. There will have been advertising campaigns, brand building and customer loyalty to nurture. Word of mouth advertising does not spring up overnight, even in the internet age. Exporters are chary of risking all that effort by widening a price differential when compared with foreign competitors just because the domestic currency has strengthened in the foreign exchange markets. As a sort of quid pro quo, exporters are less likely to reduce prices just because their domestic currency has weakened in the foreign exchange markets. Periods of currency weakness will boost an exporter's profit margin (they sell the same amount of goods, but at a higher price when translated back into domestic currency terms).

Currencies move all the time, and it is not good business sense to leave one's pricing strategy at the mercy of foreign exchange dealers. What this means, however, is that the movement of the foreign exchange markets has less importance to domestic inflation than is popularly supposed. Too many investors and policymakers seem stuck in a time warp of currency theory, not recognising the revolution that the past forty-five years have wrought on corporate behaviour in this regard. There will be a domestic inflation response to a foreign exchange market move, but it is a reaction that seems to be largely confined to commodity prices. We are back to the concept of foreigners influencing relative price shifts more than they influence absolute price levels.

Investors should not assume *general* inflation will follow in the wake of a domestic currency depreciation. Investors should consider the cost pressures of those companies that are heavy users of imported commodities in the wake of domestic currency depreciation. Investors should also recognise that foreign competitive pressures are unlikely to abate for those domestic companies that face overseas competition, just because the home currency has depreciated.

Foreigners might not be at fault

It is always terribly tempting to blame foreigners. The British have been blaming the French for pretty much everything that has ever gone wrong for Britain since roughly speaking 1066. Blaming foreigners (especially the French) is just so easy to do, and it has the wonderful and utterly beneficial consequence of absolving domestic policymakers from any share of blame for anything that has gone wrong. However, when it comes to inflation, blaming foreigners is in fact very difficult to do. It may be unpopular to say, but inflation is normally an exclusively domestic concern.

Foreign monetary policy, even the monetary policy of the world's reserve currency, has very little pass-through to domestic inflation rates. Any currency is a claim on the goods and services of a domestic economy, and the monetary policy that regulates that currency does not normally translate through in a way that will affect other prices. Foreign countries, through their impact on patterns of global supply and demand, will obviously have some bearing on domestic inflation rates, but remember that domestic inflation is largely a matter of domestic labour costs. Domestic labour costs can be affected by the fear of outsourcing to foreign climes, but rarely by the reality. The fear is fanned into an irrational inferno by sensationalism and ignorance – as with most xenophobia. The impact of foreign patterns of supply and demand has a bearing on relative prices, rather than overall domestic price levels. Relative prices should not be ignored – the wise investor will pay close attention to them, as they can have an important bearing on investment strategies – but it cannot be repeated often enough: relative price changes do not constitute inflation.

Finally, there is the vexed issue of currencies. Floating exchange rates used to be relevant to domestic inflation, but that was over a generation ago. The world has moved on from the imperial model of trade to something that is at once infinitely more complex and more insular (with the growth of trade *within* companies rather than *between* countries). Commodity prices will react to the fluctuations of foreign exchange markets, so the commercial fates of traders in commodities are partly in the hands of foreign exchange dealers (and may God have mercy on their souls). But manufactured products and services are not nearly so subject to the whims of the foreign exchange markets, with general agreement that for large economies 30 per cent is the upper limit on the proportion of currency fluctuation that will find its way through to consumer prices. Politicians like to cite moves in foreign exchange markets as being the cause of moves in domestic price levels and inflation rates (and thus competitiveness); the economics profession can only observe such rhetoric with an air of bemusement.

What does this all add up to? It means that foreigners have a role in the rate of domestic inflation, but it is not nearly so great a role as most investors seem to suppose. Because of the misinterpretation of the international element of inflation, there is a repeated risk that investors will misjudge the consequence of foreign inflation or deflation pressures on the domestic inflation rate, and in so doing make errors in their investment strategies.

With that it is time to turn our attention to the financial markets and investment in the modern, complex inflation environment. The next chapter starts this process by looking at one of the most sacred of sacred cows in the world of inflation – the interaction of debt and inflation.

Notes

1 Rathbone and Wheatley (2012).
2 Levi (1867) p xxxi. This is actually an early elaboration of what economists now call the Balassa-Samuelson effect, which is an interesting topic in its own right but something of a distraction from the matter at hand.
3 It should be noted that these exchange rates, which are based off the polite fiction of purchasing power parity, are not without controversy. Some alternatives would substantially reduce the share of the Chinese economy. Even with that reduction,

however, the increased importance of the Chinese economy over the past quarter century is still impressive.

4 These figures refer to the 16GB Wi-Fi iPad as sold in 2010, and are taken from Kraemer *et al.* (2011).

5 These figures and the subsequently cited International Monetary Fund analysis are from Roache (2012).

6 Ashworth (1952) p 165.

7 See, for instance, Lanz & Miroudot (2011).

8 Baxter and Landry (2012).

9   The debt–inflation myth

Annual income twenty pounds, annual expenditure nineteen six, result happiness.
Annual income twenty pounds, annual expenditure twenty pounds ought and six,
result misery.

(Wilkins Micawber in *David Copperfield* by Charles Dickens)

So far, the chapters of this book have discussed inflation generally in the
context of economics, and how that might influence investors. This is only right.
Economics should take its proper place of pre-eminence in the natural order of
things. This chapter differs somewhat from the preceding chapters. This chapter
covers the role of inflation and debt, and this is a topic in which economics and
investing are intimately bound up together. The economics of debt relies on
investors, because debt requires credit, and creditors are investors.

The perceived relationship of debt and inflation is the greatest misconception
that surrounds inflation. Time and time again an economist will hear
'governments will inflate their way out of debt' being asserted with a complete
certainty as to the belief that inflation will automatically reduce a government's
debt burden. This is just not true. The idea that inflation *automatically* reduces
government debt is the great debt–inflation myth that has been sold to credulous
investors for decades.

In most circumstances in twenty-first-century financial markets inflation
will tend to either maintain or increase a modern government's debt, both in
absolute terms and relative to GDP over the longer term. The debt–inflation
myth is wrong but the myth has been extrapolated, moving from the specific
case of government debt to be applied more widely to corporate or to consumer
debt where there is generally even less justification for the assertion. In the
wake of the significant increase in government debt levels and the persistence
of consumer and corporate debt levels in some economies in the aftermath of
the global financial crisis, this is an increasingly important topic for investors
to understand.

Before getting into this contentious topic let us cover a few key concepts,
starting with the most basic: what is debt? In economic terms, debt is the
means by which we (as individuals, corporates or as society at large) consume

tomorrow's income today. Another way of thinking about it is to say that the borrower is voluntarily accepting a lower future standard of living in order to raise the standard of living that they enjoy today.[1] In financial terms that means that money is borrowed against the belief that the borrower will have the income to repay the debt, with interest, in the future.

This is where the famous *David Copperfield* quote that heads this chapter becomes so apt. Debt is about spending more than one has as income right now, of course. But the mechanics of debt are also about the ease with which debt can be repaid, which means making some kind of judgement about future levels of income and future levels of spending. Borrowers borrow because their current spending exceeds their current income. The rational lender will only lend because they have some belief that the borrower's future income will exceed the borrower's future spending. If the lender does not believe that the borrower's future income can grow faster than the borrower's future spending then it is highly irrational to consider lending. Creating debt depends on the future ability of the borrower to repay, and the future ability of the borrower to repay depends on the future income and future spending of the borrower, and the future income and future spending of the borrower depend on inflation in its various forms.

Throughout any analysis of debt and inflation it is absolutely critical to be clear as to what sort of inflation is being talked about. This is a common error in investment circles – inflation is treated as a generic and homogenous concept, and it is very, very far from being that. Different inflation measures are appropriate for different circumstances. It is also important to discern the different levels of inflation that have a bearing on debt management. As a rule this chapter will ignore hyperinflation. Hyperinflation will generally reduce a debt burden in real terms in almost any circumstances, but it brings with it other social and political consequences that policymakers will tend to shy away from. For the most part this analysis confines itself to considering the main route of inflation rates of up to around 30 per cent per year, with only occasional forays of exploration down the dark side-alleys of hyperinflation.

The debt–inflation myth needs to be carefully deconstructed. This chapter will therefore follow a fairly set format. Consumer, corporate and government debt will be examined in their turn. In each instance there will be a discussion of how inflation impacts a debtor's income, and a debtor's expenditure, and thus the debtor's ability to pay. In each case the investment implications will be drawn out. Finally, the issue of financial repression will be considered – something that is peculiar to government debt, and is not about governments inflating their way out of debt so much as regulating (or in a sense, taxing) their way out of debt. Nevertheless, financial repression is bound up with concepts of debt and inflation, and it is extremely important for investors across all asset classes – not just government bonds.

Let us begin with consumer debt, an issue that is of relevance to investors mainly through the impact consumer debt burdens will have on economic performance.

Consumers, debt and inflation

In a sense a consumer who has borrowed should be supremely unconcerned about the rate of consumer price inflation. The consumer who borrows has, by definition, consumed the good (or service) *now*. Why should the consumer care what happens to the price of that good or service in the future? If one buys a car today, and the price of a car suddenly rises 10 per cent a year after one has bought it, the happy car owner should not care. There may be a certain amount of smug self-congratulation at having had the foresight to have bought the car before the price went up, but that is it. Consumers can drive around in their credit-financed vehicles with supreme indifference to what is happening to the future price of the car.

The indifference of the consumer to the price of a *single* item is justified. What is less justified is consumer indifference to general inflation levels. Consumers who have incurred debts today are going to be concerned with inflation in the way that it affects their future incomes and their future spending, and thus their future ability to consume.

The income level depends, generally speaking, on the wage inflation rate. Technically, what economists will look at is household disposable income (that is to say income after taxes and transfer payments). Wage income is a large part of that, albeit a somewhat diminishing part given ageing societies will become more dependent on investment income. The ability of a consumer to repay their debt in the future is going to be dependent on their household disposable income.

In considering consumer debt from the perspective of the borrower, therefore, the real interest rate is not the nominal interest rate less consumer price inflation. The real interest rate will be the nominal interest rate less the rate of wage growth (or disposable income growth). This has become highly pertinent in the aftermath of the global financial crisis, when the growth of household disposable income has generally been quite subdued. Although interest rates have been reduced to very low levels, the indebted consumer has not generally benefited as much as the headline nominal interest rate would suggest. If interest rates (in the sense of the interest rates charged to consumers by commercial banks, not central bank policy interest rates) are set at 1 per cent, and household disposable income is rising at 2 per cent per year, then the income level means that the consumer is more readily able to repay their debt out of future income. If on the other hand interest rates are 1 per cent and household disposable income is falling at 1 per cent per year (because of unemployment, or increased taxation, or reduced benefit transfers) then the consumer is going to find it harder and harder to meet their future interest payments.

The real interest rate for borrowers thus requires discounting by the level of income. It is worth noting that the real interest rate for savers will still require discounting by consumer price inflation. This is because of the difference in the behaviour of the two groups. Borrowers are consuming today, and accepting a lower income and a lower ability to consume in the future. Hence, real borrowing rates need to be discounted with income growth. Savers are voluntarily choosing not to consume today, in the hope of a higher income and a higher ability to consume in the future. Savers' real interest rates need to be discounted against consumer price inflation, because the consumption is being deferred. Thus, people who borrow and people who save are very likely to simultaneously face different real interest rates. Policymakers may need to decide if they wish to primarily influence saving *or* borrowing when setting interest rate policy.

There is then the second consideration that must be taken into account when thinking about the future income that a consumer has available to pay back debt. Consumer price inflation does have a bearing on debt service in that it reflects the change in the overall cost of living that the consumer has to bear. Consumers do not surrender their desire to consume everything in the future when they agree to take out debt today. Consumers still need to eat, live somewhere and generally have some kind of a life. In fact, consumers are normally very reluctant to compromise their future standard of living just to pay off old debts, unless compelled by circumstances. A moment contemplating the inclination of consumers to keep 'rolling over' their debts, particularly debts like credit card debts, will give substance to the truth of this.

While the real interest rate for the consumer should properly be calculated with reference to the growth of consumer income, the general cost of living of the consumer does still have relevance via borrowers' inconvenient desire to continue eating in the future. It might be added that this should be as close to the cost of living that is actually faced by the consumer as is possible – that is, the income-specific inflation rate is what needs to be applied. If the cost of living is rising faster than household income (if household disposable income is falling in real terms) then the consumer's ability to repay their debt is significantly impaired. An interest rate of 1 per cent, household disposable income growth of 1 per cent but (household-specific) inflation of 3 per cent is a troubling combination for an indebted consumer. The traditional interpretation of real interest rates, using interest rates less inflation, would suggest that the consumer is benefiting significantly – for the traditional method of calculating a real interest rate would give a -2 per cent real rate.

Adapting to judge the consumer's ability to spend more generally gives a less positive picture – the consumer has a real interest rate of 0 per cent when the nominal interest rate is adjusted by the consumer's income growth. However, if the consumer wishes to maintain their standard of living they are in trouble. Consumer real incomes are falling (nominal income less consumer price inflation), and the consumer real interest rate on existing debt (nominal interest rates less nominal income growth) is not actually negative.

How should the investor think about all of this? Carefully. An investor is generally unlikely to be investing directly in consumer debt. For the most part it is banks and finance companies that are exposed to consumer debt, with the notable exception of household mortgage bonds that exist in the Nordic region, the United States and a few other places. Investor concerns around consumer debt must instead focus on the broader macroeconomic consequences of indebted consumers. There are two points that should be the basis of investor analysis:

- Are real interest rates (nominal consumer interest rates less nominal income growth) positive or negative?
- Are real incomes (nominal income less an appropriate consumer price measure) growing or not?

If the gap between borrowers' income growth and the interest rate on their debt is widening, and especially if real income for borrowers is weak, an investor should be cautious about expected strong consumer demand in that economy. The value of income-specific and age-specific inflation rates for consumers is also evident; borrowing is more likely amongst the younger age cohorts, and it is less likely amongst the wealthy. Knowing the true real income of borrowing consumers could be important.

Corporate debt and inflation

Debt is a vital part of any company doing business. Companies borrow because they believe that they can invest that money in their company and earn a higher rate of return than the cost of borrowing. There is a risk in that assumption, as the future is never certain. In addition, companies may borrow because they want cash, and with no intention of investing at all. This is actually a very common form of borrowing, and for small businesses is generally the single most important form of credit.

Traditional economic models tend to look at corporate borrowing in terms of investment and not of cash flow borrowing. There is a bias in these models to consider borrowing for a project against the prospective return for that project – it is all done on a case by case basis. That is all very well for micro analysis, but a financial investor trying to decide whether to purchase the equity or debt of a listed company is unlikely to be privy to that sort of detail. Their judgement must rest on broader macro assumptions – income and expenditure.

What is income growth for a company? There is very little point using consumer price inflation as a gauge. Most companies do not sell direct to consumers, even in the internet age, but instead sell to other companies. Even retailers, however, are not likely to have their incomes rise in line with the consumer price index because the consumer price index contains utility bills, an estimation for housing costs, services and the like. A food retailer will not see their income increase because healthcare costs are rising, or because the cost of housing is rising. Indeed, in both instances, the impact of rising costs in other parts of the household budget may cause consumers to reduce their spending on food in order to meet other demands on their budget. The UK's British Retail Consortium publishes a 'shop price index' which details the price rises retailers can get away with. This frequently diverges from the consumer price index (in 2014 the shop price index indicated outright deflation, when overall consumer price inflation was positive).

For the most part financial investors need to consider not consumer prices, or even shop prices, but some form of producer price data when trying to get a sense of potential income growth for a company. Several economies assist in this analysis by giving producer price indices that break down the prices by stage of production or even by industry. This is never going to be perfect, as each of these indices are aggregations, but they are better indications of corporate earning power than consumer price inflation could ever be.

For expenditure, the same producer price data can be helpful. As was briefly mentioned in the opening chapter, one categorisation of producer price inflation divides the statistic into 'input' and 'output' producer prices – basically raw materials (what goes into a factory) and finished product (what comes out of a factory). Inevitably, the raw materials that a company uses will vary from industry to industry. The second input that is used by companies is the more important. As we saw in Chapter 4 the most important component to inflation is labour, and that applies right along the supply chain in most sectors of the economy. Labour costs are generally available at an industry level, and ideally the financial investor needs to contemplate the level of unit labour costs that a specific company is likely to face.

The financial market investor considering the debt of a company and the interaction inflation is likely to have on that debt cannot just assume consumer price inflation will work to a company's advantage by increasing that company's revenue. Even macro analysis must be more specific than that. Income is likely to be governed by producer prices, and expenditure by a blend of labour costs and (different) producer prices. The importance of relative price shifts can be seen once again in this analysis. A labour-intensive industry is a very different financial investment proposition from a more commodity-intensive industry if the relative prices of labour and raw materials are shifting.

Government debt and inflation

The relationship between government debt and inflation is one of the 'Big Topics' in economics. The capitalisation is intentional, because the relationship between government debt and inflation seems to carry such significance in the minds of investors as to merit capitalisation. This is particularly the case since the establishment of fiat currencies, which allowed the debt–inflation myth to appear as star witness in the gold bugs' prosecution of the nefarious actions of politicians around the world. The government debt and inflation relationship blends together lots of prejudices into one subject: mistrust of government, loss aversion, government interference in the economy – it is all here.

As we saw way back in Chapter 2, historically politicians and governments have been inclined to cheat on the pursuit of sound economic principles and print money to cover their bills whenever the need arose. That leads to the problem of printing too much money, and as successive Chinese dynasties found out printing too much money will in turn lead to inflation (and the downfall of Chinese dynasties, but that lies outside the sphere of economics). Despite instance after instance of economic failure arising from printing excessive amounts of cash, politicians will always be attracted to the short-term solution of printing too much money to meet short-term spending needs, in order to achieve short-term political goals.

Because the government is normally the monopoly supplier of fiat currency, the short-term solution of setting the printing presses rolling normally lies in the hands of the government (although self-denial may put the power of the printing press out of harm's way under the supervision of an independent central bank, this governmental abstinence can normally be reversed if desired). The fact that governments 'can't be trusted' is one of the reasons why investors are so nervous about governments 'inflating their way out of debt'. It is a long-held belief, as well it might be. The Duc de Saint-Simon warned against establishing a central bank in France as long ago as 1716, because France was an absolute monarchy and the necessary checks to provide monetary discipline could not therefore be established. One hopes the Duc's implied *lèse-majesté* was delivered in a suitably tactful manner.

Government debt is peculiar in two characteristics. First, government debt is disproportionately fixed rate debt – that is to say, the interest charges do not vary over the life of the debt. Interest charges tied to changeable policy or market rates are logically enough known as variable or floating rate debt, and are generally a very small part of a government's obligations. Consumer and corporate debt can be fixed rate, but for the most part it tends not to be. Corporate bonds can be fixed rate debt, it is true, but an overwhelming number of companies do not have access to the corporate bond market. In the United States over 99.9 per cent (literally) of companies are not in a position to borrow in the corporate bond market.[2] Such companies are too small to borrow via bonds and will therefore have to borrow either from their bank or from their suppliers at a variable rate. In contrast, a majority of government debt is nearly always fixed rate.

Second, government debt is nearly always rolled over. There is an expectation that the government will have some stock of outstanding debt in the future – and indeed with modern financial structures being what they are there is almost a necessity of the government having some outstanding stock of debt in the future. Because governments are generally seen as perpetual entities (although the realities of modern politics may disagree) there is an assumption that an individual debt instrument will be paid off, but the government debt in its entirety is unlikely to be repaid. Government debt rolls over in perpetuity, and indeed some individual instruments of government debt are explicitly perpetual and will only pay interest without ever repaying the capital.

In contrast, a consumer borrowing money has to demonstrate that they can pay off the entirety of their debt burden within a reasonable period. At the very least the consumer needs to show that they can repay the debt before they are likely to die – which is precisely why so many mortgage contracts require the borrower to take out a life insurance policy alongside the contract; it gives the lender certainty that the debt will be repaid.

The idea that governments can inflate their way out of debt rests on the first characteristic; that most government debt is fixed rate. If the government borrows $100 for ten years at 10 per cent fixed interest, then the government will repay the lender $10 per year for nine years and $110 in year ten at the conclusion of the loan. If inflation means that the real value of the dollar halves, then the government should find it easier to meet its debt obligations. The government's income in nominal dollar terms will have doubled while its debt service charges and the repayment of the original loan amount will have remained unchanged in nominal terms.

The ability to inflate out of debt is therefore derived from the income side of the income and expenditure argument (it is the expenditure side which kills off the ability of a government to inflate its way out of debt). Nominal income rises while the nominal value of existing debt instruments stays unchanged. Government income is pretty much down to taxes, and taxes are generally nominal in their nature because they are expressed as a fixed proportion of something nominal like income, profit or sales revenue. Governments tend to make up a relatively large part of an economy (generally somewhere between a third and a half of economic activity), so a government's tax-raising power tends to be very closely correlated with the size of the economy in nominal terms. This is why most government debt and deficit metrics are expressed as a ratio of the government's nominal debt or nominal deficit to nominal GDP. The GDP measure stands as a proxy for the government's potential income or potential income source, and so the ratio of debt to GDP for a government is similar to the ratio of debt to income for an individual.

Inflation will increase nominal GDP, all things being equal, although it does nothing to increase real GDP. As nominal GDP increases there should be an increase in nominal tax revenue for the government. In an inflationary episode a government will benefit from increased nominal revenues, but provided its debt is conventional fixed rate debt the government's nominal debt interest payments will not increase (at least not initially). The stock of government debt outstanding is also a nominal amount and should not increase as a direct result of inflation. Fixed debt payments are by definition fixed. The result is that the government's debt-to-GDP ratio should fall, as should the cost of servicing debt expressed as a proportion of GDP.

Let us turn to the caveats, because caveats are always fun. In normal circumstances it is right to assume that the government's revenue-raising power is tied to GDP, but there may be circumstances when this is not the case. If inflation is particularly high, taxpayers may try to avoid paying their taxes as long as possible (in the knowledge that the real value of their tax liabilities will fall in such circumstances). This was the case in Germany immediately before and during the hyperinflation episode of the Weimar Republic. If inflation is particularly high, it may even be worth being fined for non-payment of taxes, if the drop in the real value of one's tax liability exceeds the real cost of the fine.

Correlating tax revenues to GDP (and by extension, government debt metrics to GDP) also assumes that the government has the ability to tax the economy fully. This may not be the case. In the years after the global financial crisis the Greek government was subjected to a great deal of criticism about the relatively low proportion of the economy that it was able to tax, because of the prevalence of outright tax evasion (a more serious situation than delayed tax payments). It has also become fashionable for governments to include illegal activities in their calculation of GDP. Italy, rather memorably, was one of the first economies to do this. In 1987, Italy leapt up the international league table of economies overnight, overtaking the UK and coming close to France in terms of the size of its annual economic activity at that time. A proud moment for any nation. This surge in economic activity was not, of course, the result of a productivity miracle or sudden economic renaissance in Italy. Italy simply included an estimate for the economic efforts of tax evaders and illegal workers. The economic efforts of Italian tax evaders and illegal workers are apparently prodigious. That prodigious but illegal activity swelled the size of the country's GDP overnight.

There is a rather obvious problem when calculating a government's debt-to-GDP ratio where illegal activities are included in the GDP part of the calculation. The problem is that the government is unlikely to be able to raise taxes on those illegal activities, and so that part of GDP does *not* act as a proxy for government income. Tax evaders by definition evade paying taxes. Illegal workers are unlikely to contribute too much to the government revenue. What this means, inevitably, is that the improvement in the debt-to-GDP ratio, or the deficit-to-GDP ratio, caused by adding illegal activity to the GDP number, is entirely misleading. The ratio has improved, but the solvency of the government has not. The Italian government was no more solvent in 1987 than it had been in 1986. An accounting sleight of hand does not actually change economic fundamentals.

Lest the inclusion of illegal activities be thought an exclusively Italian issue, it is worth noting that in 2014 the British government welcomed illicit drug dealers into its calculation of GDP (as part of a plan to help bring the British statistics into line with those of the rest of the EU). Of course, Her Majesty's Revenue and Customs officers do pursue illicit drug dealers in the UK. The pursuit of Her Majesty's Revenue and Customs is not generally with the objective of getting them to pay corporation tax on the profits of their drug dealing and value added tax on their sales of heroin, however. Including drug dealers in UK GDP will lower the UK debt-to-GDP ratio, but as with the Italian government in 1987 this action will not improve the solvency of the British government.

Allowing for the caveats specified, generally speaking inflation raises nominal GDP, generally speaking higher nominal GDP raises government nominal tax revenue, and (assuming that the nominal payment on debt is fixed) higher nominal tax revenue generally works to a government's advantage in inflating its way out of debt.

So far, so simple. Against that simple 'inflation reduces indebtedness' mantra there are some strong counterarguments that come from the expenditure side. It is not just the government's revenue that rises with inflation. Spending will rise too, certainly in nominal terms and probably in real terms as well.

From the 1960s governments of developed economies moved to a process of automatically increasing their spending on an annual basis. Key parts of government budgets, generally related to social welfare, were tied into the aggregate consumer price index. The idea behind this was to depoliticise the process of maintaining a constant standard of living. In 1962, the retirement benefits of American civil servants were linked to consumer price inflation. In 1969, with President Nixon's encouragement, poverty levels were tied to consumer price inflation. By 1975, around half the American population had at least part of their income affected by consumer price inflation rates.

With some irony, Nixon was keen to index benefits to consumer prices as an attempt at controlling costs for the government, because hitherto benefits had tended to increase at a faster rate than inflation had done. The result was that around 30 per cent of government spending was tied to aggregate consumer price index, and this indexation process became an important part of the rise in government spending that followed the high inflation period of the 1970s. As inflation rose, so government spending also automatically rose.

This was not just a phenomenon in the United States. Rising inflation became a source of increased government spending via indexation across the developed world – government on automatic pilot, in a sense. Of course, governments could choose to change indexation – the Thatcher government in the United Kingdom changed the indexation of state pensions so that they no longer automatically increased in line with wage inflation but instead were tied to the generally lower growth in retail prices (it was changed back to wages by the later Blair government). While governments *can* change the principle of indexation, there are political costs to such changes: indexation seems 'fair'; it is difficult to agree on alternatives (and per Nixon's motives the alternatives may end up being more costly); and above all else the voters may not like the change. As a result, indexation tends to bring with it quite a lot of inertia as to the structure of indexation. Once indexation is in place, the principle is hard to abandon.

Other areas of government spending may not rise automatically with inflation, but they will still rise with inflation. If a government has decided to invest in the economy, for example by constructing new buildings for economics faculties at universities (a worthwhile aim), the budget for that building programme will probably not be indexed. Even without formal indexation, if there is inflation in the construction sector the chances are that the costs of that building programme will increase. Unless the contract with the builder is very strict as to its terms, those costs will be incurred by the government – governments are much like private citizens in this regard. The government's builders mutter about 'unforeseen complications' and all of a sudden there is another 20 per cent added onto the bill.

The government as monopoly supplier of money can create inflation, but the government as consumer of goods and services may fall victim to that same inflation. Of course, the government could choose to stop purchasing goods and services in order to avoid the cost inflation it has generated. That will reduce the deficit and debt, but that is fiscal management through reduced spending, not fiscal management through inflating out of debt.

The United States has another slight quirk that should be mentioned, though it is an income rather than a spending issue. Tax brackets and the innumerable special exemptions of the US tax code are indexed to consumer price inflation so as to prevent people moving into higher tax brackets as a result of nominal income increases without real income increases.[3] This removes a potential source of revenue. If a government does not index such things then it can increase its revenue by increasing the number of higher-rate taxpayers (as the thresholds for higher rates fall in real terms) and reducing the real value of tax exemptions. In the case of the US this revenue source has been specifically denied to the government.

So, there is an element of government spending that will rise automatically with inflation and thus constrain a government's ability to inflate its way out of debt. If political expediency prevents the indexation of whole swathes of government spending from being changed, then government spending increases will automatically persist through higher inflationary periods. The British government's irritation with food price inflation in the UK in the early years of the global financial crisis is a good illustration of this – higher food prices were undermining the government's attempts to bring the deficit under control. The government could cut spending in certain areas, and did, but it felt unable to change the principles of price indexation that underpinned much of the welfare budget. The fact that food prices were dragging up consumer prices, which dragged up indexed government spending, undermined British government attempts at budget deficit control. In addition a further part of government spending will rise with inflation, not as part of an automatic process but because the government's suppliers will raise their prices. The government is a consumer in the same way that the private sector is a consumer, and so it will have to pay the price for inflation in at least some of its services, just like the private sector.

The second element that undermines a government's ability to inflate its way out of debt is a little more complex than indexation of spending; it lies in the behaviour of government debt markets. Spending on 'stuff' is a major part of government spending, but nowadays debt service costs are also a very significant part of a government's budget. If we look back to the nineteenth and early twentieth centuries, a government could inflate its way out of debt because much of the debt was perpetual (meaning it never matured) or very long duration (it took years to mature). Some economies that would now be termed emerging markets were not able to borrow longer term, but the established markets with a track record for paying their debts were able to borrow with bond issues that would take decades to mature. The purchasers of these bonds implicitly assumed that inflation would not be a problem over the lifetime that they held them. If inflation came along unexpectedly, then the bond holder would suffer and the government would benefit – because both parties had committed to nominally fixed payments over a very long period.

The world has moved on over the course of the last hundred years, and even government bond markets have managed to evolve over the course of that period. Very few governments issue perpetual debt – the longest maturity tends to be thirty years, and even that is the exception rather than the rule for the most part. The government that has the longest average maturity of its outstanding debt is the United Kingdom, and there is a specific reason for that.

The United Kingdom was the first major economy to create a sizeable government bond market tied to the rate of inflation – what are known in Britain as index-linked gilts, and what the Americans call TIPS. Fairly obviously, the point of inflation-linked debt instruments is that the capital and interest rate is linked to the level of inflation. This is the aggregate level of inflation, and as discussed in Chapter 7 that may not be much use to specific investors who may face a very different inflation rate from the average, but for the purposes of this argument this is not terribly relevant. The fact that part of the government's debt (around a quarter of the UK government debt, indeed) is tied to the rate of inflation means that it is impossible for the government to inflate its way out of this portion of its debt burden. Indeed, this was cited as being a motive for issuing inflation-linked securities by the British Chancellor of the Exchequer in the 1981 budget: 'This innovation [inflation-linked securities] demonstrates the confidence that we have in our strategy for bringing inflation down. It will also reduce uncertainty about future real rates of return... We will have more flexibility in the market place and thus greater assurance of meeting the Government's borrowing needs.'[4]

The structure of index-linked securities means that they tend to be issued with longer maturities – partly because they are designed to appeal to long-term investors with a desire to protect their investments, such as pension funds, against aggregate consumer price inflation. This is why the UK national debt has the longest average maturity of the developed world. Obviously, the total size of the inflation-linked securities market is something that constrains the ability of the UK government to inflate its way out of debt. While other governments have inflation-linked securities, they tend to be a smaller proportion of the outstanding national debt and therefore are less of a constraint. It also explains why the debt of other governments has a shorter maturity than that of the UK. That shorter maturity means that other governments are still sensitive to inflation costs in servicing their debt. This comes from the combination of short maturity debt, and a need to roll over that debt.

Looking at the United States today, around half of the total outstanding publically traded government securities will mature and need to be repaid within the next three years. The issue for the government is that it will want to borrow the money again, once the debt has been repaid. Only if a government is running a budget surplus is there any possibility of not rolling over government debt, and it would have to be an unfeasibly large government surplus to avoid rolling over debt entirely.

This is really the critical force preventing modern governments from inflating away their debt. Governments no longer issue the perpetual bonds of the nineteenth century. Debt is short term, which means that the power of financial markets over governments is increased. Existing government debt holders will suffer if inflation rises – because they locked themselves into a fixed nominal rate of return before the inflation rate started to increase, and increasing inflation will reduce the real value of their rate of return. Bad luck on the existing holders of government debt – with a lesson, perhaps, not to be so trusting of government promises in the future.

Just because *existing* holders of government debt suffer from higher inflation, there is no necessity for *prospective* government debt holders to suffer the same real losses. Prospective holders of government debt can simply withhold their cash and refuse to buy government debt instruments in the absence of adequate compensation for the inflation that has been created. Indeed, prospective holders of government debt can insist on compensation not only to cover the higher inflation rate, but for more than that. If a government has attempted to inflate away its debt, then prospective holders of government debt can demand compensation for inflation uncertainty. Way back in the opening chapter it was inflation uncertainty that was highlighted as the critical problem arising from inflation. If prospective bond holders have seen existing bond holders ravaged by an inflation shock, they are a lot less likely to believe government assertions that 'this time we will behave'. Instead, prospective bond holders are likely to demand not only a higher interest rate to compensate for higher inflation, but also an additional risk premium to compensate them for the risk that their forecasts of inflation turn out to be inaccurate.

Because governments have to roll over debt so frequently, any increase in the inflation uncertainty risk premium will very rapidly raise not just the nominal cost of funding new borrowings, but also the real cost of funding new borrowings (the effect of the added risk premium for inflation uncertainty). Taking all this together, higher inflation will generate the following consequences for a government's spending:

- Higher nominal government spending where spending is inflation linked (real spending unchanged).
- Higher nominal government spending where cost overruns are passed to the government (real spending unchanged).
- Higher nominal debt service costs for inflation-linked securities (real spending unchanged).
- Higher nominal debt service costs to refinance maturing debt (real spending unchanged).
- Higher real debt service costs to refinance maturing debt (real spending rises).

The first four effects combined should not raise the government debt-to-GDP ratio in and of themselves, but they will act to prevent inflation from *reducing* the debt-to-GDP ratio. The first four effects neuter any benefit higher inflation may give in terms of debt and deficit reduction. The final effect, raising the real debt finance cost, will raise the debt-to-GDP ratio. To the extent that this risk premium outlasts the inflation shock it will give a positive impulse to the debt-to-GDP ratio for several years. Inflation uncertainty risk can add up to 1 per cent to the real cost of borrowing, which is a significant amount. Inflation uncertainty risk can linger for well over a decade – because investors need to be convinced inflation risks are under control to remove the risk premium fully, and it is likely to take more than a single economic cycle to achieve that.

With some complicated calculations – the sort of calculations that require economists to lock themselves away with a spreadsheet for days before emerging, blinking blearily in the sunlight and calling weakly for alcohol – it is possible to model what will happen to government debt ratios in the event of an inflation increase. The results will vary from economy to economy, because the maturity profile of government debt and the amount of index-linked debt will vary from country to country. For a developed economy, an inflation rate between around 5 per cent and somewhere between 25 per cent and 30 per cent will tend to raise the debt-to-GDP ratio over the course of a three-year period. The debt-to-GDP ratio may fall in the first year (because not enough debt has matured to trigger the full force of the inflation uncertainty risk premium). Thereafter, the debt-to-GDP ratio will tend to rise.

Why those boundaries? Below 5 per cent inflation and investors will assume that the inflation rate is operating in a range around the central tendency (of roughly 2.5 per cent in most advanced economies). Noise around a trend does not require uncertainty risk, as a rule. Over 25 per cent to 30 per cent and the speed with which inflation corrodes the real value of debt will overtake the market's ability to do anything about it through higher risk premiums. Of course, over 25 per cent to 30 per cent inflation would take an economy very close to what would generally be considered hyperinflation.

There are exceptions to the model. A brief spell of 5 per cent inflation may be ignored by investors, who fail to demand an inflation uncertainty premium, if it is genuinely believed to be a brief episode. A prolonged period of 4 per cent inflation could raise inflation uncertainty risk, if the higher inflation period lasts long enough so as to undermine investors' belief that inflation will revert to a lower rate. As a general rule, however, investors should bear in mind that higher inflation is not an automatic solution to a government's debt problem, and could well make it worse over time. Inflation is not a magic solution to indebted sovereign states. Today, something like 60 per cent of the US national debt is either tied to the level of inflation, or it will mature in less than three years. It is going to be quite difficult for the US to contemplate inflating its way out of that situation.

This whole situation can be summarised into one pithy phrase. Bond markets can punish governments faster than inflation can help governments.

Except... there is one way governments can hinder the avenging sword of the bond market. It does not mean that governments will deliberately seek to inflate their way out of debt. Instead, this method provides a means for governments to reduce their debt without inflation. The method is known as financial repression, and it is alive and well and increasingly being used in the twenty-first century.

Financial repression – inflating away debt without inflation

Governments raise funds by selling debt, and in selling debt they compete with other governments and other financial instruments to provide a rate of return that investors will find attractive. However, governments have an additional attribute that gives them something of an edge in finding investors for their debt. Governments are not just borrowers. Governments are also regulators.

The role of the government as a regulator of the financial sector is potentially extraordinarily powerful. Over the course of the past twenty years, the fashion in financial regulation has been to encourage financial risk management through a process of portfolio diversification. Governments have regulated with a relatively light touch, and left it to life insurers and pension funds to manage risk through

Box 9.1 The debt–inflation myth: the British example

The inflation experience of the British economy in the 1970s was not good. As Chapter 2 mentioned, consumer price inflation rose to nearly 27 per cent in 1975, and was high for the entire decade. Instinctively, one would assume that the government's debt-to-GDP ratio would fall. Nominal GDP in 1975 was receiving a significant boost from inflation, so surely the level of debt would fall at least relative to the size of the economy? Also this was an era before the British government had started to issue inflation-linked government bonds, further adding to the supposition that debt levels would fall relative to GDP.

Of course, the British government was subject to all the inflation problems on the expenditure side that have been identified. There was a serious attempt to limit public sector wage increases, but the real wage declines of the public sector were not that extreme – and as inflation rose the government's pay bill rose with it. Welfare payments rose with indexation or the demands for social justice. But above all else, the cost of borrowing rose for the British government over this period.

If the British government had been successful in inflating its way out of debt, we should expect to see the debt service cost (interest payments) of the British government declining as a share of GDP. That would be a critical signal that the bond markets were unable to punish the British government for inflation. In fact, the reverse happened. The government's public sector net debt service costs rose as a share of GDP, from 3 per cent of GDP in 1972 to a record high of just over 4.6 per cent in 1982.[5] Adding inflation uncertainty risk to the British government's bond yield cost the British government dearly.

There were other changes taking place. Government fiscal policy was tightened through the 1970s. But the punishment of the bond markets and the impact of inflation on government spending (independent of the cuts) meant that in spite of extraordinarily high inflation levels the British government was not able to meaningfully reduce its net debt burden in the 1970s – the net debt level was essentially static from 1976 onwards.

The point of this is that, had the British economy experienced a lower inflation rate in the 1970s than it did, the British government's debt-to-GDP ratio would have been lower than it was.

holding a wide range of assets in their portfolios. If something goes wrong with one asset, then hopefully the performance of other, diverse assets that are held will offset the loss and give an overall return for the portfolio as a whole.

In the wake of the global financial crisis, the pendulum is swinging back. Rather than risk management through portfolio diversification, there is now a trend for risk management through regulation. Under this scheme certain institutional investors will be either required, or alternatively given a very strong incentive, to hold a portion of their investment portfolio in certain assets that are designated as being low-risk assets.

Assets like government bonds.

Governments can, through regulation, create what amounts to a captive pool of investors. These are generally large institutions (life insurers, pension funds and, particularly in the current climate, banks). In more extreme situations, virtually anyone can be coerced into investment captivity – the government of Germany during the 1930s gave itself legal authority over all aspects of the credit system in order to direct funds towards government programmes.[6] It is also worth pointing out that formal regulation can be supplemented by more subtle forms of suasion. A quiet word from the local ministry of finance can be powerful in banking circles – the financial market equivalent of waking up to find the severed head of a horse lying in one's bed. The message is clear, even if informally delivered.

The stated objectives, maybe even the honestly held objectives of this regulation and suasion, may well be a genuine attempt to reduce risk and promote financial stability. However, regulation always brings with it unintended consequences, and one of those consequences is financial repression.

Financial repression is so called because one consequence of all this financial regulation is to repress, that is to say lower, the interest charges that the government has to pay. If there is a captive pool of investors in the bond market, then those investors will be buying bonds not because they believe these bonds represent good value or an attractive rate of return, but because these bonds have to be bought to satisfy the demands of the regulatory authority. It is not considered polite to mention that the regulatory authority making the demands that result in bond purchases is but an arm of the government that is also selling the bonds to the financial institutions.

Financial repression is about lowering the real cost of borrowing to the government, by lowering the nominal cost of borrowing to the government. Inflation may lower the real cost of borrowing to the government (initially) but leave the nominal cost of borrowing unchanged. Governments are likely to have a preference for repression rather than inflation, because the costs of repression are more narrowly focused than are the costs of inflation. To paraphrase Master Yoda, inflation leads to inflation uncertainty, inflation uncertainty leads to inflation uncertainty risk premiums, and inflation uncertainty risk premiums lead to the economic dark side. Inflation (unless combined with financial repression) will raise real interest rates through raising inflation uncertainty risk. Inflation uncertainty risk can also directly affect other business decisions in the economy, and raise the cost of capital across the board.

Financial repression will also raise the cost of capital in an economy, because investors that are forced into purchasing certain assets cannot invest that money elsewhere (this is a variation of what economists call 'crowding out', although crowding out is conventionally considered to be a result of market forces and here it is a consequence of coercion). However, as long as the repression is relatively narrowly defined, the damage of this crowding out is limited. Investors not subject to financial repression – private investors, for instance – will still be able to lend money where they choose.

The rather obvious question in all of this is who bears the cost? There must be a cost to the whole process of financial repression – there is no such thing as a free lunch, nor is there any such thing as a free reduction in government borrowing costs. Financial repression can perhaps best be thought of as a tax on specific investors or savers – life insurance policy holders, pension plan participants and bank depositors. These investors or savers will receive a lower rate of return than they could theoretically hope to enjoy, because the managers to whom they have entrusted their funds are being forced to invest those funds in government debt that generates a rate of return that is less than 'fair'.

Governments are able to get away with this sort of tax because it is generally quite subtle, and the government is one stage removed from the process. If pensioners are unhappy with the return on their assets, their first instinct will be to blame the pension fund manager and not to see the regulatory regime as being a tax masquerading under another name. There may also be limited alternatives for investors. There are, of course, alternatives to keeping one's money in a bank, but most of them are inconvenient or insecure, and the relatively small 'tax' that financial repression represents to the individual depositor is something that they may be prepared to accept in the circumstances.

Financial repression was a key part of the way in which the British government reduced its debt burden after the Second World War. The British government's debt level was around 240 per cent of GDP in 1945. By 1970, the government debt level was around 50 per cent of GDP. The government debt level came down in part because of increased taxation (inheritance tax was one way – taxing the dead being politically useful, as the dead can no longer vote). The government debt level also came down in part because of reduced government spending in some areas. The government debt level did not come down because inflation was particularly high – inflation was not particularly high in the UK in the post-war years (not until the 1970s). However, real interest rates, though generally positive, were low. This was because of financial repression. It worked.

Because the costs of financial repression are more akin to additional taxation, they should be considered more manageable than the broader risks associated with letting the inflation genie out of the bottle. More importantly, financial repression is likely to work, as long as the repressed investor still has the money to invest in the government debt. Inflation is less likely to work, unless eventually also combined with financial repression.

The oft heard accusation that 'governments must inflate their way out of debt' can be countered with the idea that it is more rational and more practical for governments to repress their way out of debt. And that is what they are tending to do at the moment.

The investment implications of financial repression are complicated. Investors should accept that financial managers who are repressed will likely earn a lower rate of return than financial managers who are not repressed. Whether that lower return is considered an adequate compensation for the *alleged* reduction in risk is for the investor to decide. Financial repression goes beyond that direct effect, however. Financial repression will reduce the nominal rate of return on government debt – that is, after all, rather the point. The problem with that is that the nominal rate of return on government debt is often used as a proxy for the risk free rate of return by equity strategists when they engage in the dark arts and alchemy of their profession. What economists are suggesting is that government bonds do not represent a risk free rate, but are distorted so as to be permanently below a risk free rate. Where does that leave equity strategists and their models? Covered in confusion (well, covered in more confusion than normal).

It does not help that repression is not a static concept. It has waxed and waned over the past seventy years or so, and no doubt it will continue to wax and wane. Moreover, some of the more subtle forms of repression are difficult to spot – the quiet word, the subtle hint; these are not to be found in lists of regulation or on the statute book. The shrewd investor will simply have to be vigilant that, in seeking to manage risk through regulation for certain investors, governments will create a distortion in bond markets that will have shifting implications for other asset classes.

The debt–inflation myth

The belief that 'inflation reduces debt' has pervaded and perverted financial markets for too many years. Under the right circumstances for a borrower, or wrong circumstances for a lender, inflation can lead to a real reduction in the debt burden. However, the relationship between debt and inflation is complex, and investors must be very, very wary of falling into the trap of subtracting consumer price inflation rates from the interest rate costs of debt to get a sense of whether inflation is eroding real debt values.

The consumer is, in the developed world at least, the most important part of the economy. For the most part an investor is not going to be concerned with consumer debt as an investable asset class, but should focus on consumer behaviour in the economy and how consumer debt may impact that.

Corporate debt is a different matter. Most corporate debt is not investable, because small and medium-sized companies – and even some quite large companies – are not able to borrow from the corporate bond markets. These corporates are important to the overall performance of the economy, as the recent global financial crisis has demonstrated. This last recession has been a small-business recession, and the unusually sluggish nature of the recovery owes much to the reluctance of small businesses to take on debt.

In the wake of the increase in public sector debt that the developed and several emerging economies have experienced, it has to be government debt that attracts most attention. The debt–inflation myth is a concern here because it gives rise to a fear that governments will, indeed that governments are able to, inflate their way out of debt. In the nineteenth and early twentieth centuries it was perfectly possible for governments to inflate their way out of debt; debt was long duration or perpetual, and little if any spending was tied to the level of inflation. There were still elements of this structure in the great inflation of the 1970s. The world today is not the same as it was nearly a half century ago, and governments will find inflation a problem, in particular if it raises inflation uncertainty risk.

Government debt management today seems to be moving in a different direction from inflation. Financial repression may be a by-product of other, more worthy aims (risk management and prudential regulation generally have the most moral of objectives, at least in theory). The consequence is that the government is able to lower its costs of borrowing in nominal terms without resorting to inflation. As long as some investors can be held captive, governments seem likely to incline their policies towards repression rather than inflation.

Notes

1 If the borrowed money is used for investment, there may be a hope that it will generate an offsetting income in the future, but this cannot be certain.
2 99.9 per cent of companies by number of companies, are small and medium-sized businesses that do not have access to financial markets.
3 This was introduced with the Economic Recovery Tax Act of 1981.
4 Sir Geoffrey Howe 1981 Budget speech, Hansard, retrieved from http://www. margaretthatcher.org/document/109499 on 8 August 2014.
5 Data from Crawford *et al.*(2009).
6 Nathan (1944).

10 Inflation and the modern investor

> With our inmost feelings we despise that low, yet pernicious trick, of some Journalists, who, however difficult, however complex a subject may be, however it may have divided the opinions of the wisest and best informed men, still address the mass of their readers on it, as if it were 'as plain as a pike-staff'.
>
> (Samuel Coleridge, *Essays on His Times in the Morning Post and Courier*)

As was hopefully made clear from the outset, the aim of this book has been to explain inflation and not to predict inflation. There is no point an economist trying to publish a book that offers predictions on the future course of inflation for a global audience – it would be out of date before it reached the bookshelf or the e-book reader. Inflation is going to vary from country to country. Inflation is going to vary from age group to age group. Inflation is going to vary from income group to income group. Inflation is one thing for a company, another for a consumer, and something else entirely for a borrower. Inflation will depend on wildly different economic circumstances, and it will ebb and flow over time. Confronted by this kaleidoscope of inflation possibilities, no investor should put blind faith in simple predictive models of a single variable like the consumer price index as being the answer to all inflation concerns. What is of most use to investors is trying to understand the complexity of inflation, to better inform their own opinions in their own time and place.

What this book has hopefully demonstrated is that inflation is a recurrent feature of the global economy. The second chapter showed that human civilisation has been littered with inflation from at least Ancient Byzantium onwards. The remarkable history of those medieval Chinese dynasties, falling like dominoes one after another in the wake of an endless loop of excess money printing and rising inflation, demonstrates that governments are not necessarily terribly adept at learning the lessons of history. Whatever the outlook for inflation in the near term, inflation will be a feature at some point in the future, somewhere in the world, for at least a certain subsection of an economy.

The history of inflation does serve a useful purpose. Governments may not learn from the lessons of history (or forget the lessons of history more often than they should), but the investor does not have to live in such ignorance. Looking at historical episodes of inflation can provide the investor with signposts, at the very least, as to how inflation may be expected to arise. The most cursory of glances at history tells the intelligent observer that inflation will arise either from too little supply of goods and services in the face of too much demand for goods and services, or from the supply of too much money in the face of too little demand for money. Policymakers must know this too, but policymakers will from time to time have a different agenda from that which investors would wish to see. The most important lesson of history is perhaps that when monetary policy is taken out of the hands of impartial economists (selflessly pursuing an appropriately stable inflation objective with the altruism of that noble profession), bad things will happen in the realm of inflation.

Modern economies also present the investor with a rather neat irony about inflation. Modern technology, like barcode scanners and the internet, give economists an unprecedented amount of information about pricing behaviour. If we take the trouble to analyse this information properly we can learn more and more about how prices actually change, what company strategies towards inflation are, and how this all comes together in the consumer price index. This allows ever more sophisticated economic analysis of pricing. At the same time, the technology of modern communication allows the dissemination of myths and half-truths – stories asserted with such force that they acquire the status of 'urban legends', and become so prevalent as to distort the behaviour of investors. Economists are undoubtedly prejudiced against the blogosphere – not because it challenges economics as a profession, but because it is mind-numbingly wearying to keep refuting the innumerable inaccuracies that are peddled to suit a political prejudice rather than economic reality.[1] It is tiring to repeatedly have to defeat a simple lie through the reiteration of a more complex truth.

Just as history shows that there is nothing new in inflation, so history also shows that there is nothing new in the problems of wilful misinterpretation and gross oversimplification. The Coleridge quote that graces the start of this chapter was made with reference to the adoption of the gold standard in Britain at the start of the nineteenth century; an extraordinarily complex issue wrapped up in concerns about inflation, value and foreign exchange. Two hundred years later and the technology by which information is disseminated has changed; little else has. Inflation and its attendant problems seem to be treated in as cavalier a fashion in the twenty-first century as they were in Coleridge's day.

The remainder of this concluding chapter, by way of a reward for having made it this far in the book, is not going to introduce new ideas. Rather, this chapter is going to take the mass of information from the previous chapters and try to distil it into something that will help investors in the twenty-first century. This is not a strategy for investing in the twenty-first century as such, but a way of structuring one's thought process so as to inform one's strategy in the best way possible.

The foundations of thinking about inflation

Before thinking about how inflation may impact asset allocation or investment specifics, the wise investor will try to pin down why it is that they are investing.

Obviously, an investor is investing to generate an income that will support a certain standard of living in the future – but what sort of standard of living? And whose standard of living? Is the investor trying to finance retirement? College education for one's children? Or is the aim to create an income stream for philanthropic purposes? Is the future income stream to meet expenses in one country or more than one country? Deciding the investment objective, and constantly having the investment objective in mind, can make a great deal of difference to the rationality of subsequent investment decisions.

Serious consideration needs to be given to these questions because the reason for investing will dictate the sort of inflation that the investor needs to 'beat' if they are to preserve the value of their investments in the future. There is no point in beating the consumer price index as published by the government if relative price changes in the economy mean that the relevant inflation rate the investor faces in the future is significantly different from the headline official data. With the demographics of most developed and several emerging markets having an ageing population, this is likely to be especially relevant for investors who are looking to finance retirement or future medical costs.

Narrowing down the inflation rate to something that approximates future cost changes does not make the task of investing any easier. Indeed, if the inflation rate the investor needs to beat is above the headline inflation figure, it is likely to make the task of investing considerably more difficult. Understanding the right inflation target to pursue simply helps the investor to avoid disappointment or 'real' real standard of living shocks and the conclusion of the investment process.

Having discerned the inflation rate that matters, the investor needs to try and purge themselves of the prejudice of anecdotal evidence and other distorted perceptions. Everyone is subject to these risks, but the twinge of annoyance one feels in having to write out a larger monthly cheque or of having to scramble for more change because the price of one's favourite chocolate bar in the vending machine has risen yet again should be suppressed. Pundits who attempt to sway the investor's views on inflation with anecdotal evidence should be kept a healthy distance from any investment portfolio. It is important to have faith in the statistics, rather than putting trust in the narrowness of immediate experience. Decisions should be arrived at on the basis of data, not on the basis of anecdote or 'gut instinct'.

Having faith in inflation numbers rather than inflation anecdote could become even more important in future years, because the technological improvements already referenced may lead to more changes in the calculation of inflation data. These changes should improve the accuracy of the inflation figures, moving the aggregate proxy for inflation to a more specific, more precise figure – and potentially allowing the creation of more customised inflation indices. A lot of the changes in inflation data in the immediate past have tended to *initially* reduce the aggregate consumer price inflation number – because sophisticated analysis allows price effects to be separated from other non-price effects (like quality changes) that had previously been caught up in the numbers. Future changes may have the same effect – at first. The fact that statistical improvements have reduced inflation in the past does not mean that the changes should be seen as some sinister plot to steal money from the investor through the creeping effects of an 'inflation tax' that is disguised by statistical manipulation. These changes are increasing accuracy. That increased accuracy may or may not reduce inflation today, but equally the increased accuracy of inflation data may or may not *increase* inflation in the future. The angst that quality adjustment of the consumer price basket causes in modern America is just as forceful as the angst that quality adjustment of the consumer price basket caused in the 1940s; the difference of course is that the popular desire for inflation quality adjustment has completely turned on its head over that period.

Complexity and inflation

Once investors have decided what inflation rate it is that they are trying to hedge against, and once they have done their best to purge themselves of the natural prejudice and bias that human nature subjects all of us to, investors need to reflect on the complexity of the task at hand. As was noted right back in the opening chapter, inflation is simple in that we should all be able to readily understand the topic. Inflation is not simplistic; inflation is not a topic that can be reduced to a single line on a chart.

This means that simplistic measures for protecting oneself against inflation need to be rejected. Indeed, 'rejected' is too weak a term. The discerning investor should run screaming in the opposite direction from any single investment that promises to safeguard one's assets from the ravages of inflation, threatening dire retribution on those that try to persuade them otherwise. Nothing – not gold, not even inflation-linked securities – can provide guaranteed inflation protection; in the case of gold because the perfection of its inflation-fighting credentials is one of the biggest myths of investment economics, and in the case of inflation-linked securities because the guarantee is against an aggregate inflation rate that is highly unlikely to match the inflation rate that matters to the investor. If inflation is not a simplistic concept, why on earth should a simplistic solution protect the investor against inflation? There is no 'golden bullet', no single asset nor even single asset class that will provide security.

This does not mean that assets like gold or inflation-linked securities should be rejected in the attempt to manage inflation risk – very far from it. Such assets can provide a valuable contribution *to a diverse portfolio* that aims to manage inflation risk. What the complexity of inflation means, however, is that investors who put all their investments into a single asset class – investors who sit smugly atop a pile of gold, or who wrap themselves in US TIPS bonds, and declare themselves to be safe – are likely to have a rude awakening as to just how unreal their 'real' asset class is.

The complexity of inflation means, in short, that we need more complex asset strategies. This means that the modern investor should consider how inflation will impact the performance of the main asset classes over time. Perhaps more importantly, the modern investor needs to consider what inflation rate matters to what asset class over time.

Inflation and equities

Equity investors are mainly interested in profit, as the driver of equity return. For all the sophisticated equity investment theories that abound, this is what the focus of an equity investor boils down to. Equity investors need to consider the impact of inflation as it operates through three broad channels on the profitability of the companies they are looking at: costs, pricing power, customers' ability to spend. This does mean that there are at least three separate inflation rates that need to be considered – our first glimpse at the complexity of inflation that was mentioned earlier. It also means that to equate a higher consumer price index with the idea that this is 'good for equities' is dangerously simplistic.

For most companies the dominant cost inflation is going to come from labour. We have already seen how labour is the most important component of overall consumer price inflation, and this importance of labour holds pretty much across the entire supply chain. Looking at generalised labour, cost inflation is not necessarily going to help too much, however. One of the global economic themes of the past quarter century has been the relative price shifts that the world economy has experienced. Those relative price shifts have included adjustments in the relative price of different forms of labour. A quick glance at income inequality statistics will show that the price of higher-skilled labour has tended to rise relative to the price of lower-skilled labour over the past twenty or thirty years. What sort of labour a company is using, and what the price of that specific form of labour is doing are thus important considerations for an equity investor.

As well as labour costs there are other inputs into a corporate cost structure. Producer price data, if it is sufficiently detailed, may give some good indications of likely cost pressures. If there is enough detail in macro wage data and producer price data, an investor will have a reasonable if somewhat generic approximation of the cost pressures that a company is facing.

Having developed some sense of what is happening with cost pressures, the investor then needs to turn their attention to pricing power. There are a couple of important observations to make here. The first point to reiterate is that most companies do not participate directly in the consumer price inflation rate. *Companies sell to companies*, in the main, not to consumers. Of course, the retail sector does sell to consumers and the role of the internet in allowing direct selling to the consumer needs to be remembered. Where this is the case consumer prices are relevant to the corporate's pricing power. The creeping advance of direct selling from companies to consumers via the internet may make consumer prices more important to more companies in the future; this may be an evolving concept investors need to keep track of. As a general rule, however, investors need to focus on producer price inflation as an indicator of corporate pricing power. It will require some finesse, as companies will have one form of producer price inflation, plus wage inflation, when considering cost inflation, but then a different form of inflation when considering their own pricing power.

Investors should also not expect companies' price changes to be smooth. In the abstract world of economic theory prices smoothly adjust over time in tiny increments (up a bit, down a bit), allowing economists to draw those pretty supply and demand charts that are so pleasing to the eye. Unfortunately, the reality is a lot uglier than those charts. Price changes tend to follow a model known as 'menu cost pricing', which basically means that if a company's costs rise by 1 per cent then the company's management is extremely unlikely to raise the price of the products being sold. It is just all too much hassle for the sake of 1 per cent. Instead, the company's management will tend to wait until the cost pressures have built up a bit, and once the cost pressures justify a price move of somewhere between 3 per cent and 5 per cent, the company will raise prices.[2]

The pattern of a company's price changes in relation to a company's cost changes also cautions against reading too much into small or short-term fluctuations in the cost–price gap. Companies expect the gap between cost inflation and price inflation to narrow and widen over time. What matters is what the average difference is over the investor's time horizon.

Finally, equity investors should consider the spending power of the consumer in their more general considerations about inflation and companies. The consumer's ability to buy a product does not just depend on the price of the product, but on the amount of cash that they have available to spend on everything. That means that income levels are important, of course. Equally important will be the price of other goods that are higher priority on the consumer's shopping list. Thus, if a company makes products that are predominantly sold to lower-income consumers, then the price of food could matter a great deal to the future earnings of that company – because consumers will tend to prioritise food over other products, and food is a large part of a low-income consumer's budget. If the food price rises there may not be enough spare money in the budget of a low-income household to spend on other products. In a world of inflation inequality this is becoming an ever more important consideration for investors to factor in.

An investor considering the relationship between equity and inflation has a complete set of inflation statistics to consider. Investing in equities on the back of changes in the generic consumer price index alone is dangerous. More sophistication is required if the investor is to avoid unpleasant surprises.

Inflation and debt

As Chapter 9 was at some pains to demonstrate, the relationship between inflation and debt is complex. For an investor, the debt that is most likely to matter as an investable asset class is going to be government debt – bonds and bills. Analysis of corporate debt can essentially be treated in the same way as equity, as far as the inflation relationship goes. This is because the creditworthiness of corporate debt depends on the issuing company's ability to pay, and that depends on their income and expenditure. It is when we come to consider government debt that we must re-examine the inflation rates used.

Having been very dismissive about the generic consumer price index as a guide to equities, it is right to restore the consumer price index to some semblance of usefulness for investors considering the relationship between government debt and inflation. The reason the generic consumer price index has a relevance to government debt is that it has a relevance to monetary policy. Monetary policymakers are usually concerned with generic consumer price targets. Unlike investors, monetary policymakers arguably should frame their decisions in the context of an aggregate price index, as their aim is to 'beat' inflation in the economy as a whole (while the investor represents a subsection of the economy as a whole, and thus has a different inflation rate to 'beat'). Indeed, when other targets are set (for example, unemployment), the normal response of a monetary policymaker is to say 'the best way we can meet the other target is by meeting our consumer price inflation target and creating suitably stable economic conditions'.

This means that as generic consumer price inflation is going to be a factor in determining the monetary policy interest rate, consumer price inflation will have some bearing in determining the performance of short-dated government bonds (bonds which will mature in a relatively short period of time, and whose interest rates tend to be quite closely linked to the official monetary policy interest rate).

Generic consumer price inflation is also going to be an important factor in determining the budget deficit, through the impact of consumer price inflation on government spending. The precise importance of this is going to vary from economy to economy. Not all government spending is tied to inflation and parts of a government's spending will be tied to different forms of inflation, like wage inflation. Nevertheless, the indexation of government spending, explicitly tying certain forms of expenditure to the level of the generic consumer price index, means that the size of the government's borrowing requirement and therefore the performance of the government bond market must in some way be tied to consumer prices.

This does mean that a rise in inflation has the potential to be a triple negative for a government bond investor. To the extent that the rise in the generic consumer price index encompasses a rise in the bond investor's own consumer price index, their real return is diminished. To the extent that a rise in the generic consumer price index prompts monetary policy tightening, their bond portfolio is at risk from rising short-term interest rates. To the extent that a rise in the generic consumer price index produces a weaker fiscal position, the credit quality of the government bond portfolio may be diminished.

Perhaps the two most salient points to remember as a bond investor, however, are that the changes in the generic consumer price index are very unlikely to match the bond investor's own inflation rate. This means that an investor may have a very different real rate of return from the simplistic real yield that is calculated by subtracting consumer prices from bond yields. This could be either good or bad – if an investor is confident that their inflation rate will run below the generic consumer price inflation, the real returns on bonds could be flattered. With inflation inequality, for instance, higher-income investors have enjoyed an enhanced real rate of return on government bonds relative to their less well-off peers. However, it also means that instruments like the US TIPS or the UK index-linked gilt offer far from perfect protection from the inflation that an *individual* investor is facing.

The second point to keep bearing in mind is that governments will find it very difficult to inflate their way out of debt without rushing to the extreme of hyperinflation (which has, other, adverse consequences). The instinctive reaction of investors to the fiscal consequences of the recent global financial crisis has been 'there must be inflation because debt is high, and that is how governments get rid of debt'. This is not true. There may be inflation, but unless it is very mild and very short-lived, it is unlikely to reduce debt. To base an overall investment strategy on the unreliable foundations of the debt–inflation myth would be foolish.

Inflation and foreign exchange

The final issue for investors to consider is how foreign exchange markets respond to inflation. A reliable foreign exchange model has evaded economists over the course of the profession's entire history – perhaps the movement of foreign exchange markets will remain one of the eternal mysteries of humanity. Any investor who thinks that the foreign exchange markets determine the price of currencies in an environment of perfect rationality is strongly urged to spend a few minutes observing a foreign exchange dealing room in operation; they will soon be disabused of the rational markets hypothesis.

Inflation is supposed to have a bearing on foreign exchange movements through the law of one price – at least, so monetarists would have us believe. A product sold in the US, converted into sterling at the prevailing foreign exchange rate, should in theory have the same price as the equivalent product sold in the United Kingdom. The problem is that so much of local prices are driven by local labour costs that the law of one price is not necessarily going to hold. Moreover, global companies seem to have less faith in foreign exchange markets than do economic theorists, and tend to ignore fluctuations in foreign exchange rates – as we saw with the example of IKEA. This means that the relationship between price, inflation and foreign exchange markets is tenuous at best.

There is a less direct series of impacts that inflation can have on foreign exchange pricing. If generic consumer price inflation influences monetary policy, then that may have an impact on foreign exchange markets. Similarly, if other asset prices like equities and bonds are influenced by consumer price inflation changes, then the foreign exchange markets may well respond to the investment opportunities created by the relative shifts of asset prices. Thus, capital flows, which help to determine the relative prices of foreign exchange markets, can be driven by expectations about what inflation will do to relative asset returns in different economies. It is all a little second-hand, but there is a foreign exchange–inflation relationship.

Perhaps rather than expecting inflation to influence foreign exchange as an asset class, investors should turn the relationship on its head and focus on how foreign exchange influences inflation (and through that, other investment decisions). The tendency to assume 'weak currency = generic inflation' is well embedded into at least the political psychology. The weakness of the relationship does not seem to influence the tenacity with which some policymakers and indeed some investors cling to the concept. Investors need to consider exactly *how* foreign exchange movements will influence local inflation.

This then loops back to the equity market. A weaker currency may not boost real economic activity (as measured by GDP). However, a weaker currency could boost profits for exporters, by allowing them to translate foreign earnings into the local currency at a favourable rate. That could be an important aspect in judging a company's profitability. At the same time, if the price of imported commodities (especially energy) starts to rise as a result of higher inflation that will impact other companies, and may impact the consumer's willingness to spend. Foreign exchange market shifts are likely to encourage relative price shifts that impact different companies in different ways – good for exporters, bad for those that import commodities.

So what is the true story of inflation?

In the aftermath of the global financial crisis, inflation has been subdued in most of the major industrialised economies. Indeed, the fear of deflation has emerged in some economies. This does not mean that inflation can now be pushed to one side by an investor as some kind of quaint anachronism of times past. In a world where overall investment returns are likely to be lower than they have been in the past, small differences in the inflation rate can play a far more important role in determining relative standards of living than in the past. In a world where investment returns of 7 per cent are easy, a 1 per cent difference in inflation is not necessarily a major concern. In a world where investment returns of 4 per cent are more normal, a 1 per cent difference in inflation suddenly assumes more importance in the mind of the investor. In all likelihood, phenomena such as inflation inequality are going to continue in the future. This makes 1 per cent variations in inflation – at least in the true inflation faced by a discriminating investor – just as probable in the future as in the past. The difference from the past is that in the modern world those relatively small inflation variations matter more to investment strategies.

The modern investor should not be afraid of inflation, but it does pay to try and understand as much as possible about the concept. Everyone likes simplicity, but blindly applying the consumer price measure as an inflation metric is almost certain to be the wrong approach. Investors will be rewarded for thinking about inflation in a more sophisticated way, recognising the complexity of the concept and rejecting the single-line charts that oversimplify the issue.

When it comes to inflation, perhaps the most useful weapon the modern investor has in their arsenal is the ability to fire off questions. 'Why?' or 'How do we know that?' can be a very strong attack to the baseless assertions that litter the fringes of the world of economics. Central banks and government statistical agencies put out a wealth of information on inflation. It can be somewhat tedious to wade through, but reliable answers can normally be found with a little perseverance.

The message of this book is that for inflation, the truth is out there. The modern investor should rigorously question every anecdote, assertion and statement on inflation to test the robustness of the analysis. The wise investor will not accept any assertions on inflation without question. Except, of course, the assertions of this book. Those, you can believe.

Notes

1 The blogosphere is relatively easy to attack because it has, as economists would say, 'low barriers to entry', which encourages the dissemination of views that are rarely fact checked before they are published. It would be remiss not to acknowledge that even more traditional forms of media are on occasion inclined to put forward misinformation. Even errors as basic and as glaring as 'the chocolate bar is getting smaller, and inflation does not capture it' have found their way into the pages of published texts. It is all a little dispiriting.
2 See Eichenbaum *et al.* (2014).

Bibliography

Abrams, Burton A. (2006), How Richard Nixon Pressured Arthur Burns: Evidence from the Nixon Tapes, *Journal of Economic Perspectives*, Volume 20, Issue 4, Fall, pp. 177–188

Ahamed, Liaquat (2009), *Lords of Finance*, Random House, London

Ahnert, Henning & Kenny, Geoff (2004), *Quality Adjustment of European Price Statistics and the Role for Hedonics*, ECB Occasional Paper Series 15, European Central Bank, Frankfurt

Allen, Robert C. (2007), *How Prosperous Were the Romans?*, Working Paper 363, Oxford University Economics Department, Oxford

Altig, David E. & Nosal, Ed (eds) (2009), *Monetary Policy in Low-Inflation Economies*, Cambridge University Press, Cambridge

Antonides, Gerrit (2008), How is Perceived Inflation Related to Actual Price Changes in the European Union?, *Journal of Economic Psychology*, Volume 29, pp. 417–432

Ashworth, William (1952), *A Short History of The International Economy 1850-1950*, Longmans, Green and Co., London

Babson, Roger W. (1937), *If Inflation Comes – What You Can Do about It*, Frederick A. Stokes Company, New York

Baxter, Marianne & Landry, Anthony (2012), *IKEA: Product, Pricing, and Pass-Through*, Federal Reserve Bank of San Francisco, San Francisco, CA

Bernanke, Ben S., Laubach, Thomas, Mishkin, Frederic S. & Posen, Adam S. (1999), *Inflation Targeting*, Princeton University Press, Princeton, NJ

Berndt, Ernst R. (2006), The Boskin Commission Report After a Decade, *International Productivity Monitor*, Volume 12, pp. 61–73

Biggeri, Luigi & Ferrari, Guido (eds) (2012), *Price Indexes in Time and Space*, Physica-Verlag, Berlin

Bodenhorn, Howard (2000), *A History of Banking in Antebellum America*, Cambridge University Press, Cambridge

Bowles, Nigel (2005), *Nixon's Business: Authority and Power in Presidential Politics*, Texas A&M University Press, College Station, TX

Brenner, Y. S. (1962), The Inflation of Prices in England, 1551–1650, *The Economic History Review,* Volume 15, Issue 4, pp. 266–84

Bresciani-Turroni, Constantino (1937), *The Economics of Inflation*, George Allen & Unwin Ltd, London

Broadberry, S., Campbell, B., Klein, A., Overton, M. & van Leeuwen, B. (2011), British Economic Growth 1270 to 1870 – an output based app.roach, retrieved 1 December 2014 from http://www.lse.ac.uk/economicHistory/pdf/Broadberry/BritishGDPLongRun16a.pdf

Buelens, Christian (2012), *Inflation Forecasting and the Crisis*, European Commission Economic Papers 451, March

Bullock, Charles J. (1930), Dionysius of Syracuse – Financier, *The Classical Journal*, Volume 25, Issue 4, January, pp. 260–76

Burdekin, Richard C. K. & Siklos, Pierre L. (eds) (2004), *Deflation*, Cambridge University Press, Cambridge

Bureau of Labor Statistics (2007), *Handbook of Methods*, BLS, Washington, DC, Chapter 17, as updated June 2007, retrieved 4 June 2014 from http://www.bls.gov/opub/hom/pdf/homch17.pdf

Cage, Robert, Greenlees, John & Jackman, Peter (2003), *Introducing the Chained Consumer Price Index*, paper presented at the seventh meeting of the International Working Group on Price Indices

Capie, Forrest (2010), *The Bank of England 1950s to 1979*, Cambridge University Press, Cambridge

Capie, Forrest & Wood, Geoffrey (2012), *Money over Two Centuries*, Oxford University Press, Oxford

Cassel, Gustav (1936), *The Downfall of the Gold Standard*, Oxford University Press, Oxford

Colavecchio, Roberta, Fritsche, Ulrich & Graff, Michael (2011), *Inflation Inequality in Europe*, University of Hamburg Department of Economics and Politics Discussion Papers, 2/2011

Copeland, Lois S. (1982), Consumer Price Indexes for the Elderly: British Experience, *Social Security Bulletin*, Volume 45, Issue 1, US Department of Social Security, Washington, DC

Coyle, Diane (2014), *GDP – A Brief but Affectionate History*, Princeton University Press, Princeton, NJ

Crawford, Rowena, Emmerson, Carl & Tetlow, Gemma (2009), *A Survey of Public Spending in the UK*, IFS Briefing Note BN43, Institute for Fiscal Studies, London

Daniel, T. Cushing (1924), *Real Money versus False Money – Bank Credits*, Monetary Educational Bureau, Washington. DC

Davies, Glyn (2002), *A History of Money*, University of Wales Press, Cardiff

DeCarlo, Scott (2013), Cost of Living Extremely Well Index, *Forbes Magazine*, 7 October, retrieved from June 2014 http://www.forbes.com/sites/scottdecarlo/2013/09/18/cost-of-living-extremely-well-index-the-price-of-the-good-life.

De Foe, Daniel (1841), *The Complete English Tradesman*, Volume II, Oxford University Press, Oxford

Del Giovane, Paolo, Fabiani, Silvia & Sabbatini, Roberto (2008), *What's behind 'Inflation Perceptions'? A Survey-based Analysis of Italian Consumers*, Banca D'Italia Working Papers No. 655, Rome

Dick, Alexander (2013), *Romanticism and the Gold Standard*, Palgrave Macmillan, Basingstoke

Dubois, Pierre, Griffith, Rachel & Nevo, Aviv (2014), Do Prices and Attributes Explain International Differences in Food Purchases?, *American Economic Review*, Volume 104, Issue 3, pp. 832–67

Dulles, Eleanor Lansing (1933), *The Dollar, The Franc and Inflation*, Macmillan, New York

Duncan, Richard (2003), *The Dollar Crisis*, John Wiley and Sons, Singapore

Easterly, William & Fischer, Stanley (2000), *Inflation and the Poor*, World Bank Research Working Paper No. 2335, World Bank, Washington, DC

Eichenbaum, Martin, Jaimovich, Nir, Rebelo, Sergio & Smith, Josephine (2014), How Frequent are Small Price Changes?, *American Economic Journal*, Volume 6, Issue 2, pp. 137–55

Eichengreen, Barry (1995), *Golden Fetters*, Oxford University Press, Oxford

Eichengreen, Barry (2011), *Exorbitant Privilege – The Rise and Fall of the Dollar*, Oxford University Press, Oxford

Eichengreen, Barry & Flandreau, Marc (eds) (1985), *The Gold Standard in Theory and History*, Routledge, London

Euromonitor Group (2013), *World Consumer Income and Expenditure Patterns 2014*, Euromonitor International, London

Evans, D. Morier (1859, reprinted 1969), *The History of the Commercial Crisis 1857-58*, Sentry Press, New York

Farrell, Chris (2005), *Deflation*, HarperCollins, New York

Feldman, Gerald D. (1977), *Iron and Steel in the German Inflation 1916-1923*, Princeton University Press, Princeton, NJ

Ferguson, Niall (2008), *The Ascent of Money*, Allen Lane, London

Fergusson, Adam (2010), *When Money Dies*, Old Street Publishing, London

Fetter, Frank Whitson (1931), *Monetary Inflation in Chile*, Princeton University Press, Princeton, NJ

Fischer, David Hackett (1996), *The Great Wave: Price Revolutions and the Rhythm of History*, Oxford University Press, New York

Fischer, Stanley, Sahay, Ratna & Végh, Carlos A. (2002), Modern Hyper- and High Inflations, *Journal of Economic Literature*, Volume XL, September, pp. 837–80

Fisher, F. J. (1965), Influenza and Inflation in Tudor England, *The Economic History Review*, Volume 18, Issue 1, August, pp. 120–9

Fox News (2014), Bacon Prices Hit an All-Time High, retrieved 11 August 2014 from http://www.foxnews.com/leisure/2014/08/05/bacon-prices-rise-to-new-all-time-high

Friedman, M. (1963), *Inflation: Causes and Consequences*, Asia Publishing House, New York

Friedman, Milton (1970), First Wincott Memorial Lecture, September 1970, Institute of Economic Affairs Occasional Paper 33, London

Gagnon, Etienne, Mandel, Benjamin R. & Vigfusson, Robert J. (2014), Missing Import Price Changes and Low Exchange Rate Pass-Through, *American Economic Journal*, Volume 6, Issue2, pp. 156–206

Galati, Gabriele, Heejmeijer, Peter & Moessner, Richhild (2011), *How do Inflation Expectations Form? New Insights from a High-frequency Survey*, BIS Working Paper No. 349, July, Bank for International Settlements, Basel

Galbraith, John Kenneth (1995), *Money – Whence it Came, Where it Went*, Penguin Books, London

Garber, Peter M. & Spencer, Michael G. (1994), *The Dissolution of the Austro-Hungarian Empire – Lessons for Monetary Reform*, Essays in International Finance, Number 191, Economics Department, Princeton University, Princeton, NJ

Geishecker, Ingo & Görg, Holger (2011), Services Offshoring and Wages: Evidence from Micro Data, *Oxford Economic Papers*, Volume 65, pp. 124–46

Georganas, Sotiris, Healy, Paul J. & Li, Nan (2014), Frequency Bias in Consumers' Perceptions of Inflation: An Experimental Study, *European Economic Review*, Volume 67, pp. 144–58

Gough, Julian (2013), On-line Retailers versus the High Street: An Analysis of Pricing, *The Business Economist*, Volume 44, Issue 2, pp. 18–29

Gould, J. D. (1964), The Price Revolution Reconsidered, *The Economic History Review*, Volume 17, Issue 2, December, pp. 249–266

Gould, J. D. (1968), F. J. Fisher on Influenza and Inflation in Tudor England, *The Economic History Review*, Volume 21, Issue 2, August, pp. 361–368

Graeber, David (2011), *Debt: The First 5,000 Years*, Melville House, New York

Granville, Brigitte (2013), *Remembering Inflation*, Princeton University Press, Princeton, NJ

Groen-Vallinga, M. J. & Tacoma, L. E. (2014), The Value of Labour: Diocletian's Prices Edict, retrieved 18 March 2014 from http://www.academia.edu/4101823/M.J._Groen-Vallinga_and_L.E._Tacoma_The_value_of_labour_Diocletians_Price_Edict

Gross, Bill (2004), *Haute Con Job*, PIMCO Investment Outlook, October, PIMCO, Newport Beach

Hanke, Steve H. & Krus, Nicholas (2012), *World Hyperinflations*, Cato Institute Working Papers 15 August 2012, Washington, DC

Hardy, Charles O. (1940), *The Wartime Control of Prices*, The Brookings Institute, Washington, DC

Hobijn, Bart & Lagakos, David (2003), *Inflation Inequality in the United States*, Federal Reserve Bank of New York Staff Reports, Number 173, October

Horne, Alistair (1967), *The Fall of Paris*, The Reprint Society, Suffolk

Howson, Susan (1974), The Origins of Dear Money 1919-20, *The Economic History Review*, Volume 27, Issue 1, February pp. 88–107

Ipswich Journal (1795), Friday's Post, 8 August, retrieved 23 December 2013 from http://www.britishnewspaperarchive.co.uk/

Jackson, Ben & Saunders, Robert (eds) (2012), *Making Thatcher's Britain*, Cambridge University Press, Cambridge

Jacobs, David, Perera, Dilhan & Williams, Thomas (2014), *Inflation and the Cost of Living*, Reserve Bank of Australia Bulletin, March Quarter

Johnson, David S. & Reed, Stephen B. (2006), Price Measurement in the United States, *Monthly Labor Review*, May, pp. 10–19

Jones, A. H. M. (1953), Inflation under the Roman Empire, *The Economic History Review*, Second Series, Volume V, Issue 3, pp. 293–317

Kraemer, Kenneth L., Linden, Greg & Dedrick, Jason (2011), Capturing Value in Global Phone Networks: App.le's iPad and iPhone, retrieved 4 December 2014 from econ. sciences-po.fr/sites/default/files/file/Value_iPad_iPhone.pdf

Kumar, Manmohan S., Baig, Taimur, Decressin, Jörg, Faulkner-MacDonagh, Chris & Feyziogùlu, Tarhan (2003), *Deflation – Determinants, Risks, and Policy Options*, IMF Occasional Paper 221, International Monetary Fund, Washington, DC

Lanz, R. & Miroudot, S. (2011), *Intra-Firm Trade: Patterns, Determinants and Policy Implications*, OECD Trade Policy Papers, No. 114, OECD Publishing, Paris

Levi, Leone (1867), *Wages and Earnings of the Working Classes*, John Murray, London

Lewis, W. Arthur (1950), *Economic Survey 1919-1939*, George Allen & Unwin Ltd, London

Loomis, William T. (1998), *Wages, Welfare Costs and Inflation in Classical Athens*, University of Michigan Press, Ann Arbor, MI

Magnusson, Niklas & Gustafsson, Katarina (2013*), Swedish Banks Make Money by Saying No to Cash*, Bloomberg news article, 11 April

Marcet, Jane (1817), *Conversations on Political Economy*, 2nd Edition, Longman, Hurst, Rees, Orme, and Brown, London

Meltzer, Allan, H. (2003), *A History of the Federal Reserve*, Volume 1, The University of Chicago Press, Chicago, IL

Meltzer, Allan, H. (2005), *Origins of the Great Inflation*, Federal Reserve Bank of St Louis, March/April (Part 2), pp. 145–76

Michell, H. (1947), The Edict of Diocletian – A Study of Price Fixing in the Roman Empire, *The Canadian Journal of Economics and Political Science*, Volume XIII, Issue 1, February, pp. 1–12

Mishkin, Frederic S. (2007), Globalization, Macroeconomic Performance, and Monetary Policy, speech delivered on 27 September, retrieved 11 August 2014 from http://www.federalreserve.gov/newsevents/speech/mishkin20070927a.htm

Miskimin, Harry A. (1989), *Cash, Credit and Crisis in Europe 1300-1600*, Variorum Reprints, London

Mitchell, B. R. (2003), *International Historical Statistics: Europe 1750-2000*, Palgrave Macmillan, London

Mouré, Kenneth (1991), *Managing the Franc Poincaré*, Cambridge University Press, Cambridge

Munro, John H. (1992), *Bullion Flows and Monetary Policies in England and the Low Countries, 1350-1500*, Variorum, Hampshire

Nathan, Otto (1944), *The Banking System in the Nazi Military and War Economy*, National Bureau of Economic Research, Washington, DC

National Industrial Conference Board (1926), The Cost of Living in the United States 1914-1926, NICB New York, retrieved August 2014 from http://babel.hathitrust.org/cgi/pt?id=coo.31924052141094;view=1up;seq=144

Nicholson, J. Shield (1919), *Inflation*, P. S. King and Son Ltd, London

Noyes, Alexander Dana (1898), *Thirty Years of American Finance*, G. P. Putnam's Sons, New York

Office for National Statistics (2012), *Briefing Note Consumer Price Indices*, ONS London, October

Paarlberg, Dan (1993), *An Analysis and History of Inflation*, Praeger, Westport, CA

Parker, Geoffrey (2013), *Global Crisis – War, Climate Change and Catastrophe in the Seventeenth Century*, Yale University Press, London

Rathbone, John Paul & Wheatley, Jonathan (2012*)*, Brazilian Finance Minister [Brazil's Finance Chief] Attacks US over QE3, *Financial Times*, London, 20 September, retrieved August 2014 from http://www.ft.com/cms/s/0/69c0b800-032c-11e2-a484-00144feabdc0.html#axzz39OoNuUTU

Rees, Albert (1961), *Real Wages in Manufacturing 1890-1914*, Princeton University Press, Princeton, NJ, pp. 74–119. Retrieved August 2014 from http://nber.org/chapters/c2286

Roache, Shaun K. (2012), *China's Impact on World Commodity Markets*, IMF Working Paper WP/12/115, Washington, DC

Rogers, James E. Thorold (1884), *Six Centuries of Work and Wages* (Volumes I and II), W. Swan Sonnenschein and Co., London,

Rogers, James Harvey (1934), *The Process of Inflation in France 1914-1927*, Columbia University Press, New York

Rostow, W. W. (1949), *British Economy of the Nineteenth Century*, Clarendon Press, Oxford

Rowlinson, Matthew (2013), *Real Money and Romanticism*, Cambridge University Press, Cambridge

Sargent, Thomas J. & Velde, François R. (2002), *The Big Problem of Small Change*, Princeton University Press, Princeton, NJ

Schenk, Catherine R. (2010), *The Decline of Sterling*, Cambridge University Press, Cambridge

Shibley, Geo. H. (1896), *The Money Question*, Stable Money Publishing Company, Chicago, IL

Shiller, Robert J. (1996), *Why Do People Dislike Inflation?*, NBER Working Paper 5539, National Bureau of Economic Research, Cambridge, MA

Slotsky, Alice Louise (1997), *The Bourse of Babylon: Market Quotations in the Astronomical Diaries of Babylonia*, CDL Press, Bethesda, MD

Sparling, Earl (1933), *The Primer of Inflation*, The John Day Company, New York

Stapleford, Thomas A. (2009), *The Cost of Living in America*, Cambridge University Press, Cambridge

Stockbridge, Frank Parker (1939), *Hedging against Inflation*, Barrons, Boston, MA

Taylor, Frederick (2013), *The Downfall of Money: Germany's Hyperinflation and the Destruction of the Middle Class*, Bloomsbury Publishing, London

Tomlinson, Jim (2014), British Government and Popular Understanding of Inflation in the Mid-1970s, *The Economic History Review*, Volume 67, Issue 3, pp. 750–68

Tooke, Thomas (1838), *A History of Prices and the State of the Circulation from 1793 to 1837*, Longman, Orme, Brown, Green, and Longmans, London

Trentman, Frank (ed.) (2012), *The Oxford Handbook of the History of Consumption*, Oxford University Press, Oxford

Trevithick, J. A. (1988), *Inflation – A Guide to the Crisis in Economics*, 2nd Edition, Penguin Books, London

Tullock, Gordon (1957), Paper Money – A Cycle in Cathay, *The Economic History Review*, Second Series, Volume IX, Issue 3, pp. 393–407

Wells, James & Restieaux, Ainslie (2014), *Review of Hedonic Quality Adjustment in UK Consumer Price Statistic and Internationally*, Office for National Statistics, London, 13 March

Wheelock, David C. (1991), *The Strategy and Consistency of Federal Reserve Monetary Policy, 1924-1933*, Cambridge University Press, Cambridge

White, Michael V. & Schuler, Kurt (2009), Who Said 'Debauch the Currency': Keynes or Lenin?, *Journal of Economic Perspectives*, Volume 23, Issue 2, Spring, pp. 213–222

Woodward, Donald B. & Rose, Marc A. (1933), *Inflation*, McGraw-Hill Book Company Inc., New York

World Gold Council (2013), *The Direct Economic Impact of Gold*, World Gold Council & Pricewaterhouse Coopers, October

Index